Exploring Biblical Backgrounds

A Reader in Historical and Literary Contexts

Derek S. Dodson
Katherine E. Smith
Editors

BAYLOR UNIVERSITY PRESS

Cover Design by Savanah Landerholm

Cover image: "The Hero Overpowering a Lion," and human-headed winged bull, Louvre Museum, Department of Near Eastern Antiquities. Photograph courtesy of Ninara, CC BY 2.0 license.

This title has been registered with the Library of Congress with the ISBN
978-1-4813-0854-0.

Printed in the United States of America on acid-free paper with a minimum of 30 percent post-consumer waste recycled content.

CONTENTS

PART II
The New Testament Background

PREFACE

The texts of the Bible were written thousands of years ago and originated from various ancient cultures. An informed reading of the Bible recognizes this historical distance and seeks to understand the biblical text in its historical and literary contexts. One way to reconstruct (at least partially) those contexts is to compare the biblical text with other written materials coming from generally the same time period. Just as scientists use underwater soundings to measure sea depths and to create maps of the ocean floor, this comparative approach allows interpreters to "measure" (i.e., analyze) how a biblical text participated in the cultural, ideological, literary, and rhetorical conventions of its time and how meaning may have been created for the text's first readers/hearers. This approach can also guard against an anachronistic reading: reading into the biblical text the interpreter's modern notions and suppositions.

This source book intends to assist undergraduate students (and the interested reader) in a comparative reading of the Bible that emphasizes its historical and literary analogs. The selections are not exhaustive, but are representative of a wide range of material encompassing the entire Bible. The editors have selected readings that they consider (for the most part) standard comparable material in biblical studies.

How to use this book: The organization of the book's material generally follows the arrangement of the Christian Bible, particularly the division between the Old Testament and the New Testament. Introductions to the sections and/or individual readings provide general descriptions of how the readings relate to the biblical material, even referencing specific biblical texts. The Scripture index provides an easy tool for identifying the biblical texts referenced in the introductions. Though specific questions and assignments can be made for particular readings, students should generally look for similar themes, concepts, and literary features between the biblical texts and comparable material. Students should also consider what is distinctive or different for both the biblical text and comparable material. Attention to the interplay between continuity and discontinuity can yield significant insights. Students should avoid asking questions of "borrowing"—that is, whether the comparable material served as a source for the biblical text (and vice versa). Such questions are mostly futile and can distract from more fruitful discoveries and understandings.

A note on the texts: brackets and braces, and occasionally parentheses, represent textual reconstruction at places where the original documents were damaged; ellipses stand in for portions of texts too damaged to be recovered or in some cases portions of texts that have been omitted from a selection. Parentheses typically mark words that have been supplied in the translation to facilitate reading while parenthetical question marks and in some instances italics indicate uncertainty in the translation.

The editors are profoundly grateful to Dr. Carey Newman, director of Baylor University Press, and his staff for their guidance and assistance in bringing this project to fulfillment. We are also thankful to Dr. W. H. Bellinger Jr., chair of the Department of Religion (Baylor University), and Dr. James Nogalski, director of graduate studies, for their various means of support that made our work on this volume possible.

Derek S. Dodson
Katherine E. Smith
Christmastide 2017

PART I

The Old Testament Background

A. CREATION AND DELUGE

The Hebrew Bible has several creation stories, including the two that it opens with in Genesis 1 and 2–3 (see also for example: Prov 8:22-31; Pss 33; 74; 104; Isa 27; 40:12-26; 45; Job 38–41). There are multiple creation myths from the ancient Eastern Mediterranean world. The texts in the selection below are from Mesopotamia, Egypt, and Greece, and date from the third millennium BCE to the seventh century BCE. The themes in the creation myths mirror those from the Hebrew Bible, including creation from nothing, the ordering of watery chaos, and creation by a single deity, among others. The primeval history in the Hebrew Bible also contains an account of a worldwide flood, common to many traditions around the world, including the Mesopotamian story given below.

1

ENUMA ELISH

The Mesopotamian poetic account of creation, the Enuma Elish (early second millennium BCE), bears resemblances to creation accounts in the Hebrew Bible. The poem, recorded on seven tablets, describes Marduk's (the preeminent Babylonian god) rise to the top of the pantheon through his battle with the watery goddess of chaos, Tiamat, and her band of monsters. Through this battle with chaos, Marduk establishes order. He divides Tiamat's body in two halves, using the upper half to create the sky and the lower to create the earth. Afterwards, using his own body, the god creates humanity to be the servants of the gods. This ordering of chaos, depicted as the defeat of a watery chaos monster, resembles the accounts in Genesis 1; Isaiah 27; Psalm 74; 104; and Job 38–41.

When in the height of heaven was not named,
And the earth beneath did not yet bear a name,
And the primeval Apsu, who begat them (heaven and earth),
And chaos, Tiamat (the ocean), the mother of them both,
Their waters were mingled together,
When no field was formed, no marsh was to be seen;
When no gods had been called into being,
And none bore a name, and no destinies were ordained;
Then the gods were created in the midst of heaven,

. . .

They were troublesome to Tiamat

. . .

Their way was evil . . .
Then Apsu, the begetter of the great gods,
Cried to Mummu, his minister, and said to him:
"O Mummu, minister that rejoices my spirit,
Come, let us go to Tiamat!"
So they went, and before Tiamat they lay down;
They consulted on a plan with regard to the gods, their sons.
Apsu opened his mouth,
And he addressed Tiamat, the glistening one . . .
"By day I cannot rest, by night I cannot lie down in peace.
But I will destroy them . . .
Let there be lamentation, and let us lie down again in peace."
When Tiamat heard these words,
She raged and cried aloud . . .
She uttered a curse, and to Apsu she spoke:
"What then shall we do?
Let their way be made difficult, and let us lie down in peace."
Mummu answered, and gave counsel to Apsu,

. . .

"Come, their way is strong, but you shall destroy it . . ."

. . .

Apsu listened, and his countenance grew bright,
Since he (Mummu) planned evil against the gods his sons.

. . .

Then Ea, who knows all, went up and he beheld their mutterings.

. . .

[He bound Apsu and killed him;
He confined Mummu]

. . .

And Tiamat . . . said,
". . . Let us wage war!"

They banded themselves together and, at the side of Tiamat, they advanced;
They were furious; they devised mischief without resting night and day.
They prepared for battle, fuming and raging;
They joined their forces and made war.
Ummu-Hubur, who formed all things,
Made in addition weapons invincible, she spawned monster-serpents,
Sharp of tooth, and merciless of fang;
With poison instead of blood she filled their bodies.
Fierce monster-vipers she clothed with terror.

. . .

After this fashion, huge of stature, she made eleven monsters.
Among the gods who were her sons, inasmuch as he had given her support,
She exalted Kingu; in their midst she raised him to power,
To march before the forces, to lead the host,
To give the battle signal, to advance to the attack,
To direct the battle, to control the fight,
To him she entrusted; in costly raiment she made him sit, saying:
"I have uttered your spell; in the assembly of the gods I have raised
     you to power.
The dominion over all the gods I have entrusted to him.
Be exalted, my chosen spouse,
May they magnify your name over all . . ."

. . .

Tiamat made weighty her handiwork,
She wrought evil against the gods her children.
To avenge Apsu, Tiamat planned evil,
But how she had collected her forces . . . to Ea she divulged.
Ea listened to this thing, and
He was grievously afflicted, and he sat in sorrow.
The days went by, and his anger was appeased,
And to the place of Anshar his father he took his way.
He went and standing before Anshar, the father who begat him,
All that Tiamat had plotted he repeated to him,
Saying, "Tiamat our mother has conceived a hatred for us,
With all her force she rages, full of wrath.
All the gods have turned to her,
With those, whom you created, they go at her side.
They are banded together, and at the side of Tiamat they advance;
They are furious, they devise mischief without resting night and day.
They prepare for battle, fuming and raging."

. . .

"Tiamat has exalted Kingu, and where is one who can oppose her?"

. . .

His (Marduk's) heart exulted, and he spoke to his grandfather,

"O Lord of the gods, Destiny of the great gods,
If I, your avenger,
Conquer Tiamat and give you life,
Appoint an assembly, make my fate preeminent and proclaim it.
In Upshukkinaku seat yourselves joyfully together,
With my word in place of you will I decree fate.
May whatsoever I do remain unaltered,
May the word of my lips never be changed nor made of no avail."
. . .
The great gods, all of them, who decree fate,
They entered in before Anshar . . .
They kissed one another, in the assembly.
They made ready for the feast, at the banquet they sat;
They ate bread, they mixed sesame wine.
. . .
They were drunk with drinking, their bodies were filled.
They were wholly at ease, their spirit was exalted;
Then for Marduk, their avenger, did they decree the fate.
They prepared for him a lordly chamber,
Before his fathers as prince he took his place.
"You are chief among the great gods,
Your fate is unequaled, your word is Anu!
. . .
None among the gods shall transgress your boundary.
Abundance, the desire of the shrines of the gods,
Shall be established in your sanctuary, even though they lack offerings.
O Marduk, you are our avenger!
We give you sovereignty over the whole world.
Sit down in night, be exalted in your command.
Your weapon shall never lose its power, it shall crush your foe.
O lord, spare the life of him that puts his trust in you,
But as for the god who began the rebellion, pour out his life."
Then they set in their midst a garment,
And to Marduk their firstborn they spoke:
"May your fate, O lord, be supreme among the gods
To destroy and to create; speak the word, and your command shall be
    fulfilled.
Command now and let the garment vanish;
And speak the word again and let the garment reappear!"
Then he spoke with his mouth, and the garment vanished;
Again he commanded it, and the garment reappeared.
When the gods, his fathers, beheld the fulfilment of his word,
They rejoiced, and they paid him homage, saying, "Marduk is king!"
They bestowed upon him the scepter, and the throne, and the ring;

They gave him an invincible weapon, which overwhelmed the foe.
"Go, and cut off the life of Tiamat,
And let the wind carry her blood into secret places."
After the gods, his fathers had decreed for the lord his fate,
They set him on a path of prosperity and success.
He made ready the bow, he chose his weapon,
He slung a spear upon him and fastened it . . .
He raised the club, in his right hand he grasped it,
The bow and the quiver he hung at his side.
He set the lightning in front of him,
With burning flame he filled his body.
He made a net to enclose the inward parts of Tiamat,
The four winds he stationed so that nothing of her might escape;
The South wind and the North wind and the East wind and the West wind
He brought near to the net, the gift of his father Anu.
He created the evil wind, and the tempest, and the hurricane,
And the fourfold wind, and the sevenfold wind, and the whirlwind, and the
     wind which had no equal;
He sent forth the winds which he had created, the seven of them;
To disturb the inward parts of Tiamat, they followed after him.
Then the lord raised the thunderbolt, his mighty weapon,
He mounted the chariot, the storm unequalled for terror,
. . .
Then they beheld him, the gods beheld him,
The gods, his fathers, beheld him, the gods beheld him.
And the lord drew near, he gazed upon the inward parts of Tiamat,
He perceived the muttering of Kingu, her spouse.
As Marduk gazed, Kingu was troubled in his gait,
His will was destroyed and his motions ceased.
. . .
Then the lord raised the thunderbolt, his mighty weapon,
And against Tiamat, who was raging, he sent the word:
"You have become great, you have exalted yourself on high,
And your heart has prompted you to call to battle.
. . .
Stand! You and I, let us join battle!"
When Tiamat heard these words,
She was like one possessed, she lost her reason.
Tiamat uttered wild, piercing cries,
She trembled and shook to her very foundations.
She recited an incantation, she pronounced her spell,
And the gods of the battle cried out for their weapons.
Then Tiamat and Marduk advanced, the counselor of the gods;

To the fight they came on, to the battle they drew nigh.
The lord spread out his net and caught her,
And the evil wind that was behind him he let loose in her face.
As Tiamat opened her mouth to its full extent,
He drove in the evil wind, while as yet she had not shut her lips.
The terrible winds filled her belly,
And her courage was taken from her, and her mouth she opened wide.
He seized the spear and burst her belly,
He severed her inward parts, he pierced her heart.
He overcame her and cut off her life;
He cast down her body and stood upon it.
When he had slain Tiamat, the leader,
Her might was broken, her host was scattered.
And the gods her helpers, who marched by her side,
Trembled, and were afraid, and turned back.
They took to flight to save their lives;
But they were surrounded, so that they could not escape.
He took them captive, he broke their weapons;
. . .
And to Tiamat, whom he had conquered, he returned.
And the lord stood upon Tiamat's hinder parts,
And with his merciless club he smashed her skull.
He cut through the channels of her blood,
And he made the North wind bear it away into secret places.
His fathers saw, and they rejoiced and were glad;
Presents and gifts they brought to him.
Then the lord rested, gazing upon her dead body,
While he divided the flesh . . . he devised a cunning plan.
He split her up like a flat fish into two halves;
One half of her he established as a covering for heaven.
He fixed a bolt, he stationed a watchman,
And bade them not to let her waters come forth.
He passed through the heavens, he surveyed its regions,
And over against the Deep he set the dwelling of Nudimmud.
And the lord measured the structure of the Deep,
And he founded E-shara, a mansion like it.
The mansion E-shara which he created as heaven,
He caused Anu, Bel, and Ea in their districts to inhabit.
He made the stations for the great gods;
The stars, their images, as the stars of the Zodiac, he fixed.
He ordained the year and into sections he divided it;
For the twelve months he fixed three stars.
. . .

The Moon-god he caused to shine forth, the night he entrusted to him.
He appointed him, a being of the night, to determine the days;
Every month without ceasing with the crown he covered him, saying:
"At the beginning of the month, when you shine on the land,
You command the horns to determine six days,
And on the seventh day to divide the crown."

. . .

When Marduk heard the word of the gods,
His heart prompted him and he devised a cunning plan.
He opened his mouth and to Ea he spoke,
That which he had conceived in his heart he imparted:
"My blood will I take and bone will I fashion,
I will make man . . .
I will create man who shall inhabit the earth,
That the service of the gods may be established, and that their shrines may
    be built."

. . .

Source: L. W. King, *The Seven Tablets of Creation: Or, the Babylonian and Assyrian Legends Concerning the Creation of the World and of Mankind* (London: Luzac and Co., 1902), 2–89, with modifications.

※

2

THE HISTORY OF CREATION

The selection below is from an Egyptian ritual text that describes the belief that Ra, the Egyptian sun god, made a daily trip to the underworld, at which time the god had to overcome the chthonic dragon, Apep. The selected excerpt speaks to beliefs not only about the daily ritual of Ra, but also to Egyptian beliefs concerning Ra's creation of the world (cp. the creation accounts in Gen 1 and 2). The tradition likely dates back to the third millennium BCE.

The Book of Knowing the Evolutions of Ra, and of Overthrowing Apep

[These are] the
words which the god Neb-er-tcher spake after he had
come into being: "I am he who came into being in

the form of the god Kheperà, and I am the creator
of that which came into being, that is to say, I am
the creator everything which came into being;
now the things which I created, and which came
forth out of my mouth after that I had come into
being myself were exceedingly many. The sky (or,
heaven) had not come into being, the earth did not
exist, and the children of the earth, and the creeping
things, had not been made at that time. I
myself raised them up from out of Nu, from a state
of helpless inertness. I found no place whereon I
could stand. I worked a charm upon my own
heart (or, will), I laid the foundation [of things] by
Maāt (a watery mass), and I made everything which had form. I
was [then] one by myself, for I had not emitted from
myself the god Shu, and I had not spit out from
myself the goddess Tefnut; and there existed no
other who could work with me. I laid the
foundations [of things] in my own heart, and
there came into being multitudes of created
things, which came into being from the created
things which were born from the created things
which arose from what they brought forth. I
had union with my closed hand, and I embraced
my shadow as a wife, and I poured seed into
my own mouth, and I sent forth from myself
issue in the form of the gods Shu and Tefnut.
Saith my father Nu: My Eye was covered up
behind them (Shu and Tefnut), but after
two *hen* periods had passed from the time when
they departed from me, from being one god I
became three gods, and I came into being in
the earth. Then Shu and Tefnut rejoiced from
out of the inert watery mass wherein they
were, and they brought to me my Eye (i.e.,
the Sun.) Now after these things I gathered
together my members, and I wept over them,
and men and women sprang into being from
the tears which came forth from my Eye.
And when my Eye came to me, and foundthat I had made another [Eye]
        in the place where
it was (i.e., the Moon), it was wroth with (or,
raged at) me, whereupon I endowed it (the

second Eye) with [some of] the splendor which
I had made for the first [Eye], and I made it
to occupy its place in my Face, and henceforth
it ruled throughout all this earth. When there fell
on them their moment through plant-like clouds,
I restored what had been taken away from them,
and I appeared from out of the plant-like clouds.
I created creeping things of every kind, and every
thing which came into being from them. Shu and
Tefnut brought forth Osiris, and Ḥeru-khent-ȧn-maati,
and Set, and Isis, and Nephthys at one birth, one
after the other, and they produced their multitudinous
offspring in this earth."

SOURCE: E. A. Wallis Budge, *Legends of the Egyptian Gods: Hieroglyphic Texts and Translations* (London: Kegan Paul, 1912), 4–7, with modifications.

3

THE CREATION LEGEND OF RA WORSHIPERS

The following text is the story of creation as told by Ra worshipers reconstructed from Egyptian myths dating to the second millennium BCE. In brief, the account unfolds as follows: first was Nu, the primeval, chaotic waters, and he begat Ra, the sun, who was greater than his father. Next came wind and rain, and then Seb, the earth, and Nut, the firmament. Nut was raised above Seb, her fingertips and toes meeting Seb at the eastern and western horizons (cp. Gen 1).

At the beginning the world was a waste of water called Nu. And it was the abode of the Great Father. He was Nu, for he was the deep, and he gave being to the sun god who has said: "Lo! I am Khepera at dawn, Ra at high noon, and Tum at eventide." The god of brightness first appeared as a shining egg which floated upon the water's breast, and the spirits of the deep, who were the Fathers and the Mothers, were with him there, as he was with Nu, for they were the companions of Nu.

Now Ra was greater than Nu from whom he arose. He was the divine father and strong ruler of gods, and those whom he first created, according to his desire, were Shu, the wind god, and his consort Tefnut, who had the head of a lioness and was called "The Spitter" because she sent the rain. In aftertime these two deities shone as stars amidst the constellations of heaven, and they were called "The Twins."

Then came into being Seb, the earth god, and Nut, the goddess of the firmament, who became the parents of Osiris and his consort Isis and also of Set and his consort Nepthys.

Ra spoke at the beginning of Creation, and bade the earth and the heavens to rise out of the waste of water. In the brightness of his majesty they appeared, and Shu, the uplifter, raised Nut upon high. She formed the vault, which is arched over Seb, the god of earth, who lies prostrate beneath her from where, at the eastern horizon, she is poised upon her toes to where, at the western horizon, bending down with outstretched arms, she rests upon her finger tips. In the darkness are beheld the stars which sparkle upon her body and over her great unwearied limbs.

When Ra, according to his desire, uttered the deep thoughts of his mind, that which he named had being. When he gazed into space, that which he desired to see appeared before him. He created all things that move in the waters and upon the dry land. Now, mankind were born from his eye, and Ra, the Creator, who was ruler of the gods, became the first king upon earth. He went about among men; he took form like unto theirs, and to him the centuries were as years.

SOURCE: Donald Mackenzie, *Egyptian Myth and Legend*, Myth and Legend in Literature and Art (London: Gresham, 1907), 1–2, with modifications.

4

THE HISTORY OF CREATION

The Egyptian Book of the Dead is a collection of mortuary texts often found in tombs with the dead. The texts were written by numerous people over time from the mid-third millennium BCE forward. One such text describes a myth of creation that begins in darkness and watery chaos (cp. Gen 1). Temu (Atum), the text claims, then spoke himself into being, parted the waters, and created the light, the rest of the earth, and all life.

The Egyptian Book of the Dead

At first a voice cried against the darkness, and the voice grew loud enough to stir black waters. It was Temu rising up—his head the thousand-petaled lotus. He uttered the word and one petal drifted from him, taking form on the water. He was the will to live. Out of nothing he created himself, the light. The hand that parted the waters, uplifted the sun and stirred the air. He was the first, the beginning, then all else followed, like petals drifting into the pool.

And I can tell you that story.

It was in a world out of time, for there was neither sun nor moon and nothing to mark the night from day until Temu reached down into the abyss and uplifted Ra. The sun shone on Temu's bright face, day began and Ra lived with him from the beginning of time. That was the first day of the world. In gratitude, the sun raised itself and marked the days' flow.

But on that first day, when Temu held the sun, a spark flew out from him. The globe he held caught and reflected first light. The light flew back and he saw the light was himself, he saw that he was god and only after Temu created Ra was he visible even to himself.

In the beginning the earth languished with the sky, nothing lay between them, neither height nor depth, and they were not separate. Each encompassed the other like a lover, and the power of life pulsed between. At a word, Temu parted them and they became heaven and earth so that the sun might move between, that it might ride over and under the bodies of two worlds giving both its light. There was space above and below and between and on all four sides so that all of the things Temu thought might take shape—beast and stone and season.

Yet because they had lain so long together, heaven and earth were still part of each other. Spirit manifested in matter and matter was infused with spirit. Between them ran three pillars of air, earth and water, and these were named thought, form and desire. The spark of his fire pulsed in all of them and this Temu called life. He created himself and his body burned, writhing with dark shapes. Out of himself he created everything else—in a word: the skies, the oceans, the mountains, the plants, the gods and men, and he named them. Of his fire, made of fire, each held fire of its own; therefore, they created and perpetuated life, a cycle of being without end. Man he gave the power to create himself, to name himself and his destiny and to be in it, living eternally in the company of gods. And Temu is with him.

SOURCE: Normandi Ellis, *Awakening Osiris: A New Translation of The Egyptian Book of the Dead* (Newburyport, Mass.: Phanes Press, 1988), 64–66. © 1988 Normandi Ellis. Used by permission from Red Wheel Weiser, LLC. www.redwheelweiser.com.

5

HESIOD AND CREATION

The Greek poet Hesiod (late eighth–early seventh century BCE), known by many as the "father of Greek didactic poetry," has two surviving works, *Theogony* and *Works and Days*. In the two selections below, Hesiod describes how things came to be. In the *Theogony* excerpt, he explains the birth of the gods, beginning with Chaos, who gave way to the "ever-sure foundation," Earth (cp. Gen 1). In *Works and Days*, the poet addresses his brother, Perses, in an attempt to dissuade him from the pursuit of deceitful gain. He relates the story of Pandora who, out of curiosity, opens a box releasing all manners of woe upon humanity (cp. Gen 2–3).

Hesiod, *Theogony* 104–239

Hail, children of Zeus! Grant lovely song and celebrate the holy race of the deathless gods who are forever, those that were born of Earth and starry Heaven and gloomy Night and them that briny Sea did rear. Tell how, at the first, gods and earth came to be, and rivers, and the boundless sea with its raging swell, and the gleaming stars, and the wide heaven above, and the gods who were born of them, givers of good things, and how they divided their wealth, and how they shared their honors amongst them, and also how at the first they took many-folded Olympus. These things declare to me from the beginning, you Muses who dwell in the house of Olympus, and tell me which of them first came to be.

In truth, at first Chaos came to be, but next, wide-bosomed Earth, the ever-sure foundation of all the deathless ones who hold the peaks of snowy Olympus, and dim Tartarus in the depth of the wide-pathed Earth, and Eros, fairest among the deathless gods, who unnerves the limbs and overcomes the mind and wise counsels of all gods and all men within them. From Chaos came forth Erebus and black Night; but of Night were born Aether and Day, whom she conceived and bore from union in love with Erebus. And Earth first bore starry Heaven, equal to herself, to cover her on every side, and to be an ever-sure abiding place for the blessed gods. And she brought forth long hills, graceful haunts of the goddess Nymphs who dwell amongst the glens of the hills. She bore also the fruitless deep with his raging swell, Pontus, without sweet union of love. But afterwards she lay with

Heaven and bore deep-swirling Oceanus, Coeus and Crius and Hyperion and Iapetus, Theia and Rhea, Themis and Mnemosyne and gold-crowned Phoebe and lovely Tethys. After them was born Cronos the wily, youngest, and most terrible of her children, and he hated his lusty sire.

And again, she bore the Cyclopes, overbearing in spirit, Brontes, and Steropes and stubborn-hearted Arges, who gave Zeus the thunder and made the thunderbolt: in all else they were like the gods, but one eye only was set in the midst of their foreheads. And they were surnamed Cyclopes because one orbed eye was set in their foreheads. Strength and might and craft were in their works. And again, three other sons were born of Earth and Heaven, great and doughty beyond telling, Cottus and Briareos and Gyes, presumptuous children. From their shoulders sprang a hundred arms, not to be approached, and fifty heads grew from the shoulders upon the strong limbs of each, and irresistible was the stubborn strength that was in their great forms. For of all the children that were born of Earth and Heaven, these were the most terrible, and they were hated by their own father from the first. And he used to hide them all away in a secret place of Earth so soon as each was born, and would not suffer them to come up into the light: and Heaven rejoiced in his evil doing. But vast Earth groaned within, being straitened, and she thought a crafty and an evil wile. Forthwith she made the element of grey flint and shaped a great sickle, and told her plan to her dear sons. And she spoke, cheering them, while she was vexed in her dear heart: "My children, gotten of a sinful father, if you will obey me, we should punish the vile outrage of your father; for he first thought of doing shameful things." So she said; but fear seized them all, and none of them uttered a word. But great Cronos the wily took courage and answered his dear mother: "Mother, I will undertake to do this deed, for I reverence not our father of evil name, for he first thought of doing shameful things."

So he said, and vast Earth rejoiced greatly in spirit, and set and hid him in an ambush, and put in his hands a jagged sickle, and revealed to him the whole plot. And Heaven came, bringing on night and longing for love, and he lay about Earth spreading himself full upon her. Then the son from his ambush stretched forth his left hand and in his right took the great long sickle with jagged teeth, and swiftly lopped off his own father's members and cast them away to fall behind him. And not vainly did they fall from his hand; for all the bloody drops that gushed forth Earth received, and as the seasons moved round she bore the strong Erinyes and the great Giants with gleaming armor, holding long spears in their hands and the Nymphs whom they call Meliae all over the boundless earth. And so, as soon as he had cut off the members with flint and cast them from the land into the surging sea, they were swept away over the main a long time: and a white foam spread around them from the immortal flesh, and in it there grew a maiden. First she drew near holy Cythera, and from there, afterwards, she came to sea-girt Cyprus, and came forth an awful and lovely goddess, and grass grew up about her beneath her shapely feet. Her gods and men call Aphrodite, and the foam-born goddess and rich-crowned Cytherea, because she grew amid the foam, and Cytherea because she reached Cythera, and Cyprogenes because she was born in billowy Cyprus, and Philommedes because she sprang from the members. And with her went Eros, and comely Desire followed her at her birth at the first and as she went into the assembly of the gods. This honor she has from the beginning, and this is the portion allotted to her amongst men and undying gods, the whisperings of maidens and smiles and deceits with sweet delight and love and graciousness.

But these sons whom he begot himself great Heaven used to call Titans in reproach, for he said that they strained and did presumptuously a fearful deed, and that vengeance for it would come afterwards. And Night bore hateful Doom and black Fate and Death, and she bore Sleep and the tribe of Dreams. And again the goddess murky Night, though she lay with none, bare Blame and painful Woe, and the Hesperides who guard the rich, golden apples and the trees bearing fruit beyond glorious Ocean. Also she bore the Destinies and ruthless avenging Fates, Clotho and Lachesis and Atropos, who give men at their birth both evil and good to have, and they pursue the transgressions of men and of gods: and these goddesses never cease from their dread anger until they punish the sinner with a sore penalty. Also deadly Night bore Nemesis to afflict mortal men, and after her, Deceit and Friendship and hateful Age and hard-hearted Strife. But abhorred Strife bore painful Toil and Forgetfulness and Famine and tearful Sorrows, Fightings also, Battles, Murders, Manslaughters, Quarrels, Lying Words, Disputes, Lawlessness, and Ruin, all of one nature, and Oath who most troubles men upon earth when anyone willfully swears a false oath. And Sea begat Nereus, the eldest of his children, who is true and lies not: and men call him the Old Man because he is trusty and gentle and does not forget the laws of righteousness, but thinks just and kindly thoughts. And yet again he got great Thaumas and proud Phorcys, being mated with Earth, and fair-cheeked Ceto and Eurybia who has a heart of flint within her.

Hesiod, *Works and Days* 27–105

Perses, lay up these things in your heart, and do not let Strife, who delights in mischief, hold your heart back from work, while you peep and peer and listen to the wrangles of the courthouse. Little concern has he with quarrels and courts who has not a year's victuals laid up in the meantime, even that which the earth bears, Demeter's grain. When you have got plenty of that, you can raise disputes and strive to get another's goods. But you shall have no second chance to deal so again: nay, let us settle our dispute here with true judgment. We divided our inheritance, but you seized the greater share and carried it off, greatly swelling the glory of our bribe-swallowing lords who love to judge such a cause as this. Fools! They know not how much more the half is than the whole, nor what great advantage there is in mallow and asphodel (poor man's fare).

For the gods keep hidden from men the means of life. Else you would easily do work enough in a day to supply you for a full year even without working; soon would you put away your rudder over the smoke, and the fields worked by ox and sturdy mule would run to waste. But Zeus in the anger of his heart hid it, because Prometheus the crafty deceived him; therefore he planned sorrow and mischief against men. He hid fire; but that the noble son of Iapetus stole again for men from Zeus the counsellor in a hollow fennel stalk, so that Zeus who delights in thunder did not see it. But afterwards Zeus who gathers the clouds said to him in anger:

"Son of Iapetus, surpassing all in cunning, you are glad that you have outwitted me and stolen fire, a great plague to you yourself and to men that shall be. But I will give men as the price for fire an evil thing in which they may all be glad of heart while they embrace their own destruction."

So said the father of men and gods, and laughed aloud. And he bade famous Hephaestus make haste and mix earth with water and to put in it the voice and strength of human kind, and fashion a sweet, lovely maiden shape, like to the immortal goddesses in face; and Athene to teach her needlework and the weaving of the varied web; and golden Aphrodite to shed grace upon her head and cruel longing and cares that weary the limbs. And he charged Hermes the guide, the Slayer of Argus, to put in her a shameless mind and a deceitful nature. So he ordered. And they obeyed the lord Zeus the son of Cronos. Forthwith the famous Lame God molded clay in the likeness of a modest maid, as the son of Cronos purposed. And the goddess bright-eyed Athene girded and clothed her, and the divine Graces and queenly Persuasion put necklaces of gold upon her, and the rich-haired Hours crowned her head with spring flowers. And Pallas Athene bedecked her form with all manners of finery. Also the Guide, the Slayer of Argus, contrived within her lies and crafty words and a deceitful nature at the will of loud thundering Zeus, and the Herald of the gods put speech in her. And he called this woman Pandora (All Endowed), because all they who dwelt on Olympus gave each a gift, a plague to men who eat bread.

But when he had finished the sheer, hopeless snare, the Father sent glorious Argus-Slayer, the swift messenger of the gods, to take it to Epimetheus as a gift. And Epimetheus did not think on what Prometheus had said to him, bidding him never take a gift of Olympian Zeus, but to send it back for fear it might prove to be something harmful to men. But he took the gift, and afterwards, when the evil thing was already his, he understood. For ere this the tribes of men lived on earth remote and free from ills and hard toil and heavy sickness which bring the Fates upon men; for in misery men grow old quickly. But the woman took off the great lid of the jar with her hands and scattered all these and her thought caused sorrow and mischief to men. Only Hope remained there in an unbreakable home within under the rim of the great jar, and did not fly out at the door; for ere that, the lid of the jar stopped her, by the will of Aegis-holding Zeus who gathers the clouds. But the rest, countless plagues, wander amongst men; for earth is full of evils and the sea is full. Of themselves diseases come upon men continually by day and by night, bringing mischief to mortals silently; for wise Zeus took away speech from them. So is there no way to escape the will of Zeus.

Source: Hugh Evelyn-White, *Hesiod, Homeric Hymns, Epic Cycle, Homerica*, Loeb Classical Library 57 (Cambridge, Mass.: Harvard University Press, 1914), 4–9, 85–97. Loeb Classical Library® is a registered trademark of the President and Fellows of Harvard College.

6

THE FLOOD

The Mesopotamian Epic of Gilgamesh (second millennium BCE) describes the life of Gilgamesh, the demigod king of Uruk and his best friend, Enkidu. Towards the end of the epic (tablets 10–11), Gilgamesh, on a search for the secret of eternal life, encounters immortal Utnapishtim (elsewhere called Atrahasis) who recounts to Gilgamesh the story of the gods flooding the earth, an event of which he and his wife were the only survivors. The flood story in the Gilgamesh epic has striking similarities to the account of Noah and the flood in Genesis (6–9). The excerpt below is from the Akkadian (Semitic-speaking region of northern Mesopotamia; modern-day central Iraq) version of the Gilgamesh epic based on earlier, Mesopotamian sources.

The Epic of Gilgamesh, Tablet 11

Gilgamesh spoke to him, to Utnapishtim the Distant:
"Utnapishtim, upon you I gaze, yet in no way is your presence
Strange; you are like me, and in no way are you different.
You are like me; a stomach for fighting makes you consummate,
. . . on your back you lie. O tell me, how could you
Stand in the Assembly of Gods to petition for life everlasting?"
Utnapishtim answered Gilgamesh:
"Gilgamesh, to you I will reveal the hidden story.
Aye, and the council of the Gods I will tell you.
The City Shurippak,
It is a city you know—set on the Euphrates,
Old is this city, with gods in its midst. Now, the great gods a deluge
Purposed to bring: . . . there was Anu, their sire; their adviser,
Warrior Enlil; Ninurta, their herald; their leader Ennugi;
Nin-igi-azag—that is Ea—conspirator with them,
To a reed hut their counsel he betrayed: 'O Reed-hut, O Reed-hut!
Wall, wall! Listen, O Reed-hut, consider, O Wall! O you Mortal,
You of Shurippak, you scion of Ubara-Tutu, pull down
A dwelling, and with it fashion a vessel; abandon possessions,
Life do you seek, and your hoard disregard, and save life; every creature
Make to enter into the vessel. The vessel, which you are to fashion,
Apt be its measure; its beam and its length be in due correspondence,
Then launch it on the deep.' And I, apprehending,
wisdom to Ea, my lord, did I speak: 'Lord, what you say
Thus, will I honor, I'll do this, but to city, to people, and elders
Am I, able to explain?' Then Ea made answer in speaking,
Saying to me, me, his henchman, 'You mortal, shall speak to them this way:
"It is me alone whom Enlil so hates that I in your city
No more may dwell, nor turn my face to the land which is Enlil's.
I will go down to the Deep, there dwelling with Ea, my lord,
Wherefore on you he will shower down plenty, fowl in great number,

Plenty of fish . . . . and great harvest.
. . . causing a plentiful rainfall to come down upon you." '
Then when morning had dawned . . .
The children provided pitch, while the strong brought all that was needed.
Then on the fifth day, after I laid out the shape of my vessel,
Ten *gar* each was the height of its sides, in accord with its planning,
Ten *gar* to match was the size of its deck, and the shape of the forepart
I laid down, and I fashioned the same; six times cross-pinned it,
Sevenfold I divided it . . . divided its inwards
Ninefold: hammered the caulking within it, and found a quant pole,
All that was needed I added; the hull with six *shar* of bitumen
I smeared, and three *shar* of pitch I smeared on the inside; some people,
Bearing a vessel of grease, brought me three *shar* of it; and one *shar*
Out of this grease I left, which the tackling consumed; and the boatman
Stowed away two *shar* of grease; cattle . . . I slaughtered,
Each day I slaughtered lambs: mead, beer, oil, wine, too, the workmen
Drank as though they were water, and made a great feast like the New Year.
All I possessed I laded on it; the silver I laded
All I possessed; gold, all I possessed I laded aboard it,
All I possessed of the seed of all living I laded aboard it.
Into the ship I embarked all my kin and family,
Cattle and beasts of the field and all handicraftsmen embarking.
Then Shamash decreed the hour: . . .
'In the night let a plentiful rainfall pour down . . .
Then you shall enter the vessel, and shut down your hatchway.'
Then the appointed hour came . . .
In the night let a plentiful rainfall pour down . . .
 I viewed the aspect of day: to look on the day bore a horror,
I entered the vessel, and shut down my hatchway,
So, too, to shut down the vessel to Puzur-Amurri, the boatman,
Did I deliver the deck of the ship, besides its equipment.
Then, when dawn appeared, on the horizon
A cloud rose darkling; lo, Adad (the storm god) was rumbling within it,
Nabu and Sharru were leading the vanguard, and coming as heralds
Over the hills and the levels: then Irragal wrenched out the bollar
Havoc Ninurta let loose as he came, the Anunnaki their torches
Brandished, and shriveled the land with their flames; desolation from Adad
Stretched to Heaven, and all that was bright was turned into darkness.
Nor could a brother distinguish his brother, from heaven mortals
Were not seen. O, the gods were stricken with terror at the Deluge.
Fleeing, they rose to the Heaven of Anu, and crouched in the outskirts,
The gods were cowering like curs, like a woman in childbirth
Ishtar cried, she shrieking aloud, the sweet-spoken Lady:

'May that day turn to dust, because I spoke evil
In the Assembly of Gods! O, how could I utter such evil
In the Assembly of Gods, so to blot out my people, ordaining
Havoc! Sooth, then, am I to give birth, to my own people
Only to glut with their bodies the Sea as though they were fish spawn?'
Gods—Anunnaki—wept with her, the gods were sitting humbled
In their weeping, and their lips were closed in the Assembly.
Six days, and six nights the hurricane, deluge, and tempest continued
Sweeping the land: when the seventh day came, the warfare was quelled,
Tempest and deluge like to an army embattled were fighting.
The sea was lulled, the gale was spent, the deluge was assuaged.
I looked on the day; sound was stilled; and all humanity
Was returned to clay, and fen was level with tree.
I opened a hatchway, and sunlight streamed down on my cheek.
Bowing, I sat weeping, my tears overflowing my cheek,
Into the distance I gazed, to the furthest bounds of the Ocean,
Land was upreared at twelve points, and the Ark on the Mountain of Nisir
Settled; the Mountain of Nisir held fast, and did not give lease to
    its shifting.
One day, two, did Nisir hold fast, and did not give lease to its shifting.
Three days, four, did Nisir hold fast, and did not give lease to its shifting.
Five days, six, did Nisir hold fast, and did not give lease to its shifting.
When the seventh day dawned, I put forth a dove, and released it.
To and fro went the dove, and returned for there was not a resting place.
I put forth a swallow and released it; to and fro went the swallow.
She too returned, for there was not a resting place; I put forth a raven.
Her, too, releasing; the raven went, too, and saw the abating waters,
And she ate as she waded and splashed, not returning.
Unto the four winds I freed all the beasts, and an offering I
Sacrificed, and a libation I poured on the peak of the mountain,
Twice seven flagons devoting, and sweet cane, and cedar, and myrtle,
I heaped up beneath them; the gods smelt the savor, the gods the sweet savor
Smelt; the gods did assemble like flies over him making the offering.
Then, on arriving, the Queen of the gods the magnificent jewels
Lifted on high, which Anu had made in accord with her wishes:
'O Gods! I would rather forget my necklet of sapphires
Than not maintain these days in remembrance, nor ever forget them.
Though the rest of the gods may present themselves at the offering,
Enlil may himself not come to the offering,
Because he, unreasoning, brought on a deluge, and therefore my people
Consigned to destruction.'
Then Enlil, on his arrival,
Spied out the vessel, and Enlil burst into anger,

Swollen with wrath against the gods, the Igigi: 'Has any mortal
Escaped? Sooth, never a man could have lived through ruin.'
Then Ninurta made answer and spoke to warrior Enlil,
Saying: 'O, who can there be to devise such a plan, except Ea?
Surely, Ea is privy to every design.' Ea
Answered and spoke to Enlil, the warrior, saying: 'O chieftain
You of the gods, thou warrior! How, forsooth, how all uncounseled
Could you bring on a deluge? Visit his sin on the sinner,
Visit his guilt on the guilty, but O, have mercy, that
He shall not be cut off; be clement, that he may not perish.
O, instead of making a flood, let a lion come, man to diminish;
O, instead of making a flood, let a jackal come, man to diminish;
O, instead of making a flood, let a famine occur, that the country
May be devoured; instead of making a flood, let the Plague-god
Come and the people be overwhelmed;
Sooth, indeed it was not I of the Great Gods who revealed the secret,
But to the Abounding in Wisdom I vouchsafed a dream, and in this way
He of the gods heard the secret. Deliberate, now, on his counsel.'
Then Enlil came up to the Ark; he grasped my hand, and uplifted
Me, even me, and my wife, too, he raised, and, bent-kneed beside me,
Made her to kneel; our foreheads he touched as he stood there between us,
Blessing us: 'Utnapishtim has hitherto only been mortal,
Now, indeed, Utnapishtim and his wife shall be equal
Like to us gods; in the distance afar at the mouth of the rivers
Utnapishtim shall dwell.' So they took me and there in the distance
Caused me to dwell at the mouth of the rivers . . ."

SOURCE: R. Campbell Thompson, *The Epic of Gilgamish: A New Translation from a Collation of the Cuneiform Tablets in the British Museum Rendered Literally into English Hexameters* (London: Luzac & Co., 1928), 49–54, with modifications.

B. LAW AND RITUAL

The Torah contains numerous individual law codes such as the Covenant Code (Exod 20–23), the law code in Deuteronomy, and the Holiness Code (Lev 17–26). The laws in these codes contain regulations on a wide range of topics, such as (but not limited to) family relationships, ritual stipulations for priests and the general population, food, agricultural and business practices, relationships with foreign powers, religious practices, and ordinances against various social behaviors. There are numerous law codes from the ancient Near East that have both similar regulations and literary formats. The selections below are Amorite, Sumerian, Hittite, Assyrian, Egyptian, Ugaritic, and Hurrian, and date from the third millennium BCE to the seventh century BCE.

7

CODE OF HAMMURABI

Hammurabi was an Amorite (Old Babylonian Dynasty ruling southern Mesopotamia) king in the second millennium BCE. The following text claims that the gods commissioned Hammurabi to write down the law code, an excerpt of which is given below, in order to establish justice in the land. The code includes laws concerning theft, property ownership, loans and debts, marriage and family, slaves, and commerce. The code has parallels to many of the laws in Exodus 20–23 as well as similarities to the marriage customs demonstrated in the stories of the biblical ancestors (see for example Gen 16; 30; 24:53-61; 31:14-18)

Prologue

When the lofty Anu, king of the Anunnaki, and Bel, lord of heaven and earth, he who determines the destiny of the land, committed the rule of all mankind to Marduk, the chief son of Ea; when they made him great among the Igigi; when they pronounced the lofty name of Babylon; when they made it famous among the quarters of the world and in its midst established an everlasting kingdom whose foundations were firm as heaven and earth, at that time, Anu and Bell called me, Hammurabi, the exalted prince, the worshiper of the gods, to cause justice to prevail in the land, to destroy the wicked and the evil, to prevent the strong from oppressing the weak, to go forth like the Sun over the Black Head Race, to enlighten the land and to further the welfare of the people. Hammurabi, the governor named by Bel, am I, who brought about plenty and abundance; who made everything for Nippur and Durilu complete; the exalted supporter of E-kur; the wise king, who restored Eridu to its place; who purified the sanctuary of E-apsu; who stormed the four quarters of the world; who made the fame of Babylon great; who rejoiced the heart of Marduk his lord . . . when Marduk sent me to rule the people and to bring help to the country, I established law and justice in the land and promoted the welfare of the people.

Law Code

If a man brings an accusation against a man, and charges him with a capital crime, but cannot prove it, he, the accuser, shall be put to death.

If a man charges a man with sorcery, and cannot prove it, he who is charged with sorcery shall go to the river and throw himself into the river, and if the river overcomes him, his accuser will take for himself his house. If the river shows that man to be innocent and he comes forth unharmed, he who charged him with sorcery shall be put to death. He who threw himself into the river shall take for himself the house of his accuser.

If a man in a case pending judgment, bears threatening witness or does not establish the testimony that he has given, if that case is a case involving life, that man shall be put to death.

If a man bears witness for grain or money, he shall himself bear the penalty imposed in that case.

If a judge pronounces a judgment, renders a decision, or delivers a verdict duly signed and sealed and afterwards alters his judgment, they shall call that judge to account for the alteration of the judgment which he had pronounced, and he shall pay twelvefold the penalty which was in said judgment; and, in the assembly, they shall expel him from his seat of judgment, and he shall not return and with the judges in a case he shall not take his seat.

If a man steals the property of a god or palace, that man shall be put to death; and he who receives from his hand the stolen property shall also be put to death.

If a man purchases silver or gold, manservant or maid servant, ox, sheep or ass, or anything else from a man's son, or from a man's servant without witnesses or contracts, or if he receives in trust, that man shall be put to death as a thief.

If a man steals ox or sheep, ass or pig, or boat, if it is from a god or a palace, he shall restore thirtyfold; if it is from a freeman, he shall render tenfold. If the thief has nothing with which to pay, he shall be put to death.

If a man, who has lost anything, finds that which was lost in the possession of another man, and the man in whose possession the lost property is found says, "It was sold to me, I purchased it in the presence of witnesses," and the owner of the lost property says, "I will bring witnesses to identify my lost property": if the purchaser produces the seller who has sold it to him and the witnesses in whose presence he purchased it, and the owner of the lost property produces witnesses to identify his lost property, the judges shall consider their evidence. The witnesses in whose presence the purchase was made and the witnesses to identify the lost property shall give their testimony in the presence of god. The seller shall be put to death as a thief; the owner of the lost property shall recover his loss; the purchaser shall recover from the estate of the seller the money which he paid out.

If the purchaser does not produce the seller who sold it to him, and the witnesses in whose presence he purchased it, and if the owner of the lost property produces witnesses to identify his lost property, the purchaser shall be put to death as a thief; the owner of the lost property shall recover his loss. If the owner of the lost property does not produce witnesses to identify his lost property, he has attempted fraud, he has stirred up strife; he shall be put to death.

If the seller has gone to his fate, the purchaser shall recover damages in said case fivefold from the estate of the seller. If the witnesses of that man are not at hand, the judges shall declare a postponement for six months; and if he does not bring in his witnesses within the six months, that man has attempted fraud, he shall himself bear the penalty imposed in that case.

If a man steals a man's son, who is a minor, he shall be put to death.

If a man aids a male or female slave of the palace, or a male or female slave of a freeman to escape from the city gate, he shall be put to death. If a man harbors in his house a male or female slave who has fled from the palace or from a freeman, and does not bring him forth at the call of the commandant, the owner of that house shall be put to death.

If a man seizes a male or female slave, a fugitive, in the field and brings that slave back to his owner, the owner of the slave shall pay him two shekels of silver. If that slave will not name his owner, he shall bring him to the palace and they shall inquire into his antecedents and they shall return him to his owner.

If he detains that slave in his house and later the slave is found in his possession, that man shall be put to death. If the slave escapes from the hand of his captor, that man shall so declare, in the name of god, to the owner of the slave and shall go free.

If a man makes a breach in a house, they shall put him to death in front of that breach and they shall thrust him therein.

If a man practices brigandage and is captured, that man shall be put to death. If the brigand is not captured, the man who has been robbed, shall, in the presence of god, make an itemized statement of his loss, and the city and the governor, in whose province and jurisdiction the robbery was committed, shall compensate him for whatever was lost.

If it is a life that is lost, the city and governor shall pay one mana of silver to his heirs.

If a fire breaks out in a man's house and a man who goes to extinguish it casts his eye on the furniture of the owner of the house, and takes the furniture of the owner of the house, that man shall be thrown into that fire.

If either an officer or a constable, who is ordered to go on an errand of the king, does not go but hires a substitute and dispatches him in his stead, that officer or constable shall be put to death; his hired substitute shall take to himself the officer's house.

If an officer or a constable, who is in a garrison of the king, is captured, and afterward they give his field and garden to another and he conducts his business, if the former returns and arrives in his city, his field and garden shall be returned to him, and he himself shall conduct his business.

If an officer or a constable, who is in a fortress of the king, is captured and his son is able to conduct the business, they shall give him the field and garden, and he shall conduct the business of his father. If his son is too young and is not able to conduct the business of his father, they shall give one-third of the field and of the garden to his mother, and his mother shall rear him.

If an officer or a constable from the beginning of his business neglects his field, his garden, and his house, and leaves them uncared for and another after him takes his field, his garden, and his house, and conducts his business for three years; if the former returns and desires his field, his garden and his house, they shall not give them to him; he who has taken them and conducted the business shall continue to do so. If he leaves them uncared for but one year and returns, they shall give him his field, his garden, and his house, and he himself shall continue his business.

If a merchant ransoms either an officer or a constable who has been captured on an errand of the king, and enables him to reach his city; if there is sufficient ransom in his house, he shall ransom himself; if there is not sufficient ransom in his house, in the temple of his city he shall be ransomed; if there is not sufficient ransom in the temple of his city, the palace shall ransom him. In no case shall his field or his garden or his house be given for his ransom.

If a governor or a magistrate takes possession of the men of levy or accept and send a hired substitute on an errand of the king, that governor or magistrate shall be put to death.

If a governor or magistrate takes the property of an officer, plunders an officer, lets an officer for hire, presents an officer in a judgment to a man of influence, takes the gift which the king has given to an officer, that governor or magistrate shall be put to death.

If a man buys from an officer the cattle or ship which the king has given to that officer, he shall forfeit his money.

In no case shall one sell the field or garden or house of an officer, constable or tax gatherer. If a man purchases the field or garden or house of an officer, constable or tax gatherer, his deed tablet shall be broken and he shall forfeit his money and he shall return the field, garden or house to its owner.

An officer, constable or tax gatherer shall not deed to his wife or daughter the field, garden, or house, which is his business, nor shall he assign them for debt. He may deed to his wife or daughter the field, garden, or house which he has purchased and possesses, or he may assign them for debt.

A woman, merchant, or other property holder may sell field, garden, or house. The purchaser shall conduct the business of the field, garden, or house which he has purchased. If a man has bargained for the field, garden, or house of an officer, constable, or tax gatherer and given sureties, the officer, constable, or tax gatherer shall return to his field, garden, or house, and he shall take to himself the sureties which were given to him.

If a man rents a field for cultivation and does not produce any grain in the field, they shall call him to account, because he has not performed the work required on the field, and he shall give to the owner of the field grain on the basis of the adjacent fields. If he does not cultivate the field and neglect it, he shall give to the owner of the field grain on the basis of the adjacent fields; and the field which he has neglected, he shall break up with hoes, he shall harrow and he shall return to the owner of the field.

If a man rents an unreclaimed field for three years to develop it, and neglects it and does not develop the field, in the fourth year he shall break up the field with hoes, he shall hoe and harrow it, and he shall return it to the owner of the field and shall measure out ten *gur* of grain per ten *gan*.

If a man rents his field to a tenant for crop rent and receives the crop rent of his field and later Adad inundates the field and carries away the produce, the loss falls on the tenant.

If he has not received the rent of his field and he has rented the field for either one-half or one-third of the crop, the tenant and the owner of the field shall divide the grain which is in the field according to agreement. If the tenant gives the cultivation of the field into the charge of another, because in a former year he has not gained a maintenance, the owner of the field shall not interfere. He would cultivate it, and his field has been cultivated and at the time of harvest he shall take grain according to his contracts.

If a man owes a debt and Adad inundates his field and carries away the produce, or, through lack of water, grain has not grown in the field, in that year he shall not make any return of grain to the creditor, he shall alter his contract tablet and he shall not pay the interest for that year.

If a man obtains money from a merchant and gives to the merchant a field to be planted with grain and sesame and says to him: "Cultivate the field, and harvest and take for yourself the grain and sesame which is produced"; if the tenant raises grain and sesame in the field, at the time of harvest, the owner of the field shall receive the grain and sesame which is in the field and he shall give to the merchant grain for the loan which he had obtained from him and for the interest and for the maintenance of the tenant.

If he gives a field planted with grain or a field planted with sesame, the owner of the field shall receive the grain or the sesame which is in the field and he shall return the loan and its interest to the merchant. If he has not the money to return, he shall give to the merchant grain or sesame, at their market value according to the scale fixed by the king, for the loan and its interest which he has obtained from the merchant. If the tenant does not secure a crop of grain or sesame in his field, he shall not cancel his contract.

If a man neglects to strengthen his dyke and does not strengthen it, and a break is made in his dyke and the water carries away the farmland, the man in whose dyke the break has been made shall restore the grain which he has damaged. If he is not able to restore the grain, they shall sell him and his goods, and the farmers whose grain the water has carried away shall share the results of the sale.

If a man opens his canal for irrigation and neglects it and the water carries away an adjacent field, he shall measure out grain on the basis of the adjacent fields. If a man opens up the water and the water carries away the improvements of an adjacent field, he shall measure out ten *gur* of grain per *gan*.

If a shepherd has not come to an agreement with the owner of a field to pasture his sheep on the grass; and if he pasture his sheep on the field without the consent of the owner, the owner of the field shall harvest his field, and the shepherd who has pastured his sheep on the field without the consent of the owner of the field shall give over and above twenty *gur* of grain per ten *gan* to the owner of the field.

If, after the sheep have gone up from the meadow and have crowded their way out of the gate into the public common, the shepherd turn the sheep into the field, and pasture the sheep on the field, the shepherd shall oversee the field on which he pastures and at the time of harvest he shall measure out sixty *gur* of grain per ten *gan* to the owner of the field.

. . .

If a wine seller does not receive grain as the price of drink, but if she receives money by the great stone, or makes the measure for drink smaller than the measure for corn, they shall call that wine seller to account, and they shall throw her into the water.

If outlaws collect in the house of a wine seller, and she does not arrest these outlaws and bring them to the palace, that wine seller shall be put to death.

. . .

If a man is on a journey and he gives silver, gold, stones, or portable property to a man with a commission for transportation, and if that man does not deliver that which was to be transported where it was to be transported, but takes it for himself, the owner of the transported goods shall call that man to account for the goods to be transported which he did not deliver, and that man shall deliver to the owner of the transported goods fivefold the amount which was given to him.

If a man holds a debt of grain or money against a man, and if he takes grain without the consent of the owner from the heap or the granary, they shall call that man to account for taking grain without the consent of the owner from the heap or the granary, and he shall return as much grain as he took, and he shall forfeit all that he has lent, whatever it be.

. . .

If a man is in debt and sells his wife, son, or daughter, or binds them over to service, for three years they shall work in the house of their purchaser or master; in the fourth year they shall be given their freedom. If he binds over to service a male or female slave, and if the merchant transfers or sells such slave, there is no cause for complaint.

If a man is in debt and he sells his maid servant who has borne him children, the owner of the maid servant shall repay the money which the merchant paid, and he shall ransom his maid servant.

If a man stores his grain in bins in the house of another and an accident happens to the granary, or the owner of the house opens a bin and takes grain or he raises a dispute about the amount of grain which was stored in his house, the owner of the grain shall declare his grain in the presence of god, and the owner of the house shall double the amount of the grain which he took and restore it to the owner of the grain.

. . .

If a man points the finger at a priestess or the wife of another and cannot justify it, they shall drag that man before the judges and they shall brand his forehead.

If a man takes a wife and does not arrange with her the proper contracts, that woman is not a legal wife.

If the wife of a man is taken in lying with another man, they shall bind them and throw them into the water. If the husband of the woman would save his wife, or if the king would save his male servant, he may.

If a man forces the betrothed of another who has not known a male and is living in her father's house, and he lies in her bosom and they take him, that man shall be put to death and that woman shall go free.

If a man accuses his wife and she has not been taken in lying with another man, she shall take an oath in the name of god and she shall return to her house.

. . .

If a man is captured and there is no maintenance in his house, and his wife openly enters into another house and bears children; if later her husband returns and arrives in his city, that woman shall return to her husband and the children shall go to their father.

If a man deserts his city and flees and afterwards his wife enters into another house; if that man returns and would take his wife, the wife of the fugitive shall not return to her husband because he hated his city and fled.

If a man sets his face to put away a concubine who has borne him children or a wife who has presented him with children, he shall return to that woman her dowry and shall give to her the income of field, garden, and goods, and she shall bring up her children; from the time that her children are grown up, from whatever is given to her children they shall give to her a portion corresponding to that of a son and the man of her choice may marry her.

If a man would put away his wife who has not borne him children, he shall give her money to the amount of her marriage settlement and he shall make good to her the dowry which she brought from her father's house and then he may put her away.

. . .

If a man takes a wife and that gives a maid servant to her husband and she bears children; if that man sets his face to take a concubine, they shall not countenance him. He may not take a concubine.

If a man takes a wife and she do not present him with children and he sets his face to take a concubine, that man may take a concubine and brings her into his house. That concubine shall not rank with his wife.

If a man takes a wife and she gives a maidservant to her husband, and that maidservant bears children and afterwards would take rank with her mistress; because she has borne children, her mistress may not sell her for money, but she may reduce her to bondage and count her among the maidservants. If she has not borne children, her mistress may sell her for money.

. . .

If a woman, who dwells in the house of a man, makes a contract with her husband that a creditor of his may not hold her for his debts and compels him to deliver a written agreement; if that man were in debt before he took that woman, his creditor may not hold his wife, and if that woman were in debt before she entered into the house of the man, her creditor may not hold her husband.

If they contract a debt after the woman has entered into the house of the man, both of them shall be answerable to the merchant.

If a man has known his daughter, they shall expel that man from the city.

If a man has betrothed a bride to his son and his son has known her, and if the father afterward lies in her bosom and they take him, they shall bind that man and throw him into the water.

If a man has betrothed a bride to his son and his son has not known her but he himself lies in her bosom, he shall pay her one-half mana of silver and he shall make good to her whatever she brought from the house of her father and the man of her choice may take her.

. . .

If a man takes a wife and she does not present him with children and that woman dies, if his father-in-law returns to him the marriage settlement which that man brought to the house of his father-in-law, her husband may not lay claim to the dowry of that woman. Her dowry belongs to the house of her father.

. . .

If a man's wife bears him children and his maidservant bears him children, and the father during his lifetime says to the children which the maid servant bore him: "My children," and reckons them with the children of his wife, after the father dies the children of the wife and the children of the maidservant shall divide the goods of the father's house equally. The child of the wife shall have the right of choice at the division.

. . .

If a man gives his son to a nurse and that son dies in the hands of the nurse, and the nurse substitutes another son without the consent of his father or mother, they shall call her to account, and because she has substituted another son without the consent of his father or mother, they shall cut off her breast.

If a son strikes his father, they shall cut off his fingers. If a man destroys the eye of another man, they shall destroy his eye. If one breaks a man's bone, they shall break his bone. If one destroys the eye of a freeman or break the bone of a freeman, he shall pay one mana of silver. If one destroys the eye of a man's slave or breaks a bone of a man's slave he shall pay one-half his price.

. . .

Epilogue

The righteous laws, which Hammurabi, the wise king, established and by which he gave the land stable support and pure government. Hammurabi, the perfect king, am I. I was not careless, nor was I neglectful of the Black-Head people, whose rule Bel presented and Marduk delivered to me. I provided them with a peaceful country. I opened up difficult barriers and lent them support. With the powerful weapon which Za-má-má and Nana entrusted to me, with the breadth of vision which Ea allotted me, with the might which Marduk gave me, I expelled the enemy to the North and South; I made an end of their raids: I brought health to the land; I made the populace to rest in security; I permitted no one to molest them.

The great gods proclaimed me and I am the guardian governor, whose scepter is righteous and whose beneficent protection is spread over my city. In my bosom I carried the people of the land of Sumer and Akkad; under my protection I brought their brethren into security; in my wisdom I restrained them; that the strong might not oppose the weak, and that they should give justice to the orphan and the widow, in Babylon, the city whose turrets Anu and Bel raised; in Esagila, the temple whose foundations are firm as heaven and earth, for the pronouncing of judgments in the land, for the rendering of decisions for the land, and for the righting of wrong, my weighty words I have written upon my monument, and in the presence of my image as king of righteousness have I established.

The king, who is preeminent among city kings, am I. My words are precious, my wisdom is unrivaled. By the command of Shamash, the great judge of heaven and earth, may I make righteousness to shine forth on the land. By the order of Marduk, my lord, may no one efface my statutes, may my name be remembered with favor in Esagila forever. Let any oppressed man, who has a cause, come before my image as king of righteousness! Let him read the inscription on my monument! Let him give heed to my weighty words! And may my monument enlighten him as to his cause and may he understand his case! May he set his heart at ease! "Hammurabi indeed is a ruler who is like a real father to his people; he has given reverence to the words of Marduk, his lord; he has obtained victory for Marduk in North and South; he has made glad the heart of Marduk, his lord; he has established prosperity for the people for all time and given a pure government to the land." Let him read the code and pray with a full heart before Marduk, my lord, and Zarpanit, my lady, and may the protecting deities, the gods who enter Esagila, daily in the midst of Esagila look with favor on his wishes in the presence of Marduk, my lord, and Zarpanit, my lady!

In the days that are yet to come, for all future time, may the king who is in the land observe the words of righteousness which I have written upon my monument! May he not alter the judgments of the land which I have pronounced, or the decisions of the country which I have rendered! May he not efface my statues! If that man has wisdom, if he wishes to give his land good government, let him give attention to the words which I have written upon my monument! And may this monument enlighten him as to procedure and administration, the judgments which I have pronounced, and the decisions which I have rendered for the land! And let him rightly rule his Black-Head people; let him pronounce judgments for them and render for them decisions! Let him root out the wicked and evildoer from his land! Let him promote the welfare of his people!

Hammurabi, the king of righteousness, whom Shamash has endowed with justice, am I. My words are weighty; my deeds are unrivaled . . .

If that man pays attention to my words which I have written upon my monument, does not efface my judgments, does not overrule my words, and does not alter my statutes, then will Shamash prolong that man's reign, as he has mine, who am king of righteousness, that he may rule his people in righteousness.

If that man does not pay attention to my words which I have written upon my monument: if he forgets my curse and does not fear the curse of god; if he abolishes the judgments which I have formulated, overrules my words, alters my statutes, effaces my name written thereon and writes his own name; on account of these curses, commissions another to do so, as for that man, be he king or lord, or priest-king or commoner, whoever he may be, may the great god, the father of the gods, who has ordained my reign, take from him the glory of his sovereignty, may he break his scepter, and curse his fate!

May Bel, the lord, who determines destinies, whose command cannot be altered, who has enlarged my dominion, drive him out from his dwelling through a revolt which his hand cannot control and a curse destructive to him. May he determine as his fate a reign of sighs, days few in number, years of famine, darkness without light, death staring him in the face! The destruction of his city, the dispersion of his people, the wresting away of his dominion, the blotting out of his name and memory from the land, may Bel order with his potent command! . . .

SOURCE: Robert Francis Harper, *The Code of Ḥammurabi King of Babylon*, 2nd edition (Chicago: University of Chicago Press, 1904), 3–105, with modifications.

8

CODE OF LIPIT-ISHTAR

The law code of Lipit-Ishtar is a Sumerian (southern Mesopotamia; modern-day southern Iraq) law text from the second half of the third millennium BCE written by Lipit-Ishtar, it states, at the command of the gods in order to establish justice for the Sumerians and Akkadians (Semitic-speaking region of northern Mesopotamia; modern-day central Iraq). The code includes laws on topics such as real estate, land, inheritance, marriage, property damage, and slaves. The text was discovered in Nippur (modern-day southeastern Iraq), once a religious center of Mesopotamia. Like the Code of Hammurabi, this older code contains parallels to the law codes of the Hebrew Bible.

Prologue

. . . when Anu and Enlil had called Lipit-Ishtar—Lipit-Ishtar the wise shepherd whose name had been pronounced by Nunamnir—to the princeship of the land in order to establish justice in the land, to banish complaints, to turn back enmity and rebellion by force of arms, and to bring well-being to the Sumerians and the Akkadians, then I, Lipit-Ishtar, the humble shepherd of Nippur, the stalwart farmer of Ur, who abandons not Eridu, the suitable lord of Erech, [king] of I[sin], [kin]g of Sum[er and Akkad], who am f[it] for the heart of Inanna, [estab]lished [jus]tice in [Su]mer and Akkad in accordance with the word of Enlil. . . .

Law Code

If a man gave bare ground to (another) man to set out as an orchard and (the latter) did not complete setting out that bare ground as an orchard, he shall give to the man who set out the orchard the bare ground which he neglected as part of his share.

If a man entered the orchard of (another) man and was seized there for stealing, he shall pay ten shekels of silver.

If a man cut down a tree in the garden of (another) man, he shall pay one-half mina of silver.

If adjacent to the house of a man the bare ground of (another) man has been neglected and the owner of the house has said to the owner of the bare ground, "Because your ground has been neglected someone may break into my house: strengthen your house," and this agreement has been confirmed by him, the owner of the bare ground shall restore to the owner of the house any of his property that is lost.

If a slave girl or slave of a man has fled into the heart of the city and it has been confirmed that he (or she) dwelt in the house of (another) man for one month, he shall give slave for slave.

If he has no slave, he shall pay fifteen shekels of silver.

If a man's slave has compensated his slaveship to his master and it is confirmed (that he has compensated) his master twofold, that slave shall be freed.

. . .

If a man without authorization bound (another) man to a matter of which he (the latter) had no knowledge, that man is not affirmed (i.e., legally obligated); he (the first man) shall bear the penalty in regard *to the matter to which he had bound him.*

If the master of an estate or the mistress of an estate has defaulted on the tax of the estate and a stranger has borne it, for three years he (the owner) may not be evicted. (Afterwards), the man who bore the tax of the estate shall possess that estate and the (former) owner of the estate shall not raise any claim.

. . .

[I]f the secon[d wife] whom [he had] married bore him [chi]ldren, the dowry which she brought from her father's house belongs to her children (but) the children of (his) first wife and the children of (his) second wife shall divide equally the property of their father.

If a man married a wife and she bore him children and those children are living, and a slave also bore children for her master (but) the father granted freedom to the slave and her children, the children of the slave shall not divide the estate with the children of their (former) master.

. . .

If a man's wife has not borne him children but a harlot (from) the public square has borne him children, he shall provide grain, oil, and clothing for that harlot; the children which the harlot has borne him shall be his heirs, and as long as his wife lives the harlot shall not live in the house with the wife.

If a man has turned his face away *from* his first wife . . . but she has not moved out of the [house]; his wife, which he married *as his favorite,* is a second wife; he shall continue to support his first wife.

If a son-in-law has entered the house of his (prospective) father-in-law and he made his betrothal and afterwards they made him go out (of the house) and gave his wife to his companion; they shall present to him the betrothal gifts which he brought and that wife may not marry his companion.

. . .

Epilogue

Verily, in accordance with the tr[ue word] of Utu, I caused Sumer and Akkad to hold to true justice. Verily, in accordance with the pronouncement of Enlil, I, Lipit-Ishtar, the son of Enlil, abolished enmity and rebellion; made weeping, lamentations, and . . . caused righteousness and truth to shine forth; brought well-being to the Sumerians and Akkadians. . . .

Verily, when I had established the wealth of Sumer and Akkad, I erected this stele.

May he who will not commit any evil deed *with regard to it*, who will not damage my handiwork, who will [not] erase its inscription, who will not write his own name upon it—be presented with life and breath of long days; may he rise high in the Ekur; may Enlil's bright forehead look down upon him.

. . .

Source: Francis Steele, "The Code of Lipit-Ishtar," *American Journal of Archeology* 52 (1948): 425–50, translation 432–45. Used by permission of the publisher.

9

TREATY BETWEEN MURSILI II OF HATTI AND TUPPI-TESHSHUP OF AMURRU

There are several extant treaties establishing the relationship between the Hittite suzerain (overlord) and their vassal states. These treaties follow a basic pattern: (1) the identity of the Hittite king; (2) the history of the relationship between the two parties; (3) the rules of the relationship including the duties of the vassal country and the Hittite king; (4) a list of divine witnesses; and (5) a list of potential blessings and curses based on the vassal's adherence or nonadherence to the treaty rules (cp. Deuteronomy). The following text from the second millennium BCE is the treaty between the Hittite king Mursili and Tuppi-Teshshup, king of Amurru (Amorite kingdom spanning modern-day Syria and Lebanon).

History of the Relationship between Hatti and Amurru

[Thus says] My Majesty, Mursili, [Great King, King of Hatti], Hero, Beloved of the Storm-god; [son of] Suppiluliuma, [Great King, King of Hatti, Hero]:

Aziru, your [grandfather, Tuppi-Teshshup], became the subject of my father. When it came about that the kings of the land of Nuhashshi [and the king of the land of Kinza became hostile (to my father)], Aziru did not become hostile. [When my father made war on his enemies], Aziru likewise made war. And Aziru protected only my father, and my father protected [Aziru], together with his land. [He did not seek] to harm him in any way. [And Aziru] did not anger [my father] in any way. He always paid him [the 300 shekels of refined, first-class gold which] he had imposed [as tribute]. My father died, and I [took my seat] upon the throne [of my father]. But [as] Aziru had been in [the time of my father], so he was in my time.

. . . [And when Aziru became an old man] and was no longer able to go on military campaign as he had always gone to war [with infantry] and chariotry, [then] Ari-Teshshup [likewise went to war with the infantry and chariotry of the land of Amurru]. And My Majesty destroyed those [enemies . . .]

But when your father died, according to [the request of your father], I did not cast you off. Because your father had spoken your name before me during his lifetime(?), I therefore took care of you. But you were sick and ailing. [And] although you were an invalid, I nonetheless installed you [in] place of your father. . . .

Details of the Treaty

And as I took care of you according to the request of your father, and installed you in place of your father, I have now made you swear an oath to the King of Hatti and the land of Hatti, and to my sons and grandsons. Observe the oath and the authority of the King. I, My Majesty, will protect you, Tuppi-Teshshup. And when you take a wife and produce a son, he shall later be king in the land of Amurru. And as you protect My Majesty, I will likewise protect your son. You, Tuppi-Teshshup, in the future protect the King of Hatti, the land of Hatti, my sons, and my grandsons. The tribute which was imposed upon your grandfather and upon your father shall be imposed upon you: They paid 300 shekels of refined gold by the weights of Hatti, first-class and good. You shall pay it likewise. You shall not turn your eyes to another. . . .

[If] you commit [. . .], and while the King of Egypt [is hostile to My Majesty you] secretly [send] your messenger to him, [or you become hostile] to the King of Hatti [and cast] off the authority of the King of Hatti, becoming a subject of the King of Egypt, you, Tuppi-Teshshup, will transgress the oath.

[Whoever] is [My Majesty's] enemy shall be your enemy. [Whoever is My Majesty's friend] shall be your friend. And if [any] of the lands which are "protectorates" [of the King of Hatti should become hostile] to the King of Hatti, and if I, My Majesty, come against that [land for attack], and you do not mobilize wholeheartedly with [infantry and chariotry, and do] not [make war wholeheartedly] and without hesitation on the enemy, you will transgress the oath.

. . .

As I, My Majesty, protect you, Tuppi-Teshshup, be an auxiliary army for My Majesty and [for Hatti]. And if some [evil] matter arises in Hatti, and [someone] revolts against My Majesty, and you hear [of it], lend assistance [together with] your [infantry] and your chariotry. Take a stand immediately to help [Hatti]. But if it is not possible for you to lend assistance (personally), send aid to the King of Hatti either by your son [or] your brother, together with your infantry and your [chariotry]. If you do not send aid to the King of Hatti [by your son] or your brother, together with your infantry and your chariotry, you will transgress the oath.

If some matter oppresses you, Tuppi-Teshshup, or someone revolts against you, and you write to the King of Hatti, then the King of Hatti will send infantry and chariotry to your aid. . . .

If Hittites bring you, Tuppi-Teshshup, infantry and chariotry—because they will go up to your cities, Tuppi-Teshshup must regularly provide them with food and drink. And if any Hittite undertakes an evil matter against Tuppi-Teshshup, such as the plunder of his land or of his cities, or the removal of Tuppi-Teshshup from kingship in the land of Amurru, he will transgress the oath.

Whatever civilian captives of the land of Nuhashshi and the land of Kinza my father carried off, or I carried off—if one of these civilian captives flees from me and comes to you, and you do not seize him and give him back to the King of Hatti, you will transgress the oath. And if you should even think as follows (concerning a fugitive): "[Come] or go! Wherever you go, I don't want to know about you."—you will transgress the oath.

If someone should bring up before you, Tuppi-Teshshup, evil matters against the King or against Hatti, you shall not conceal him from the King. Or if My Majesty speaks confidentially of some matters to you: "Perform these deeds or that deed," then make an appeal right there at that moment concerning whatever among those deeds you do not want to perform: "I cannot do this deed. I will not perform it." And when the King again commands, and you do not perform a deed of which you are capable, but rebuff(?) the King, or if you do not observe the matter of which the King speaks to you confidentially, you will transgress the oath.

If some population or fugitive sets out, travels toward Hatti, and passes through your land, set them well on their way and point out the road to Hatti. Speak favorable words to them. You shall not direct them to anyone else. If you do not set them on their way and do not show them the road to Hatti, but direct them to the mountains—or if you speak evil words before them, you will transgress the oath. . . .

Divine Witnesses

[. . . The Thousand Gods shall now stand] for this [oath]. They shall observe [and listen].

[The Sun-god of Heaven, the Sun-goddess] of Arinna, the Storm-god of Heaven, the Storm-god of Hatti, [Sheri], Hurri, Mount Nanni, Mount Hazzi, [the Storm-god of the Market(?), the Storm-god of] the Army . . . the male deities and female deities of Hatti, [the male deities] and female deities of Amurru, [all] the primeval deities—Nara, Namsara, [Minki], Tuhusi, Ammunki, Ammizzadu, Alalu, Antu, Anu, Apantu, Enlil, Ninlil—the mountains, the rivers, the springs, the great sea, heaven and earth, the winds, and the clouds. They shall be witnesses to this treaty [and] to the oath.

Curses

All the words of the treaty and oath [which] are written [on] this tablet—if Tuppi-Teshshup [does not observe these words] of the treaty and of the oath, then these oath gods shall destroy Tuppi-Teshshup, [together with his person], his [wife], his son, his grandsons, his household, his city, his land, and together with his possessions.

Blessings

But if Tuppi-Teshshup [observes] these [words of the treaty and of the oath] which [are written] on this tablet, [then] these oath gods [shall protect] Tuppi-Teshshup, together with his person, his wife, his son, his grandsons, [his city, his land], his household, his subjects, [and together with his possessions].

SOURCE: Gary Beckman, *Hittite Diplomatic Texts*, edited by Harry A. Hoffner Jr., Writings from the Ancient World 7 (Atlanta: Scholars Press, 1996), 55–59. Used by permission of the publisher.

10

VASSAL TREATIES OF ESARHADDON

In 672 BCE the king of Assyria, Esarhaddon, developed a treaty and forced nine vassal princes from Persia (Iran) to sign in an attempt to secure their support for his son, the crown prince Ashurbanipal. This treaty, discovered in the palace at Nimrud (the ancient Assyrian city of Kalhu), established the relationship between Esarhaddon and the Persian princes and exhibits similarities to older vassal treaties like the Hittite suzerain treaties as well as covenant treaties in the Hebrew Bible.

> Seal of the god Ashur, king of the gods, lord of the lands—not to be altered;
>   seal of the great
> prince, father of the gods—not to be disputed.
> The treaty which Esarhaddon, king of the world, king of Assyria,
> son of Sennacherib, likewise king of the world, king of Assyria,
> with Ramataia, city ruler of Urakazabanu,
> with his sons, his grandsons, with all the Urakazabaneans
> young and old, as many as there may be—
> with (all of) you, your sons, your grandsons
> who will exist in days to come after the treaty,
> from sunrise to sunset,
> over as many as Esarhaddon, king of Assyria, exercises
> kingship and lordship—(so) he has made the treaty
> with you concerning Ashurbanipal, the crown prince,
> son of Esarhaddon, king of Assyria.
> In the presence of Jupiter, Venus,
> Saturn, Mercury,
> Mars, Sirius;
> in the presence of Ashur, Anu, Enlil, Ea,
> . . .
> the gods dwelling in [heaven and earth],
> the gods of Assyria, [the gods of Sumer and Akkad],
> the gods of the lands, all of them, have affirmed,
> have laid hold on, (and) made (this treaty).
> You [swear(?) by] Ashur, father of the gods, lord of lands,
> by Anu, Enlil, Ea,
> . . .
> by the gods of Babylon, Borsippa, Nippur,
> by the gods of Sumer and Akkad, all of them,
> by the gods of the lands, all of them; by the gods of heaven and earth.
> The treaty (which) Esarhaddon, king of Assyria, has made with you,
> in the presence of the great gods of heaven and earth,
> concerning Ashurbanipal, the crown prince,
> son of Esarhaddon, king of Assyria, your lord, whom
> he named and appointed to the crown princeship.
> When Esarhaddon, king of Assyria, dies,
> you will seat Ashurbanipal, the crown prince,
> upon the royal throne, he will exercise the kingship

(and) lordship of Assyria over you. You will
protect him in country and in town; you will fight,
and (even) will die, for him. You will speak
with him in the truth of your heart, you will give
him sound advice loyally.
You will set a fair path at his feet.
(You swear) that you will not be hostile to him nor will you
seat one of his brothers, older or younger, on the throne of Assyria
instead of him. That the word of Esarhaddon, king of Assyria,
you will neither change nor alter. That you will
serve only Ashurbanipal, the crown prince,
whom Esarhaddon, king of Assyria, your lord (hereby commends),
that he will exercise the kingship and dominion over you.
(You swear) that you will protect Ashurbanipal, the crown prince,
whom Esarhaddon, king of Assyria, has designated to you
(and of whom) he has spoken to you, and concerning whom
he has firmly imposed the treaty upon you.
That, you will not sin against him; that you will not
bring your hand against him with evil intent. That you will not
revolt (or) do anything to him which is not good, and not proper.
You will not oust him from the kingship of Assyria
by helping one of his brothers, older or younger, to seize the throne
of Assyria in his stead. You will not set over you any (other) king
or any (other) lord, nor will you swear an oath to any (other) king or any
     (other) lord.
(You swear) that you will neither listen to nor conceal any improper,
Unsuitable, or unseemly words concerning the exercise of kingship, which
are unseemly and evil against Ashurbanipal, the crown prince,
either from the mouth of his brothers, his uncles, his cousins,
his family, members of his father's line; or from the mouth of officials
or governors, or from the mouth of an officer or courtiers
or from the mouth of any skilled person or from the mouth of any of
the masses, as many as there are, but you will
come (and) report (these things) to
Ashurbanipal, the crown prince.
. . .
[(You swear) that you will fight for Ashurbanipal,]
the crown prince, son of Esarhaddon, your lord,
and will die (for him). You will seek to
do for him that which is good.
That you will not do to him (anything which) is not good.
You will not counsel him that which is improper.
You will not direct him in an unwholesome course.

You will continually treat him in a true and suitable manner.
(You swear) that should [Esarh]addon, king of Assyria, die
during the minority of his sons, (and) either an officer
or a courtier put Ashurbanipal, the crown prince,
to death, (and) take over the kingship
of the land of Assyria.
That you will not make common cause with him,
that you will not become his servant
(but) you will break away and be hostile,
you will make other lands to be hostile to him.
You will seize him and put him to death
and will then cause a son of Ashurbanipal,
the crown prince, to take the throne of Assyria.
(You swear) that you will (if necessary) await the woman pregnant
by Esarhaddon, king of Assyria (or) the wife of Ashurbanipal,
the crown prince. That, after (the son)
is born you will bring him up
and will set (him) on the throne of Assyria.
That you will seize and slay the perpetrators of
rebellion. You will destroy their name and their seed
from the land. That, by shedding blood
for blood, you will avenge
Ashurbanipal, the crown prince.
That you will neither feed
Ashurbanipal, the crown prince,
son of Esarhaddon, king of Assyria, your lord,
nor give him to drink, nor anoint him
with, a deadly (poisonous) plant
nor will you make magic against him, nor make
the gods and goddesses to be angry with him.
(You swear) that you will love Ashurbanipal, the crown prince,
son of Esarhaddon, king of Assyria, your lord
as (you do) yourselves.
That, before Ashurbanipal, the crown prince,
you will not slander his brothers, his mother's sons.
That you will not speak anything that is not good about them,
that you will not put your hands on their houses; that you will not transgress
against them. That you will not take from the gift which their
father has given them, (or) the acquisitions which they themselves
have gained.
(You swear) that the gift of lands, houses, plantations,
peoples, implements, horses, m[ules,]
donkeys, cattle, and flocks which Esarhaddon, king of Assyria,

has given to his sons, shall be theirs.
(You swear) that you will report their slaughter before
Ashurbanipal, the crown prince.
(You swear) that they shall stand before him
And be united with you.
As for these treaty provisions which Esarhaddon, king of Assyria,
has firmly made with you concerning Ashurbanipal,
the crown prince (and) his brothers, son(s) by the same mother
as Ashurbanipal, the crown prince,
he has made you take an oath
that you will relate (them) to your sons and to your grandsons,
to your seed, to your seed's seed which shall be (born) in
the future, that you will order them
as follows: "Guard this treaty.
Do not transgress your treaty,
(or) you will lose your lives,
you will be turning over your dwellings to be shattered,
your people to be carried off. May this matter
which is acceptable to god and mankind,
[be acceptable also to you]. May it last forever upon you."
[May Ashurbanipal, the crown prince,] be [preserved]
to be the ruler of the land and people,
(and) later may [he be named] for the kingship.
You will not set any (other) king or any (other) lord over you.

. . .

You will not make a claim against (a document bearing)
the [seal of] Ashur, king of the gods. It is set on in your presence,
you will serve (him) as your own god.
(You swear that) you will not alter (it), you will
not consign (it) to the fire nor throw (it) into the water,
nor [bury (it)] in the earth nor destroy it by
any cunning device, nor make [(it) disappear], nor sweep (it) away.
(If you do,) [may Ashur, king of the] gods who decrees the fates,
[decree for you] evil and not good. May he never grant
you fatherhood and attainment of old age.
[May Ninlil], his beloved wife [evilly interpret the] utterance
of his mouth evil, may she not intercede for you.
[May Sin], the brightness of heaven and earth, clothe you with
[a lep]rosy; [may he forbid your entering into the presence of the gods]
[or king (saying): "Roam the desert] like the wild ass (and) the gazelle."
[May Shamash, the light of the heavens and] earth [not]
[judge] you justly (saying): "May it be dark
in your eyes, walk in darkness."

. . .

Just as a snake and a mongoose do not
enter and lie down together in the same hole
and think (only) of cutting off each other's life,
(so) may you (and) your women folk not enter the same room
without thinking of cutting off each other's lives.

. . .

Like locusts devour . . . lice and caterpillars
may they cause your towns, your land (and) your district to be devoured.
May they treat you as a fly (caught) in the hand;
may your enemy squash you.

. . .

SOURCE: D. J. Wiseman, "The Vassal-Treaties of Esarhaddon," *Iraq* 20 (1958): i–ii, 1–99, translation 29–76. © The British Institute for the Study of Iraq 1958. Published by Cambridge University Press. Used by permission of the publisher.

11

UNCLEAN ANIMALS

Like the biblical Israelites, the ancient Egyptians considered certain animals unfit for eating or for ritual use (see for instance Lev 11). The text below provides the reasoning for the taboo against pigs in Egyptian society. It is an Egyptian coffin text, part of the Egyptian Book of the Dead, dating at least to the late third millennium BCE.

Egyptian Book of the Dead

The Efficacy of This Text

BEING DESTINED FOR FOOD IN THE NECROPOLIS. BEING FAVORED AND LOVED UPON EARTH. BEING AMONG THE FOLLOWERS OF HORUS AND HIS RETINUE. A MYSTERY WHICH ONE LEARNED IN THE HOUSE. KNOWING THE SOULS OF BUTO.

The Claim of Exceptional Knowledge

O Batit of the evening, ye swamp dwellers, ye of Mendes, ye of the Mendes nome (territory), ye of the Butine *House of Praise*, ye of the Shade of Re *which knows not praise*, ye who *brew stoppered beer*—do ye know why Buto was given to Horus? Ye do not know it, (but) I know it. It was Re who gave it to him in recompense for the injury in his eye. I know it.

The Myth

It was Re—he said to Horus: "Pray, let me see thy eye since this has happened to it." Then he saw it. He said: "Pray, look at that *(black) part*." Then Horus said: "Now I see it quite white." That is how the oryx came into being.

Then Re said: "Pray, look another time at that black pig." Thereupon Horus looked at this pig. Thereupon Horus shrieked because of the state of his eye, which was stormy. He said: "Behold, my eye is as (at) that first blow which Seth made against my eye!" Thereupon Horus swallowed his heart before him. Then Re said: "Put ye him upon his bed until he has recovered."

It was Seth—he had assumed form against him as a black pig; thereupon he shot a blow into his eye. Then Re said: "The pig is an abomination to Horus." "Would that he might recover!" said the gods.

THAT IS HOW THE PIG BECAME AN ABOMINATION TO THE GODS, AS WELL AS THEIR FOLLOWERS, FOR HORUS' SAKE.

SOURCE: John A. Wilson, "The Mythological Origins of Certain Unclean Animals," in *Ancient Near Eastern Texts Relating to the Old Testament*, ed. James B. Pritchard, 3rd edition with supplement (Princeton: Princeton University Press, 1969), 10. © 1950, 1955, 1969 by Princeton University Press. Renewed 1978 by Princeton University Press. Used by permission of the publisher.

12

INSTRUCTIONS FOR HITTITE TEMPLE OFFICIALS

The following excerpt is from a much longer Hittite instructional text dating to the second millennium BCE that outlines the regulations for temple personnel and priests. The text gives rules regarding issues such as offerings, purity of the priests, festival regulations, the care of the temple treasures, and the care of the livestock belonging to the temple (cp. the priestly regulations in Leviticus).

. . . Moreover: You are the custodians of the silver, gold, clothing, (and) bronze utensils of the deities [(th)]at you keep. It belongs to the silver, gold, clothing, (and) bronze utensils of the deity. (*As far as you are concerned*) it does not (*even*) exist! What is in the temple (simply) does not exist! Whatever (is there) belongs exclusively to the deity, so be extremely reverent! No silver (or) gold whatsoever shall belong to a temple functionary. He is not even allowed to wear it on his person. He is not allowed to make it into jewelry for his wife (or) his son. . . .

Moreover, you who are the temple personnel: if you do not celebrate the festivals at festival time, (e.g.,) you perform the spring festival [i]n autu[mn], bu[t] then you celebrate the autumn festival i[n] the spring; or when the p[(ro)]per time to celebrate a festival has arrived, and the one who is to perform it either comes to you priests, anoint[ed] ones, mother-deity priest-esses and te[mple] personnel, and he grabs your knees (crying): "The harvest is before me"; or a dowry or a journey or some other matter, (or he says): "Stand behind me! Let me take care of this matter in the meantime, and as soon as I have taken care of this matter, I will perform the festival as such." In no case shall you act according to this man's wishes! He shall not make you feel sorry for him. And do not accept payment (in a matter concerning) the will of the deities! The man will make you feel sorry for him, so that you accept payment; but the deities will avenge (it) upon you some day. They will most malevolently confront you yourselves, your wives, your sons, (and) your servants. You should act exclusively for the will of the deities. Eat bread and drink water, establish your household, too, but [in no case] shall you [d]o it according to a man's wishes! You shall not sell death, but [y]ou shall not bu[y] death either!

. . .

Furthermore: all you w[h]o are kitchen personnel of the deities: cupbearer, waiter, cook, baker, beer brewer: you must be extremely reverent with regard to the will of the deities. And main[(tain)] great respect for the bread loaf (and) wine pitcher of the deities. The kitchen shall be swept and sprayed for you. A pig (or) a dog shall not cross the threshold. And [(yo)]u yourselves must be washed, and you must [(we)]ar clean clothes. Further, your *hair* and nails must be trimmed. . . . If a pig or a dog ever does touch the wooden uten[(sil)]s (or) the ceramic wares that you have, but the kitchen foreman does not throw them out, and he gives the deities to eat from unclean (utensils/ wares), then the deities will give him feces (and) urine to eat (and) drink. Also, when someone goes to sleep with a woman, as soon as he performs the rite(s) for the deities, gives the deity to eat (and) drink, then let him thus go with the woman. Further, [. . .] and by the ti<(me)> the sun (comes) up, let him bat[he] punctually, and in the morning, by [(feedi)]ng time for the deities, let him appear punctually. If he neglects to do so, however, [(then)] he commits an offense. If, however, someone sleeps with a woman, [bu]t his *foreman*, his boss *presses* [hi]m (about it), he must certainly tell. But [i]f he does not dare to tell, then let him tell his colleague. And he shall bathe in any case. But if he knowingly *postpones* (it), he has not yet bathed, and he approaches the bread loaf (and) the wine pitcher of the deities unclean, or his colleague notices him, and you feel sorry for him, [(and)] he conceals [(him)], but it later becomes known, [(then they)] commit a capital (offense). Both shall die. . . .

Furthermore: You who are the cowherds of the deity (and) shepherds of the deity: If there is a rite for some deity during the birthing season, and you bring him a calf, a lamb, a kid, or the afterbirth . . . then you will not delay it. Bring it at the proper time. The deities should not be kept waiting for it. Before a person consumes the young animals, bring them punctually to the deities. Or if there is a mild festival for some deity, do not neglect it (the festival) while they churn the milk. Carry it out for him. If you do not bring the young animals to the deities immediately, but rather you hastily consume them yourselves, or you bring them to your foreman, and afterwards it becomes known, you commit a capital offense. . . .

Source: Jared L. Miller, *Royal Hittite Instructions and Related Administrative Texts*, ed. Mauro Giorgieri, Writings from the Ancient World 31 (Atlanta: Society of Biblical Literature, 2013), 253–63. Used by permission of the publisher.

13

PURIFYING OFFERINGS AT UGARIT

The following excerpt is from a ritual text from Ugarit (Ras Shamra) on the Mediterranean coast of Syria which was destroyed in 1200 BCE. The text describes the appropriate offerings given in order to cleanse the people of Ugarit from their ritual impurities (cp. the ritual texts in Leviticus).

(If) you transgress or (if) you sin,
Then a sacrifice or an offering,
Our sacrifices are sacrificed.
The offering is offered;

The libation is poured out.
It is brought to the father of the gods;
It is brought to the assembly of the gods;
To all of the gods.
Offer a bull . . .
For a bodily transgression
Or for a transgression of your soul
Or for any transgression you transgress,
. . .

Our sacrifice is sacrificed.
The offering is offered;
The libation is poured out.
It is brought to the father of the gods
It is brought to the assembly of the gods,
To all of the gods.
. . .

SOURCE: Translation by Katherine E. Smith.

14

CERTIFICATE OF ADOPTION

The Nuzi archives are a collection of administrative tablets from Nuzi near the Hurrian capital (modern-day northern Iraq) dating from around 1450 BCE–1350 BCE. The archives describe legal issues similar to those in Genesis dealing with inheritance, marriage, and blessings (see for example Gen 15:2; 16; 21; 29; 38; 48). The excerpt below deals with the legal issue of adoption by childless men and inheritance issues, mirroring some of the concerns of the Israelite ancestors, particularly Abraham and Sarah.

The tablet of adoption belonging to [Zike], the son of Akkuya: he gave his son Shennima in adoption to Shuriha-ilu, and Shuriha-ilu, with reference to Shennima, (from) all the lands . . . (and) his earnings of every sort gave to Shennima one (portion) of his property. If Shuriha-ilu should have a son of his own, as the principal (son) he shall take a double share; Shennima shall then be next in order (and) take his proper share. As long as Shuriha-ilu is alive, Shennima shall revere him. When Shuriha-ilu [dies], Shennima shall become the heir. Furthermore, Kelim-ninu has been given in marriage to

Shennima. If Kelim-ninu bears (children), Shennima shall not take another wife; but if Kelim-ninu does not bear, Kelim-ninu shall acquire a woman of the land of Lullu as wife for Shennima, and Kelim-ninu may not send the offspring away. Any sons that may be born to Shennima from the womb of Kelim-ninu, to (these) sons shall be given [all] the lands (and) buildings of every sort. [However], if she does not bear a son, [then] the daughter of Kelim-ninu from the lands (and) buildings shall take one (portion) of the property. Furthermore, Shuriha-ilu shall not adopt another son in addition to Shennima. Whoever among them defaults shall compensate with 1 mina of silver (and) 1 mina of gold.

Furthermore, Yalampa is given as a handmaid to Kelim-ninu and Shatim-ninu has been made co-parent. As long as she is alive, she (i.e., Yalampa) shall revere her and Shatim-ninu shall not annul the [*agreement*].

If Kelim-ninu bears (children) and Shennima takes another wife, she may *take* her dowry and leave.

(The names of nine persons and the scribe as witnesses, each preceded by the witness sign.)

The remaining sons of Zike may not lay claim to the lands (and) buildings belonging to the (above) one (portion) of the property.

The tablet was written after the proclamation.

(Sealed by eight persons, seven of whom were already named witnesses.)

SOURCE: Theophile J. Meek, "Mesopotamian Legal Documents," in *Ancient Near Eastern Texts Relating to the Old Testament*, ed. James B. Pritchard, 3rd edition with supplement (Princeton: Princeton University Press, 1969), 220. © 1950, 1955, 1969 by Princeton University Press. Renewed 1978 by Princeton University Press. Used by permission of the publisher.

C. LEGENDS AND FOLKTALES

There are a number of legends and folktales from the ancient Eastern Mediterranean that share themes in common with literature from the Hebrew Bible. Of particular popularity in this part of the world are stories of foundling kings and leaders, a selection of which are given below from Mesopotamia, the Hittite Empire, and Greece. These foundling-king stories play out in similar fashion to the birth story of Moses in Exodus 1–2. There are also Egyptian ("The Tale of Two Brothers," for instance) and Greek (Bellerophon) stories that show striking similarities to the biblical story of Joseph, and the final selection, given below, shows that the Greeks, like the Hebrews, had their own stories of figures rescued from the ocean by sea creatures. The ancient Eastern Mediterranean is rich with colorful tales, and the selections below show that the biblical stories are at home with their Mesopotamian, Greek, and Egyptian counterparts.

15

BIRTH OF SARGON THE GREAT

Sargon of Akkad (2334–2279 BCE) was the famed king of the first empire of Mesopotamia. The following text fragment, dated to the first millennium BCE, describes Sargon as a foundling king whose mother was a high priestess. The text, written in first person from Sargon's perspective, states that the emperor's mother left him in a reed basket in the Euphrates where he was discovered by Aqqi and raised as his adopted son. The motif of the abandoned infant is one common in Greek and ancient Near Eastern myth as seen also in the stories of Oedipus, Cyrus the Great, and Moses (Exod 1:8–2:10).

> I am Sargon the great king, king of Agade.
> My mother was a high priestess, I did not know my father.

My father's brothers dwell in the uplands.
My city is Azupiranu, which lies on Euphrates bank.
My mother, the high priestess, conceived me, she bore me in secret.
She placed me in a reed basket, she sealed my hatch with pitch.
She left me to the river, whence I could not come up.
The river carried me off, it brought me to Aqqi, drawer of water.
Aqqi, drawer of water, brought me up as he dipped his bucket.
Aqqi, drawer of water, raised me as his adopted son.
Aqqi, drawer of water, set (me) to his orchard work.
During my orchard work, Ishtar loved me.
Fifty-five years I ruled as king,
I became lord over and ruled the black-headed folk.
I . . . hard mountains with picks of copper,
I was wont to ascend high mountains,
I was wont to cross over low mountains.
The [la]nd of the sea I sieged three times, I conquered Dilmun.
I went up to great Der, I . . .
I destroyed [Ka]zallu and . . .
Whatsoever king who shall arise after me,
[Let him rule as king fifty-five years],
Let him become lo[rd over and rule] the black-headed folk,
Let him . . . hard mountains with picks [of copper],
Let him be wont to ascend high mountains,
[Let him be wont to cross over low mountains].
Let him siege the [la]nd of the sea three times,
[Let him conquer Dilmun].
Let him go up [to] great Der and . . .
. . . from my city Agade.

SOURCE: Benjamin R. Foster, *From Distant Days: Myths, Tales, and Poetry of Ancient Mesopotamia* (Bethesda, Md.: CDL Press, 1995), 165–66. Used by permission of the publisher.

16

THE SUN GOD AND THE COW

This text is part of the Boğazköy archives, a collection of tablets discovered at excavations in Boğazköy in Turkey, which was once the capital of the ancient Hittite Empire. The text dates to the second millennium BCE and describes the birth of the Hittite sun god from a cow, left by a stream to be adopted by a local fisherman (cp. the birth of Moses in Exod 2).

While looking down from heaven, the sun god beheld a cow ravenously grazing in a meadow. He descended to earth to find out why she was consuming so much grass. After listening to her explanation, he impregnated her in a flash of light. Nine months passed and the animal gave birth to a human child, whose appearance so surprised and frightened her that she was about to kill her own offspring.

Fortunately, the sun god intervened and chased the cow away. He then provided nourishment for the infant, who was bathed by the waters of a stream. The servant of the god was sent to place the child on a ledge overlooking another stream. There a fisherman spotted the infant near where he had earlier left his basket. Being without children of his own, he joyfully took up the foundling to return to his wife. As soon as the fisherman reached home, he shrewdly ordered his wife to withdraw to their bedroom and scream out as if in labor. After the wife had carried out the instructions, the neighbors, believing her about to give birth, brought many presents to the couple.

SOURCE: Brian Lewis, *The Sargon Legend: A Study of the Akkadian Text and The Tale of the Hero Who was Exposed at Birth,* ed. David Noel Freedman, American Schools of Oriental Research Dissertation Series 4 (Cambridge: American Schools of Oriental Research, 1980), 156–57. Used by permission of the publisher.

17

BIRTH OF IAMUS

The odes of the Greek poet Pindar (fourth–fifth century BCE) were written in celebration of athletic achievements. In the odes, Pindar often drew on myths from the victorious athlete's local legends. *Olympian Ode 6* was written for Hagesias of Syracuse, a region whose local myths included that of Iamus, son of Evadne and Apollo. In the excerpt below, Pindar describes the birth of Iamus who was hidden in the rushes after his birth by his mother (cp. the birth of Moses in Exod 2).

Pindar, *Olympian Ode 6*

. . .
We must therefore throw wide the gates of song for them
and come today in good time to Pitane,
beside the waters of Eurotas.

She it was, men say, who coupled with Cronus' son Poseidon
and bore a daughter, Euadne of the violet-colored hair.
She concealed the fruit of her unwedded labor
by the folds of her dress, and in her birth month
dispatched her maids to Aepytus, the hero son of Eilatus,
with orders to deliver the child into his keeping.
He was king of the Arcadians of Phaesane,
and had his allotted home beside the Alpheus.
Here Euadne was raised, and here she gave herself to Apollo
and first tasted the delights of Aphrodite.
But she could not hide the god's seed from Aepytus for ever;
with painful self-control he thrust down in his heart
the anger he could not speak of, and went to Pytho
to consult the oracle concerning his intolerable grief.
Meanwhile she had laid aside her purple belt and silver jug,
and in a dark copse began the birth of a son with the spirit of a god.
To help her, the golden-haired god sent the Fates
and Eleithyia, giver of gentle counsel.
Without delay, in joyful birth pangs
Iamus issued from her womb into the light.
In her distress she left him there on the ground,
but by the gods' designs two grey-eyed snakes nurtured him,
feeding him on the blameless venom of bees.
When the king had driven back from rocky Pytho
he questioned everyone in the house about the boy Euadne had borne,
because, he said, his father was Phoebus,
and he would surpass all mortals as a seer for mankind,
and his posterity would never fail. This much he revealed;
but they claimed that though the boy was five days old
they had neither seen nor heard of him.
And in truth he had been hidden on a bed of rushes
under a great bush, his tender body suffused
with the gold and purple radiance of violets;
and this is why his mother had declared that for all time
he would be known by this immortal name.
    . . .

SOURCE: Anthony Verity, *Pindar: The Complete Odes*, Oxford World's Classics (Oxford: Oxford University Press, 2007), 17–18. © 2007 Oxford University Press. Used by permission of the publisher.

18

BIRTH OF CYRUS THE GREAT

The Greek historian Herodotus, born in the Persian Empire (fifth century BCE), gives the story of the birth of Cyrus the Great, king of Persia. Herodotus presents Cyrus as a foundling king, abandoned at birth. Astyages, Cyrus' grandfather, ordered Cyrus' death at his birth after dreaming that his grandson would rule all of Asia. Harpagus, the man charged with killing the infant, however, adopted and raised the child as his own at the urging of his wife. Cyrus' birth narrative, as told by Herodotus, bears a striking resemblance to those of other foundling kings in Greek myth (such as Oedipus and Iamus) as well as ancient Near Eastern leaders like Sargon and Moses (Exod 1:8–2:10).

Herodotus, *Histories* 1.107.2–1.113.3

Astyages had a daughter, whom he called Mandane, and he dreamed that she urinated so much that she filled his city and flooded all of Asia. He communicated this vision to those of the Magi who interpreted dreams, and when he heard what they told him he was terrified. Presently, when Mandane was of marriageable age, he feared the vision too much to give her to any Mede worthy to marry into his family, but married her to a Persian called Cambyses, a man whom he knew to be wellborn and of a quiet temper, for Astyages held Cambyses to be much lower than a Mede of middle rank. But during the first year that Mandane was married to Cambyses, Astyages saw a second vision. He dreamed that a vine grew out of the genitals of this daughter, and that the vine covered the whole of Asia. Having seen this vision, and communicated it to the interpreters of dreams, he sent to the Persians for his daughter, who was about to give birth. When she arrived he kept her guarded, meaning to kill whatever child she bore, for the interpreters declared that the meaning of his dream was that his daughter's offspring would rule in his place. Anxious to prevent this, Astyages, when Cyrus was born, summoned Harpagus, a man of his household who was his most faithful servant among the Medes and was administrator of all that was his, and he said, "Harpagus, whatever business I turn over to you, do not mishandle it, and do not leave me out of account and, giving others preference, trip over your own feet afterwards. Take the child that Mandane bore, and carry him to your house, and kill him; and then bury him however you like."

"O King," Harpagus answered, "never yet have you noticed anything displeasing in your man, and I shall be careful in the future, too, not to err in what concerns you. If it is your will that this be done, then my concern ought to be to attend to it scrupulously." Harpagus answered thus. The child was then given to him, consigned to its death, and he went to his house weeping. When he came in, he told his wife the entire speech uttered by Astyages.

"Now, then," she said to him, "what do you propose to do?" "Not to obey Astyages' instructions," he answered, "not even if he should lose his mind and be more frantic than he is now. I will not lend myself to his plan or be an accessory to such a murder. There are many reasons why I will not kill him: because the child is related to me, and because Astyages is old and has no male children. Now if the sovereignty passes to this daughter of his after his death, whose son he is now killing by means of me, what is left for me but the gravest of all dangers? For the sake of my safety this child has to die, but one of Astyages' own people has to be the murderer and not one of mine." So saying, he sent a messenger at once to one of Astyages' cowherds, who he knew pastured his herds in the likeliest spots and where the mountains were most infested with wild beasts. The man's name was Mitradates, and his wife was a slave like him. Her name was in the Greek language Cyno, in the Median Spako: for "spax" is the Median word for dog. The foothills of the mountains where this cowherd pastured his cattle are north of Ecbatana, towards the Euxine sea; for the rest of Media is everywhere a level plain, but here, on the side of the Saspires, the land is very high and mountainous and covered with woods.

So when the cowherd came in haste at the summons, Harpagus said: "Astyages wants you to take this child and leave it in the most desolate part of the mountains so that it will perish as quickly as possible. And he wants me to tell you that if you do not kill it, but preserve it somehow, you will undergo the most harrowing death; and I am ordered to see it exposed."

Hearing this, the cowherd took the child and went back the same way and came to his dwelling. Now as it happened his wife too had been on the verge of delivering every day, and as the divinity would have it, she did in fact give birth while the cowherd was away in the city. Each of them was anxious for the other, the husband being afraid about his wife's labor, and the wife because she did not know why Harpagus had so unexpectedly sent for her husband. So when he returned and stood before her, she was startled by the unexpected sight and asked him before he could speak why Harpagus had so insistently summoned him. "Wife," he said, "when I came to the city, I saw and heard what I ought never to have seen, and what ought never to have happened to our masters. Harpagus' whole house was full of weeping. Astonished, I went in, and immediately I saw a child lying there struggling and crying, adorned in gold and embroidered clothing. And when Harpagus saw me, he told me to take the child in haste and bring it away and leave it where the mountains are the most infested with wild beasts. It was Astyages, he said, who enjoined this on me, and Harpagus threatened me grievously if I did not do it. So I took him and brought him away, supposing him to be the child of one of the servants, for I could never have guessed whose he was. But I was amazed at seeing him adorned with gold and clothing, and at hearing, too, the evident sound of weeping in the house of Harpagus. Very soon on the way I learned the whole story from the servant who brought me out of the city and gave the child into my custody: namely, that it was the son of Mandane the king's daughter and Cambyses the son of Cyrus, and that Astyages gave the command to kill him. And now, here he is."

And as he said this the cowherd uncovered it and showed it. But when the woman saw how fine and fair the child was, she began to cry and laid hold of the man's knees and begged him by no means to expose him. But the husband said he could not do otherwise; for, he said, spies would be coming from Harpagus to see what was done, and he would have to die a terrible death if he did not obey. Being unable to move her husband, the woman then said: "Since I cannot convince you not to expose it, then, if a child has to be seen exposed, do this: I too have borne a child, but I bore it dead. Take this one and put it out, but the child of the daughter of Astyages let us raise as if it were our own; this way, you won't be caught disobeying our masters, and we will not have plotted badly. For the dead child will have royal burial, and the living will not lose his life."

Thinking that his wife advised him excellently in his present strait, the cowherd immediately did as she said. He gave his wife the child whom he had brought to kill, and his own dead child he put into the chest in which he carried the other, and dressed it with all the other child's finery and left it out in the most desolate part of the mountains. Then on the third day after leaving the child out, the cowherd left one of his herdsmen to watch it and went to the city, where he went to Harpagus' house and said he was ready to show the child's dead body. Harpagus sent the most trusted of his bodyguard, and these saw for him and buried the cowherd's child. So it was buried: and the cowherd's wife kept and raised the boy who was afterwards named Cyrus; but she did not give him that name, but another.

SOURCE: A. D. Godley, *Herodotus: The Persian Wars,* vol. 1, Loeb Classical Library 117 (Cambridge, Mass.: Harvard University Press, 1920), 139–47. Loeb Classical Library® is a registered trademark of the President and Fellows of Harvard College.

✹

19

SEVEN LEAN YEARS IN EGYPT

The text below is from an inscription on a rock in Siheil of Egypt. The inscription dates to the second century BCE, but it is set during the reign of Djoser in the third millennium BCE. The inscription shows that there was an Egyptian tradition of seven years of drought and famine followed by fertile years, a bargain agreed upon by the pharaoh Djoser and Khnum, the god of Elephantine. The tradition of seven lean years of Egypt is mirrored in the story of Joseph in Genesis 41.

Year 18 of the Horus: Netjer-er-khet; the King of Upper and Lower Egypt: Netjer-er-khet; the Two Goddesses: Netjer-er-khet; the Horus of Gold: Djoser, *and under* the Count, Mayor, *Royal Acquaintance,* and Overseer of Nubians in Elephantine, Madir. There was brought to him this royal decree:

To let thee know. I was in distress on the Great Throne, and those who are in the palace were in heart's affliction from a very great evil, since the Nile had not come in my time for a space of seven years. Grain was scant, fruits were dried up, and everything which they eat was short. Every man *robbed* his companion. They moved without going (*ahead*). The infant was wailing; the youth was *waiting;* the heart of the old men was in sorrow, their legs were bent, crouching on the ground, their arms were folded. The courtiers were in need. The temples were shut up; the sanctuaries held [*nothing but*] *air.* Every[*thing*] was found empty.

I extended my heart back to the beginnings, and I asked him who was the *Chamberlain,* the Ibis, the Chief Lector Priest Ii-em-(ho)tep, the son of Ptah, South-of-His-Wall: "What is the birthplace of the Nile? *Who is . . .* the god there? Who is the god?"

Then he answered me: "I need the guidance of Him Who Presides over the House of the Fowling Net . . . *for the heart's confidence* of all men about what they should do. I shall enter into the House of Life and spread out the Souls of Re, (to see) if some guidance be in them."

So he went, and he returned to me immediately, that he might *instruct* me on the inundation of the Nile . . . and everything about which they had written. He uncovered for me the hidden spells thereof, to which the ancestors had taken (their) way, without their equal among kings since the limits *of time.* He *said* to me:

"There is a city in the midst of the waters [*from which*] the Nile *rises*, named Elephantine. It is the Beginning of the Beginning, the Beginning Nome, (*facing*) toward Wawat. It is the *joining* of the land, the primeval hillock *of earth, the throne* of Re, when he *reckons to cast* life beside everybody. 'Pleasant of Life' is the name of its dwelling. 'The Two Caverns' is the name of the water; they are the two breasts which pour forth all good things. It is the couch of the Nile, in which he becomes young (again). . . . He fecundates (the land) by mounting as the male, the bull, to the female; he renews (his) virility, assuaging his desire. He rushes twenty-eight cubits (high at Elephantine); he hastens at Diospolis seven cubits (high). Khnum is there as a god. . . ." . . .

. . . As I slept in life and satisfaction, I discovered the god standing over against me. I propitiated him with praise; I prayed to him in his presence. He *revealed* himself to me, *his face* being fresh. His words were:

"I am Khnum, thy fashioner . . . I know the Nile. When he is introduced into the fields, his introduction gives life to every nostril, like the introduction (of life) to the fields. . . . The Nile will pour forth for thee, without a year of cessation or laxness for any land. Plants will grow, bowing down under the *fruit*. Renenut will be at the head of everything. . . . Dependents *will fulfill* the purposes in their hearts, as well as the master. The starvation year will have gone, and (people's) *borrowing* from their granaries will have departed. Egypt will come into the fields, the banks will sparkle . . . and contentment will be in their hearts more than that which was formerly."

Then I awoke *quickly*, my heart cutting off weariness. I made this decree beside my father Khnum:

"An offering which the King gives to Khnum, the Lord of the Cataract Region, Who Presides over Nubia, in recompense for these things which thou wilt do for me:

"I offer to thee thy west in Manu and thy east (in) Bakhu, from Elephantine as far as [Takompso], for twelve *iters* on the east and west, whether arable land or desert or river in every part of these *iters* . . ."

Source: John A. Wilson, "Egyptian Myths and Tales," in *Ancient Near Eastern Texts Relating to the Old Testament,* ed. James B. Pritchard, 3rd edition with supplement (Princeton: Princeton University Press, 1969), 31–32. © 1950, 1955, 1969 by Princeton

20

THE TALE OF TWO BROTHERS

The Egyptian folktale of two brothers tells the story of Anpu (Anubis in some translations), the elder brother, and Bata, the younger brother. Bata is an upstanding, hard worker who cares for his brother's estate until Anpu's wife falsely accuses Bata of sexual assault. Bata and Anpu are then separated after Anpu attempts to kill Bata, though they are reunited after a series of fantastic events which leads to Bata ruling all of Egypt. "The Tale of Two Brothers" contains a theme central to both the account of Bellerophon in Homer's *Iliad* and the story of Joseph in Genesis 39, the blameless hero falsely accused of rape by the wife of the ruler.

Once there were two brothers, of one mother and one father; Anpu was the name of the elder, and Bata was the name of the younger. Now, as for Anpu he had a house and a wife. But his little brother was like a son to him. Anpu made for Bata his clothes, and Bata followed behind Anpu's oxen in the fields because he did the plowing, and Bata harvested the corn. Bata did for Anpu all the matters that were in the field. Behold, Bata grew to be an excellent worker; there was not his equal in the whole land. Behold, the spirit of a god was in him.

Now after this the younger brother followed his oxen in his daily manner, and every evening he returned to the house, laden with all the herbs of the field, with milk and with wood, and with all the things of the field. And he put them down before his elder brother, who was sitting with his wife, and he drank and ate, and he lay down in his stable with the cattle. And at dawn he took bread which he had baked, and laid it before Anpu, and he took his bread to the field with him, and he drove his cattle to pasture in the fields. And Bata walked behind his cattle, they said to him, "The herbage is good in that place," and he listened to all they said, and he took them to the place they desired. And the cattle before him became exceeding excellent, and they multiplied greatly.

Now at plowing time his elder brother said to him, "Let us make ready for ourselves a good yoke of oxen for plowing, for the land has come out from the water, and it is fit for plowing. Moreover, come to the field with corn, for we will begin the plowing in the morning." Thus Anpu instructed him, and Bata did all things as his elder brother had spoken to him.

And when the morning came, they went to the fields with their things, and their hearts were exceedingly pleased with their task in the beginning of their work. And it came to pass after this that as they were in the field they stopped for corn, and he sent his younger brother, saying, "Hurry, bring corn from the farm." And Bata found the wife of his elder brother, as she was sitting braiding her hair. He said to her, "Get up, and give me corn, so I may run to the field, for my elder brother hurried me saying, 'do not delay.'" She said to him, "Go, open the bin, and take for yourself what you want, so that I will not drop my locks of hair while I dress them."

The youth went to the stable. He took a large measure, for he desired to take much corn. He loaded it with wheat and barley, and he went out carrying it. She said to him, "How much of the corn is on your shoulder?" He said to her, "Three bushels of barley, and two of wheat, five in all; these are what are on my shoulder." And she conversed with him, saying, "You are very strong, for I see your might every day." And her heart desired him intimately. And she arose and came to him, and conversed with him, saying, "Come, stay with me, and it will be good for you, and I will make you beautiful garments." Then the youth became like a panther of the south with fury at the evil speech that she had made to him, and she was very afraid. And he spoke to her, saying, "Behold you are like a mother to me, your husband is like a father to me, for he who is older than I raised me. What is this wickedness that you have said to me? Say it not to me again. For I will not tell it to any man, for I will not let it be uttered by the mouth of any man." Bata lifted up his burden, and he went to the field and came to his older brother, and they took up their work.

Now afterward, at evening time, his elder brother was returning to his house, and the younger brother was following after his oxen, and he loaded himself with all the things of the field, and he brought his oxen before him, to make them lie down in their stable which was in the farm. And behold, the wife of the elder brother was afraid on account of the words that she had said. She took a parcel of fat, and she became like one who is evilly beaten, desiring to say to her husband, "It is your younger brother who has done this wrong." Her husband returned in the evening, in his typical fashion. He came to his house, and he found his wife ill of violence. She did not give him water for his hands as he was used to having; she did not make a light before him; his house was in darkness, and she was lying very sick. Her husband said to her, "Who has spoken with you?" Behold she said, "No one has spoken with me except your younger brother. When he came to get your corn he found me sitting alone. He said to me, 'Come, let us stay together; tie up your hair.' Thus he said to me. I did not listen to him, but I said to him: 'Behold, am I not your mother; is not your elder brother like a father to you?' And he was afraid, and he beat me to stop me from telling you, and if you let him live I will die. Now behold he is coming in the evening, and I complain of these wicked words, for he would have done this even in daylight."

And the elder brother became like a panther of the south. He sharpened his knife; he took it in his hand; he stood behind the door of his stable to slay his younger brother as he came in the evening to bring his cattle into the stable.

Now the sun went down, and Bata loaded himself with herbs in his daily manner. He came, and his first cow entered the stable, and she said to her keeper, "Behold your elder brother is standing before you with his knife to slay you; flee from him." He heard what his first cow had said; and the next entering, she also said likewise. He looked beneath the door of the stable, and he saw the feet of his elder brother. He was standing behind the door, and his knife was in his hand. He cast down his load to the ground, and fled swiftly; and his elder brother pursued after him with his knife. Then the younger brother cried out to Ra Harakhti, saying, "My good Lord! You are the one who divides the evil from the good." And Ra stood and heard all his cry; and Ra made a wide water between him and his older brother, and it was full of crocodiles. And the one brother was on one bank, and the other on the other bank. And the elder brother struck twice on his hands at not slaying him. And the younger brother called to the elder on the bank, saying, "Stand still until the dawn, and when Ra rises, I will judge you before him, and he will discern between the good and the evil. For I will not be with you ever again. I shall not be in the place in which you are. I shall go to the valley of the acacia."

Now when the land was lightened, and the next day appeared, Ra Harakhti arose, and one looked to the other. And the youth spoke with his elder brother, saying, "Why were you after me to slay me in craftiness, when you did not hear the words of my mouth? For I am your brother in truth, and you are to me as a father, and your wife even as a mother: is it not so? Truly, when I was sent to get us corn, your wife said to me, 'Come, stay with me;' but behold this has been turned over to you in another way." And he caused him to understand all that happened with him and his wife. And Bata swore an oath by Ra Harakhti, saying, "Your coming to slay me by deceit with your knife was an abomination." Then the youth took a knife, and cut off his phallus, and cast it into the water, and the fish swallowed it. He failed; he became faint, and his elder brother cursed his own heart greatly. He stood weeping for him from far off, but he did not know how to pass over to where his younger brother was, because of the crocodiles. And the younger brother called to him, saying, "Because you devised an evil thing, will you not also devise a good thing, even like that which I would do to you? When you go to your house you must look to your cattle, for I will not stay in the place where you are. I am going to the valley of the acacia. And now as to what you shall do for me, you shall come to seek me, if you perceive a matter, namely, that there are things happening to me. And this is what shall come to pass, that I will draw out my soul, and I will put it on the top of the flowers of the acacia, and when the acacia is cut down, and it falls to the ground, and you come to seek it, if you search for it seven years do not let your heart be wearied. For you will find it, and you must put it in a cup of cold water, and expect that I will live again, that I may make answer to what has been done wrong. And you will know of this, that is to say, that things are happening to me, when someone gives you a cup of beer in your hand, and it is troubled; stay not then, for truly it shall come to pass with you."

And the youth went to the valley of the acacia; and his elder brother went to his house. His hand was laid on his head, and he cast dust on his head. He came to his house, and he killed his wife. He cast her to the dogs, and he sat in mourning for his younger brother.

Now many days after these things, the younger brother was in the valley of the acacia. There was no one with him. He spent his time in hunting the beasts of the desert, and he came back in the evening to lie down under the acacia, which bore his soul upon the topmost flower. And after this he built himself a tower with his own hands, in the valley of the acacia. It was full of all good things, so that he might provide for himself a home.

And he went out from his tower, and he met the Nine Gods, who were walking forth to look upon the whole land. The Nine Gods talked with one another, and they said to him, "Ho! Bata, bull of the Nine Gods, are you remaining alone? You have left your village because of the wife of Anpu, your elder brother. Behold his wife is slain. You have given him an answer to all that was transgressed against you." And their hearts were vexed for him exceedingly. And Ra Harakhti said to Khnumu, "Behold, fashion a woman for Bata, that he may not remain alone." And Khnumu made him a mate to dwell with him. She was more beautiful in her limbs than any woman in the whole land. The essence of every god was in her. The seven Hathors came to see her: they said with one mouth, "She will die a sharp death."

And Bata loved her exceedingly, and she dwelt in his house. He passed his time in hunting the beasts of the desert, and brought and laid them before her. He said, "Do not go outside, lest the sea seize you, for I cannot rescue you from it, for I am a woman like you. My soul is placed on the head of the flower of the acacia, and if another finds it, I must fight with him." And he opened to her his heart in all its nature.

Now after these things Bata went to hunt in his daily manner. And the young girl went to walk under the acacia which was by the side of her house. Then the sea saw her, and cast its waves up after her. She fled from it. She entered her house. And the sea called to the acacia, saying, "Oh, would that I could seize her!" And the acacia brought a lock from her hair, and the sea carried it to Egypt, and dropped it in the place of the fullers of Pharaoh's linen. The smell of the lock of hair entered into the clothes of Pharaoh, and they were wroth with the fullers of Pharaoh, saying, "The smell of ointment is in the clothes of Pharaoh."

And the people were rebuked every day; they did not know what they should do. And the chief fuller of Pharaoh walked by the bank, and his heart was very evil within him after the daily quarrel with him. He stood still. He stood upon the sand opposite to the lock of hair, which was in the water, and he made someone go into the water and bring it to him, and there was found in it a smell, exceedingly sweet. He took it to Pharaoh, and they brought the scribes and the wise men, and they said to Pharaoh, "This lock of hair belongs to a daughter of Ra Harakhti: the essence of every god is in her, and it is a tribute to you from another land. Let messengers go to every strange land to seek her: and as for the messenger who shall go to the valley of the acacia, let many men go with him to bring her." Then his majesty said, "Exceedingly excellent is what has been said to us," and they sent them. And many days after these things the people who were sent to strange lands came to give report to the king: but not those who went to the valley of the acacia, for Bata had slain them, but he let one of them return to give a report to the king. His majesty sent many men and soldiers, as well as horsemen, to bring her back. And there was a woman amongst them, and to her had been given in her hand beautiful ornaments of a woman. And the girl came back with her, and they rejoiced over her in the whole land.

And his majesty loved her exceedingly, and raised her to high estate, and he asked her to speak to him concerning her husband. And she said, "Let the acacia be cut down, and let one chop it up." And they sent men and soldiers with their weapons to cut down the acacia, and they came to the acacia, and they cut the flower upon which was the soul of Bata, and he fell dead suddenly.

And when the next day came, and the earth was lightened, the acacia was cut down. And Anpu, the elder brother of Bata, entered his house, and washed his hands; and someone gave him a cup of beer, and it became troubled. And someone gave him another of wine, and the smell of it was evil. Then he took his staff, and his sandals, and his clothes, with his weapons of war, and he went forth to the valley of the acacia. He entered the tower of his younger brother, and he found him lying upon his mat. He was dead. And he wept when he saw his younger brother truly lying dead. And he went out to seek the soul of his younger brother under the acacia tree, under which his younger brother lay in the evening. Anpu spent three years seeking it, but did not find it. And when he began the fourth year, he desired in his heart to return into Egypt. He said, "I will go tomorrow morning." Thus he spoke in his heart.

Now when the land lightened, and the next day appeared, Anpu was walking under the acacia. He was spending his time seeking it. And he returned in the evening, and labored at seeking it again. He found a seed. He returned with it. Behold this was the soul of his younger brother. He brought a cup of cold water, and he put the seed into it, and he sat down, as he was accustomed to do. Now when the night came Bata's soul sucked up the water. Bata shuddered in all his limbs, and he looked on his elder brother. His soul was in the cup. Then Anpu took the cup of cold water, in which the soul of his younger brother was. Bata drank it; his soul stood again in its place, and he became as he had been. They embraced each other, and they conversed together.

And Bata said to his elder brother, "Behold I will become a great bull, which bears every good mark. No one knows its history, and you must sit upon my back. When the sun rises I will be in the place where my wife is, that I may return answer to her, and you must take me to the place where the king is. For all good things shall be done for you. For one shall lade you with silver and gold, because you bring me to Pharaoh, for I will become a great marvel, and they will rejoice for me in all the land. And you shall go to your village."

And when the land was lightened, and the next day appeared, Bata transformed into the form which he had told to his elder brother. And Anpu sat upon his back until the dawn. He came to the place where the king was, and they made his majesty aware of him. He saw Bata, and he was exceeding joyful with him. He made great offerings for him, saying, "This is a great wonder which has come to pass." There were rejoicings over the bull in the whole land. They presented silver and gold to his elder brother, who went and stayed in his village. They gave to the bull many men and many things, and Pharaoh loved him exceedingly above all that is in this land. And after many days after these things, the bull entered the purified place. He stood in the place where the princess was, and he began to speak with her, saying, "Behold, I am alive indeed." And she said to him, "And, pray, who are you?" He said to her, "I am Bata. I perceived when you caused them to destroy the acacia of Pharaoh, which was my abode, that I might not be suffered to live. Behold, I am alive indeed, I am an ox." Then the princess feared exceedingly because of the words that her husband had spoken to her. And he went out from the purified place.

And his majesty was sitting, making a good day with her. She was at the table of his majesty, and the king was exceedingly pleased with her. And she said to his majesty, "Swear to me by God, saying, 'Whatever you say, I will obey it for your sake.'" He hearkened to all that she said, even this. "Let me eat of the liver of the ox, because he is fit for nothing!" Thus she said to him. And the king was exceedingly sad at her words; the heart of Pharaoh grieved him greatly. And after the land was lightened, and the next day appeared, they proclaimed a great feast with offerings to the ox. And the king sent one of the chief butchers of his majesty to sacrifice the ox. And when he was sacrificed, as he was on the shoulders of the people, he shook his neck, and he threw two drops of blood against the two doors of his majesty. The one fell upon the one side, on the great door of Pharaoh, and the other upon the other door. They grew as two great Persea trees, and each of them was excellent.

And one went to tell his majesty, "Two great Persea trees have grown, as a great marvel of his majesty, in the night by the side of the great gate of his majesty." And there was rejoicing for them in all the land, and there were offerings made to them.

And when the days were multiplied after these things, his majesty was adorned with the blue crown, with garlands of flowers on his neck, and he was on the chariot of pale gold, and he went out from the palace to behold the Persea trees. The princess also was going out with horses behind his majesty. And his majesty sat beneath one of the Persea trees, and it spoke with his wife: "Oh deceitful one, I am Bata, I am alive, though I have been evilly treated. I knew who caused the acacia to be cut down by Pharaoh at my dwelling. I then became an ox, and you asked that I should be killed."

And many days after these things the princess stood at the table of Pharaoh, and the king was pleased with her. And she said to his majesty,

"Swear to me by God, saying, 'That which the princess shall say to me I will obey it for her.'" And he hearkened to all she said. And he commanded, "Let these two Persea trees be cut down, and let them be made into good planks." And he hearkened to all she said. And after this his majesty sent skillful craftsmen, and they cut down the Persea trees of Pharaoh, and the princess, the royal wife, was standing looking on, and they did all that was in her heart to the trees. But a chip flew up, and it entered the mouth of the princess. She swallowed it, and after many days she bore a son. And one went to tell his majesty, "There is born to you a son." And they brought him, and gave to him a nurse and servants, and there were rejoicings in the whole land. And the king sat making a merry day, as they were about the naming of him, and his majesty loved him exceedingly at that moment, and the king raised him to be the royal son of Kush.

Now after the days had multiplied after these things, his majesty made him heir of all the land. And many days after that, when he had fulfilled many years as heir, his majesty flew up to heaven. And the heir said, "Let my great nobles of his majesty be brought before me, that I may make them know all that has happened to me." And they brought before Bata his wife, and he judged her before him, and they agreed with him. They brought to him his elder brother. He made Anpu hereditary prince in all his land. Bata was thirty years king of Egypt, and he died, and his elder brother stood in his place on the day of his burial.

SOURCE: W. M. Flinders Petrie, *Egyptian Tales Translated from the Papyri*, First Series IVth–XIIth Dynasty, 2nd edition (New York: Frederick A. Stokes, 1899), 36–65, with modifications.

21

BELLEROPHON

In his epic poem the *Iliad*, the Greek poet Homer (ninth–eighth century BCE) tells the story of the fall of Troy. Throughout the poem, Homer often relates the stories of famed Greek heroes, including Bellerophon, recounted in the excerpt below. Bellerophon was granted beauty by the gods, and Proetus, king of Argos and Tiryns, was jealous and plotted Bellerophon's demise. Proetus' wife, Anteia, desired Bellerophon, and when spurned, she lied to Proetus, claiming that Bellerophon attempted to seduce her. Proetus, afraid to kill Bellerophon himself, sends him to his father-in-law in Lycia. The story of Bellerophon contains a theme central to both the popular Egyptian "Tale of Two Brothers" and the story of Joseph in Genesis 39, the blameless hero falsely accused of rape by the wife of the ruler.

Homer, *Iliad* 6.150–190

Howbeit, if you will, hear this also, that you may know well my lineage; and many there are that know it. There is a city Ephyre in the heart of Argos, pastureland of horses, and there dwelt Sisyphus that was craftiest of men, Sisyphus, son of Aeolus; and he had a son Glaucus; and Glaucus begat peerless Bellerophon.

To Bellerophon the gods granted beauty and lovely manliness; but Proetus in his heart devised evil against him, and drove him, seeing he was mightier, far from the land of the Argives; for Zeus had made them subject to his scepter. Now the wife of Proetus, fair Anteia, lusted madly for Bellerophon, to lie with him in secret love, but could in no way prevail upon wise-hearted Bellerophon, for his heart was upright. So she made a tale of lies, and spoke to king Proetus: "Either die yourself, Proetus, or slay Bellerophon, seeing he was minded to lie with me in love against my will." So she spoke, and wrath grabbed hold of the king to hear that word.

Slay Bellerophon he would not, for his soul had awe of that; but he sent him to Lycia, and gave him baneful tokens, graving in a folded tablet many deadly signs, and bade him show these to his own wife's father, that he might be slain. So Bellerophon went his way to Lycia under the blameless escort of the gods. And when he came to Lycia and the stream of Xanthus, then with a ready heart did the king of wide Lycia do him honor: for nine days he showed him entertainment, and slew nine oxen.

However, when the tenth rosy-fingered Dawn appeared, then at length he questioned Bellerophon and asked to see whatever token he bore from his daughter's husband, Proetus. But when he had received from him the evil token of his daughter's husband, first he bade him slay the raging Chimaera. She was of divine stock, not of men: in the forepart a lion, in the hinder a serpent, and in the midst a goat, breathing forth in terrible wise the might of blazing fire. And Bellerophon slew her, trusting in the signs of the gods. Next he fought with the glorious Solymi, and this, said he was the mightiest battle of warriors that ever he entered; and thirdly he slew the Amazons, women the peers of men. And against him, as he journeyed back therefrom, the king wove another cunning wile; he chose out of wide Lycia the bravest men and set an ambush; but these did not return home, for peerless Bellerophon slew them one and all.

SOURCE: A. T. Murray, *Homer: Iliad*, vol. 1: *Books 1–12*, Loeb Classical Library 170 (Cambridge, Mass.: Harvard University Press, 1924), 285–89. Loeb Classical Library® is a registered trademark of the President and Fellows of Harvard College.

22

ARION

The Greek historian Herodotus (fifth century BCE) tells the story of Arion, a famous Greek musician. Arion, while traveling from Italy to Corinth, found himself in danger at the hands of the Corinthian sailors who plotted to rob him and throw him overboard. Unable to convince them otherwise, Arion bargained for an opportunity to play and sing one last song, after which he flung himself into the sea, only to be saved by a dolphin (cp. the book of Jonah).

Herodotus, *Histories* 1.23–24

Periander, who disclosed the oracle's answer to Thrasybulus, was the son of Cypselus, and sovereign of Corinth. The Corinthians say (and the Lesbians agree) that the most marvelous thing that happened to him in his life was the landing on Taenarus of Arion of Methymna, brought there by a dolphin. This Arion was a lyre player second to none in that age; he was the first man whom we know to compose and name the dithyramb which he afterwards taught at Corinth.

They say that this Arion, who spent most of his time with Periander, wished to sail to Italy and Sicily, and that after he had made a lot of money there he wanted to come back to Corinth. Trusting none more than the Corinthians, he hired a Corinthian vessel to carry him from Tarentum. But when they were out at sea, the crew plotted to take Arion's money and cast him overboard. Discovering this, he earnestly entreated them, asking for his life and offering them his money. But the crew would not listen to him, and told him either to kill himself and so receive burial on land or else to jump into the sea at once. Abandoned to this extremity, Arion asked that, since they had made up their minds, they would let him stand on the half deck in all his regalia and sing; and he promised that after he had sung he would do himself in. The men, pleased at the thought of hearing the best singer in the world, drew away toward the waist of the vessel from the stern. Arion, putting on all his regalia and taking his lyre, stood up on the half deck and sang the "Stirring Song," and when the song was finished he threw himself into the sea, as he was with all his regalia. So the crew sailed away to Corinth; but a dolphin (so the story goes) took Arion on his back and bore him to Taenarus. Landing there, he went to Corinth in his regalia, and when he arrived, he related all that had happened. Periander, skeptical, kept him in confinement, letting him go nowhere, and waited for the sailors. When they arrived, they were summoned and asked what news they brought of Arion. While they were saying that he was safe in Italy and that they had left him flourishing at Tarentum, Arion appeared before them, just as he was when he jumped from the ship; astonished, they could no longer deny what was proved against them. This is what the Corinthians and Lesbians say, and there is a little bronze memorial of Arion on Taenarus, the figure of a man riding upon a dolphin.

SOURCE: A. D. Godley, *Herodotus: The Persian Wars,* vol. 1: *Books 1–2,* Loeb Classical Library 117 (Cambridge, Mass.: Harvard University Press, 1920), 25–29. Loeb Classical Library® is a registered trademark of the President and Fellows of Harvard College.

D. EPIC HEROES

The plethora of stories of ancestors, leaders, judges, and kings in the Hebrew Bible is somewhat unique in the ancient Near East given that there are not many stories of mortal heroes in the literature of Babylon, Assyria, or Egypt. There are a few exceptions, however, like Mesopotamian Enkidu, and Ugaritic literature in particular is rife with epic mortal heroes comparable to their fellow Semitic figures in the Hebrew Bible. Below are excerpts from epic poems describing the feats of the mortal heroes Enkidu, Keret, Aqhat and his father Danel, as well as an excerpt from the story of the Ugaritic deity, Baal. The poems share themes with stories of biblical figures like Abraham, Elijah, Jael, and Samson.

23

ENKIDU

The Mesopotamian Epic of Gilgamesh (second millennium BCE) describes the life of Gilgamesh, the demigod king of Uruk, and his best friend, Enkidu. The excerpt below describes the creation of the nearly invincible warrior, Enkidu, who is covered in hair and lives in the wild with the animals. When Gilgamesh hears of Enkidu, he is concerned that Enkidu is the only living being that would be able to defeat the king, and so Gilgamesh devises a plan to domesticate and subdue Enkidu through a sexual encounter with a woman. The hairy "wild man" motif in the story of Enkidu is similar to the wild men in the Hebrew Bible like Samson, Elijah, and Elisha (Jdg 13–16; 1 Kgs 17–19; 21; 2 Kgs 1–9; 13). The excerpt below is from the Akkadian (Semitic-speaking region of northern Mesopotamia; modern-day central Iraq) version of the Gilgamesh epic based on earlier Mesopotamian sources.

The Epic of Gilgamesh, Tablet 1

. . . Aruru
Fingered some clay, on the desert she molded it . . .
Enkidu she made, a warrior, born and begotten,
Of Ninurta the double, and put forth on the whole of his body
Hair: in the way of a woman he braided his locks;
Luxuriant growth of his hair sprouted like the barley,
Nor did he know the people nor land; he was clad in a garb like Sumuqan.
Even with gazelles he pastured on herbage, along with the cattle
He drank his fill, with the beasts did his heart delight at the water.
Then a hunter, a trapper, came face to face with him,
Came upon him, two, three days, at the place where the beasts drank water;
When the hunter spied him, his face over mantled with terror,
He and his cattle went to his steading, dismayed and frightened,
Crying aloud, distressed in, his heart, and his face clouded,
. . .
His face was the same as one who has gone on a far journey.
The hunter opened his mouth, and spoke, addressing his father:
"Father, there is a great fellow who came forth from out of the mountains,
But his strength is the greatest,
Like a double of Anu's own self, his strength is enormous,
He ranges at large over the mountains with cattle;
He grazes on herbage and he ever sets his foot to the water,
So that I fear to approach him. The pits which I hollowed
With my own hands he has filled in, and the traps of my setting
Torn up, and out of my clutches he has helped all the cattle escape,
Beasts of the desert. He will not allow me to work at my field craft."
His father opened his mouth and spoke, addressing the hunter:
"Gilgamesh dwells in Erech, my son, whom no one has vanquished,
Nay, but his strength is greatest,
Like a double of Anu's own self, his strength is enormous.
Go, set your face towards Erech: and when he hears of a monster,
He will say 'Go, O hunter, a courtesan girl, a hetaera
Take with you . . .
When he gathers the cattle again to the place of drinking,
So will she put off her mantle the charm of her beauty revealing;
Then he will spy her, and will embrace her, and thenceforth his cattle,
Which in his very own deserts were reared, will deny him.'"
Unto the council of his father the hunter hearkened, and straightway
He went away to Gilgamesh.
Taking the road towards Erech
He turned his steps, and came to Gilgamesh, his speech thus addressing:

"There is a great fellow who has come forth out of the mountains,
O, but his strength is the greatest, the length and breadth of the country,
Like to a double of Anu's own self his strength is enormous,
Ever he ranges at large over the mountains, and ever with cattle
He grazes on herbage, and ever he sets his foot to the water,
So that I fear to approach him. The pits which I hollowed
With my own hands he has filled in, the traps of my setting
Torn up, and out of my clutches he has helped the cattle escape,
Beasts of the desert: to work at my field craft he will not allow me."
Gilgamesh to him, to the hunter made answer:
"Go, my hunter, take with you a courtesan girl, a hetaera,
When he gathers again the cattle to the place of drinking,
So will she put off her mantle, revealing the charm of her beauty,
Then he will spy her, and will embrace her, and thenceforth his cattle
Which in his very own deserts were reared will straightway deny him."
Forth went the hunter and took with him a courtesan girl, a hetaera,
They started on their travels, went forth on their journey,
At the term of three days arrived at the place appointed.
They sat down in their ambush, the hunter and the hetaera,
One day, two days they sat by the place where the beasts drank water.
Then at last the cattle came to take their fill in their drinking.
Thither the animals came that their hearts might delight in the water.
There was Enkidu also, he whom the mountains had gendered,
Even with gazelles did he pasture on herbage, along with the cattle
He drank his fill, with the beasts did his heart delight at the water,
So he beheld the courtesan girl, the lusty great fellow,
O but a monster savage from out of the depths of the desert!
"It is he, O girl! O, discover your beauty, your comeliness show him,
So that your loveliness he may possess. O, in no way be bashful,
Ravish his soul, as soon as his eye falls on you,
He, forsooth, will approach you, and you, O, loosen your mantle,
So that he can clasp you, and with the wiles of a woman shall ply him;
Wherefore his animals, bred in his desert, will deny him,
Since to his breast he has held you."
The girl, displaying her bosom,
Showed him her comeliness, so that her beauty possessed him,
Bashful she was not, but ravished his soul, losing her mantle,
So that he clasped her, and then with the wiles of a woman she plied him,
Holding her to his breast.
So it was that Enkidu dallied
Six days, seven nights, with the courtesan girl in his mating.
Sated at length with her charms, he turned his face to his cattle.
O the gazelles, how they scampered away, as soon as they saw him!

Him, yes, Enkidu, fled from his presence the beasts of the desert!
Enkidu losing his innocence, so, when the cattle fled from him,
Failed his knees, and he slacked in his running, not as aforetime:
Nonetheless he has attained his full growth and has broadened his wisdom.
He sat again at the feet of the woman, the woman his features
Scanning, and, while she was speaking, his ears heard what she was saying:
"You are comely, even like to a god, O Enkidu, shall be,
Why with the beasts of the field do you range over the desert?
Up! for I'll lead you to Erech, the high-walled, to the Temple
Sacred, the dwelling of Anu and Ishtar, where, highest in power,
Gilgamesh is, and prevails over men like an aurochs."
Her counsel, even as she spoke it,
Found favor, for conscious he was of his longing,
Some companion to seek; so to the courtesan he spoke:
"Up, then, O girl, to the Temple, the holy and sacred, invite me,
Me, to the dwelling of Anu and Ishtar, where, highest in power,
Gilgamesh is, and prevails over men like an aurochs . . ."

SOURCE: R. Campbell Thompson, *The Epic of Gilgamish: A New Translation from a Collation of the Cuneiform Tablets in the British Museum Rendered Literally into English Hexameters* (London: Luzac & Co., 1928), 10–14, with modifications.

24

THE LEGEND OF KING KERET

The legend of King Keret is recounted in second-millennium BCE texts from Ugarit (Ras Shamra), located on the Mediterranean coast of northern Syria. The epic poem praises the life of King Keret, described as the son of El, the head of the Ugaritic pantheon, and his wife, Asherah. Keret, though, unlike his parentage, is mortal, and is deeply concerned about his lack of offspring. Keret's concern for offspring mirrors many of the ancestor stories in the Hebrew Bible, including Abraham's long wait for his heir, Isaac (Gen 11:29–18:33; 20–22), Rebekah's initial barrenness (Gen 25:21-23), and Rachel and Leah competing to have more children (Gen 29:31–30:24).

. . .

Keret in offspring is ruined,
Keret is undermined of establishment.
His lawful wife he did find,

his legitimate spouse:
he married the woman, and she "departed."
Flesh of kinship had he:
one-third died at birth,
one-fourth of sickness;
one-fifth the pestilence gathered
unto itself, one-sixth the sea
engulfed; one-seventh thereof fell
by the sword. He sees his offspring,
doth Keret; he sees his offspring ruined,
wholly undermined his seat,
and in its entirety a posterity perishing,
and in its totality a succession.
He enters his cubicle, he weeps,
an inner chamber and cries.
His tears do drop
like shekels to the ground.
His bed was soaked
by his weeping, and he slept
a slumber in his crying.
sleep prevails (over him(?))
and he lies, slumber
and he reclines. And in his dream
El descends, in his vision
The Father of Man (Adam). And he approaches
asking Keret: "What ails thee,
Keret, that he weeps,
that he cries, Naaman the Lad
of El? Is it the kingship of Bull his father
that he desires, or authority
like the Father of Man (Adam)?"
. . .
"[Grant that] I may beget [chil]dren;
[grant that] I may multiply [kins]men."
And Bull, his father El, [replied]:
"E[nough] for thee of weeping, Keret;
Of crying, Naaman, Lad of
El. Though shalt wash and rouge thyself.
Wash thy [h]and to the elbow,
[thy] fing[ers] up to the shoulder.
Enter the shade of a pavilion.
Take a lam[b in thy hand],
A lamb of sac[rifice in (thy)] right hand,

A kid in th[e other han]d,

. . .

Take a *msrr*, bird of
sacrifice. Pour wine [into a bo]wl of
silver, honey into a bowl of [g]old.
{Mount to the top of a [to]wer.}
And mount to the top of a [to]wer; be-
stride the top of the wal[l]. Lift thy hands
to heaven. Sacrifice to Bull,
thy father El. Honor Baal
with thy sacrifice, the Son of Dagon
with thine oblation. Then let Keret
descend from the housetops. Prepare thou
corn from the granaries,
wheat from the storehouses.
Let bread be baked of a fifth,
food of a sixth month.
Muster Ngb and let it come forth,
the host of the troops of Ngb.
And let come forth the assembled multitude,
thy troops, a mighty force:
three hundred myriads;
serfs uncounted,
peasants untold.
They march in thousands serried,
and in myriads massed.
After two, two march;
after three, all of them.
The solitary man closes his house;
the widow hires herself
out; the sick man is carried in
(his) bed; the one-eyed man blinks
with one eye. And even the newly wed
bridegroom goes forth: he drives to another
his wife, to a stranger
his well beloved. (They are) like the locusts
that swell on the steppe,
like grasshoppers on the borders of the desert.
March a day and a second; a third, a fourth day;
a fifth, a sixth day. Behold, at sunrise
on the seventh thou wilt arrive at Udum
the Great, even at Udum the Grand.
And do thou attack the villages, harass
the towns. Sweep from the fields

her woodcutters, from the threshing floors the straw pickers.
Sweep from the spring the women that draw, from the fountain
the women that fill. Tarry a day and a second;
a third, a fourth day; a fifth,
a sixth day: thine arrows shoot not
into the city, (nor) thy hand stone
flung headlong. And behold, at sunrise
on the seventh, King Pabel will
sleep until the noise of the neighing of his stallion,
until the sound of the braying of his ass,
until the lowing of the plough ox, the howling
of the watch dog. Then will he send
two messengers unto thee, unto Keret,
to the camp: 'Message of King Pabel:
Take silver and yellow-glittering gold;
. . . and perpetual slaves;
a groom, horses, chariots,
from the stable of the son of a handmaid.
Take, Keret, make peace,
make peace. And flee, O king,
from my house; withdraw, O Keret,
from my court. Vex not
Udum the Great, even Udum the Grand.
Udum is a gift of El, even a present
of the Father of Man (Adam).' Then send thou
the two messengers back to him: 'What need have I
of silver and yellow-glittering gold;
. . . and perpetual
slaves; a groom, horses, chariots,
from the stables of the son of a handmaid?
A possession that is not in my house shalt thou give!
Give me Lady Ḥurriya,
the fairest of the offspring of thy firstborn;
whose grace is like the grace of Anath,
[whose] beau[ty] like the beauty of Ashtoreth;
whose eyeballs are the pureness of lapis, whose pup[ils]
the gleam of garnet . . .
let me bask in the brightness of her eyes—
whom in my dream El bestowed,
in my vision the Father of Man (Adam).
And let her bear offspring to Keret,
and a lad to the Servant of El.'"
Keret looked, and (it was) a dream;
the Servant of El, and (it was) a fantasy.

He washed and rouged himself;
he washed his hands to the elbow,
his fingers up to the shoulder.
He entered the shade of a pavilion. He took
a lamb of offering in his hand,
a kid in the other hand,

. . .

He took a *msrr*, bird of sacrif[ice].
He poured wine into a bowl of silver,
honey into a bowl of gold. And he mounted
to the top of a tower, he bestrode
the top of the wall. He lifted up
his [han]ds to heaven. He sacrificed
to Bull, his father El. He honored
Baal with his sacrifice, the Son of Dagon
with his [ob]lation. Keret descended
[from the housetop]s. He prepared corn from the granaries,
wheat from the storehouses.
Bread [was ba]ked of a fifth,
[food] of a sixth mon[th].
He mu[st]ered Ngb and [it came forth, the host]
of the troops of Ng[b. And there came forth the assembled]
multitude, his [troo]ps, [a mighty force]:
thr[ee] hundred myriads.
They marched in thousands serried,
and in myriads massed.
After two, two march;
after three, all of them.
The solitary man closes his house;
the widow hires herself
out; the sick man is carried in
(his) bed; the one-eyed man
blinks with one eye.
And (to them) is added the newly wed bridegroom:
He drives to another his wife,

. . .

. . . "Give
me Lady Ḥurriya,
the fairest of the offspring of thy firstborn;
whose fairness is like the fairness
of Anath, whose beauty like the
beauty of Ashtoreth;
whose eyeballs are the pureness of lapis,
whose pupils the gleam of garnet;

whom in my dream [El] bestowed,
in my vision the Father of Man (Adam).
And let her bear offspring to Keret,
and a Lad to the Servant of
El." . . .
The gods bless (and) proceed.
The gods proceed to their tents,
the family of El to their habitations.
And she conceives and bears son<s> to him,
and conceives and bears daughters to him.
Lo! In seven years,
the sons of Keret were even as had been stipulated in the vows;
the daughters, also, of Ḥurriya
were even so. . . .

SOURCE: H. L. Ginsberg, *The Legend of King Keret: A Canaanite Epic of the Bronze Age*, Bulletin of the American Schools of Oriental Research Supplementary Series 2–3 (New Haven: American Schools of Oriental Research, 1946), 14–23. Used by permission of the publisher.

25

THE AQHAT EPIC

The legend of Aqhat is from the ancient site of Ugarit (Ras Shamra) on the Mediterranean coast of Syria which was destroyed in 1200 BCE. The poem begins by pointing out that Danel, the servant of the gods, has no children, so El decides to bless him with a son, Aqhat. Danel then feasts the gods and in return receives a bow for Aqhat. The goddess Anat covets the bow, so she kills Aqhat with the aid of Yatpan, smashing Aqhat's head. Danel's progeny is not at an end, however, because the poem reveals that Danel also has a daughter, Pughat, who plots vengeance on her brother's slayer, though whether or not she is successful is unknown given that the ending of the poem is missing. Elements of the poem bear resemblances to stories in the Hebrew Bible. For instance, the desire for male offspring parallels the biblical ancestors' struggles to have heirs (Gen 11:29–18:33; 20–22; 25:21-23; 29:31–30:24), and the female warrior Anat kills the male warrior Aqhat by smashing his head, similar to Sisera's death at the hands of Jael (Jdg 4–5).

Danel, the Rapian,
The Hero, the devoted one of the Rainmaker:
In a loincloth, he served food to the gods,

In a loincloth, he served drinks to the holy ones.

. . .

He lay down upon his mourning bed and went to sleep.
Behold, a day passed and then a second:
In a loincloth, Danel served the gods,
In a loincloth, he served the gods food,
In a loincloth, he served drinks to the holy ones.
A third, a fourth day passed:
In a loincloth, Danel served the gods,
In a loincloth, he served the gods food,
In a loincloth, he served drinks to the holy ones.
A fifth, a sixth day passed:
In a loincloth, Danel served the gods,
In a loincloth, he served the gods food,
In a loincloth, he served drinks to the holy ones.

. . .

He lay down upon his mourning bed and went to sleep.
Behold, the seventh day arrived:
In a loincloth, he served the gods food,
In a loincloth, he served drinks to the holy ones;
Then Baal approached with his request to El:
"Do you not care about Danel, the Rapian?
About the work of the Hero, the devoted one of the Rainmaker?
He has no son like his kin,
He is without a son, unlike his family,
He is without offspring, unlike his brothers.
Will you bless him, O Bull, El, my father?

. . .

So that a son may come into his house,
Offspring in his residence,
To bury his father,

. . .

To draw out his spirit from the earth,
The guardian of his resting place from the earth . . ."
El took a cup in his hand,
A goblet in his right hand.
Truly, El blessed his servant,
He blessed Danel, the Rapian,
Pronounced a benediction on the Hero, devoted one of the Rainmaker.
"By my soul: Danel the Rapian shall live on,
By my strength, the Hero, the devoted one of the Rainmaker.
No one else, will rise from his bed,
He will mount the lovemaking bed.

While kissing his wife, he will impregnate,
His breath will be heated as he embraces her.
No one else will impregnate the child bearer,
Passionately, the Lady of the Rapian.
A son will come into his house,
Offspring in his residence.
To set up his father's grave

. . .

To consume his portion in the temple of Baal,
And his allotment in the temple of El.
To take his hand when he is drunk,
To support him when he is intoxicated.
To plaster his roof after a day of rain,
To wash his garments after a dirty day."
Danel's face brightened,
His countenance shined.
He opened his mouth to laugh,
He stretched his foot to the footstool;
He raised his voice and declared:
"I will sit down to rest,
And my soul will be at ease in my chest.
For a son will be born to me like those of my brothers,
Offspring like my kin."

. . .

Danel arrived at his house,
Danel took himself home.
The Kosharot entered his house,
The radiant daughters of the Crescent Moon.
Danel, the Rapian,
The Hero, devoted one of the Rainmaker;
Slaughtered an ox for the Kosharot,
He served up food to the Kosharot;
He served up drinks to the radiant daughters of the Crescent Moon.
Behold! A day and a second passed,
He served up food to the Kosharot;
He served up drinks to the radiant daughters of the Crescent Moon.
A third, a fourth day passed,
He served up food to the Kosharot;
He served up drinks to the radiant daughters of the Crescent Moon.
A fifth, a sixth day passed,
He served up food to the Kosharot;
He served up drinks to the radiant daughters of the Crescent Moon.
Behold, the seventh day arrived;
The Kosharot departed from Danel's house,

The radiant daughters of the Crescent Moon,
The beloved, lovely attendants of the bed,
The companions, beautiful attendants of the bed.
Danel sat down to wait,
To count the months of her pregnancy.
A month, two months went by,
Three, four months;
In the tenth month, it arrived.

. . .

Danel said: "I will fashion a bow of great value,
I will construct a curve."
Then, on the seventh day:
Danel, the Rapian,
The Hero, devoted one of the Rainmaker,
Took his high seat in the gate,
Alongside the nobles on the threshing floor.
He judged the case of the widow,
He presided over the case of the orphan;

. . .

Behold! He fashioned a bow;
He constructed a curve.
Danel, the Rapian,
The Hero, devoted one of the Rainmaker,
Called to his wife:
"Hear, Lady Danty:
Prepare a lamb from the flock,
For Koshar-Hasis,
For the appetite of Hayin, the artisan.
Serve up food and drink for the god,
Wait on him with honor;
He is the Lord of Memphis,
. . ."
The Lady heard;
She prepared a lamb from the flock,
For the palette of Koshar-Hasis,
For the appetite of Hayin, the artisan.
Afterwards, Koshar-Hasis arrived,
In the hand of Danel he placed a bow,
On his knees he laid a curve.
Whereupon Lady Danty
Served up food and drinks to the gods;
She waited on him with honor.
He is the Lord of Memphis,

. . .

Koshar departed to his tent,
Hayin departed
To his resting place.
Danel, the Rapian,
The Hero, devoted one of the Rainmaker,
Bent the bow,
He stood over Aqhat, his son:
"Observe, my son, your initiation in hunting,
May you hunt well!
. . .
Eat the food, indeed;
Drink of the foamy wine, indeed.
Serve up suckling calf,
With a carving knife, the breast of a yearling."
They drank wine from goblets,
From golden cups, the juice of fruit trees
Barrels of wine, cup upon cup.
Truly the goddess Anat drank from the wine,
And the alcohol went to her head;
The wine verily swelled her waistline.
Aqhat set the bow down,
He braced his bow against his ear;
The bow sat erect.
When Anat raised her eyes, she beheld it.
Anat's muscles hardened like ice,
Her eyes flashed like lightning;
Like the sea rolling the deep,
Lightning bolts destroying a forest;
She coveted the protruding bow,
The curve standing erect;
Her eyes were like those of a snake.
She dropped her goblet to the ground,
Her cup spilled over the earth;
She raised her voice and declared:
"Hear, O Hero Aqhat:
Ask for silver, and I will give it to you,
Ask for gold, and I will grant it to you;
But give your bow to me, the Maiden Anat."
. . .
The Hero Aqhat replied:
"The finest wood from Lebanon,
The sinews of wild oxen,
The toughest horn of an antelope;
The best reeds from the Great River Valley,

The strongest tendons from the heels of a bull;
Give them all to Koshar-Hasis,
And he will fashion a bow for you, Anat."
. . .

The Maiden Anat replied:
"Ask for life, O Hero Aqhat,
Ask for life, and I will give it to you;
Immortality, and I will grant it to you.
I will let you live long with Baal,
You can count the seasons with the gods.
You will live like Baal,
Life will be served,
It is served him and he drinks it.
He is celebrated in poems and songs,
Beautiful songs are sung about him;
This is the kind of life will I give you, Hero Aqhat."
The Hero Aqhat replied:
"Tell me no lies, O Maiden;
For to a hero your tales are like thorns,
Like spikes in the ass.
. . .

For I will die as all men die,
Indeed, I shall die like a mortal.
I would speak again:
The bow is the weapon of soldiers;
Now, is hunting a pastime for weak womankind?"
On the outside Anat smiled,
But inside, she schemed:
"Now then, leave me, O Hero Aqhat,
Leave me and be gone, funny one;
I will meet you on the road of arrogance,
I will encounter you on the road of pride;
. . .

I will trample you under my foot,
O handsome offspring of Danel,
Wisest of mortals."
She leapt to her feet and shook the ground.
Then she set out,
Towards El, between the Two Rivers,
In the midst of the river beds.
She saw the camp of El,
She arrived at the domain of the King,
The father of the lofty ones.
At the feet of El she knelt and fell,

She bowed and paid him homage;
She slandered the Hero Aqhat,
Truly she blackened the name of the beloved one of Danel, the Rapian.
Then the Maiden Anat declared,
She raised her voice and called out:
"I ask that Aqhat be brought low.
In the height of your house, O El,
In the height of your house do not jest,
In the loftiness of the house.
I will seize it with my right hand,
With both my hands,
In the lengthiness of my reach.
I will smash the crown of your head,
I will make your white hair run with blood,
The whiteness of your beard with gore.
Then you can call on Aqhat for help,
On the son of Danel to deliver you
From the hand of Maiden Anat."
Then Latpan, the benevolent god, replied:
"I know, my daughter, that you are man-like,
And that no other goddess has your temper.
Let the poison depart from your heart,
Discard what is in your bowels,
Set aside what is in your breast;
The one who defies you will be trampled."
The Maiden Anat left.
She set out towards the Hero Aqhat,

. . .

The Maiden Anat smiled.
She raised her voice and declared:
"Hear, O Hero Aqhat:
You are my brother,
And I your sister.
I love the fullness of your passion;
A lustiness like that of the Bull, El my father;

. . .

I am truly a bride to you,
You shall walk at my side my man.
Hear, O you happy man,
Bend your ear, O hero;
I will teach you how to hunt!"

. . .

"Groaning and excreting Aqhat will die,
By the crushing of the Maiden Anat,

By the annihilation of the levirate wife of Lim."
The Maiden Anat departed,
Then she set out,

. . .

She raised her voice and declared:

. . .

"As soon as the moon is new,
When its tip glows,
When its right corner shines;
When the light of its crown appears,
Aqhat will come . . .
He will hold the bow in his hand,
A curve, in his right hand;
I will slay him for the sake of his bow,
I will slay him for his curve;
I will dispossess the handsome hero,
Yes, his bow will be mine."

. . .

"Aqhat will sit down to eat,
The son of Danel to dine.
Above him, hawks will fly,
A band of birds will surveille.
Among the hawks I will fly,
Over Aqhat I will release you, Yatpan.
Hit him twice on the head,
Three times upon the ear.
Spill his blood like water,
Like a slaughtered animal on its knees.
Let his soul vanish like the wind,

. . .

Like breath from his nose.
When his death throes end, I will dispossess him."
She took Yatpan, the Sutean warrior,
She put him like a falcon in her belt,
Like a bird in her pouch.
Aqhat sat down to eat,
The son of Danel to dine.
Above him hawks hovered,
A band of birds surveilled.
Among the hawks Anat flew,
Over Aqhat she placed him (Yatpan).
He hit him twice on the head,
Three times upon the ear.
He spilled his blood like water,

Like a slaughtered animal on its knees.
His soul vanished like the wind,

. . .

Like breath from his nose.
Anat watched as his convulsions ended,
She watched as Aqhat expired;
She wept like a child, like a nursing babe.
"I am responsible on account of your bow.
Culpable, because of your curve.
You did not live long enough, Aqhat,
Truly plucked, you perished like the leaves."
The bow of Aqhat broke,
Like a lyre broke,
The prize of Koshar.
Thus the Maiden Anat return to Inbab.
She climbed the mountain like a wild bull,
Her hands, like a flash of lightning,
Her fingers, like a fire.
Then she cut the gums of his mouth,
She grasped his teeth and pulled them out.

. . .

From his grave, Aqhat watched,
He saw her heart of darkness.

. . .

Danel, the Rapian,
The Hero, devoted one of the Rainmaker,
Rose to take his seat in the gate,
Alongside the nobles on the threshing floor.
He judged the case of the widow,
He presided over the case of the orphan;
Now present is his daughter, Pughat.
A girl who draws from the spring and carries water,
Who wrings dew from wool,
Who knows the course of the stars.

. . .

SOURCE: Translation by Katherine E. Smith.

26

THE BAAL CYCLE

The following text gives the story of the rise of Baal and his female counterpart, Anat, often mentioned in the Hebrew Bible, to power among his fellow deities. The story comes from the ancient site of Ugarit (Ras Shamra) on the Mediterranean coast of Syria which was destroyed in 1200 BCE. Baal, who, like the biblical Yahweh, is a storm god, has to defeat his enemies, Yamm (also referred to as "Judge River" in the poem), the sea (cp. Gen 1 and God's ordering of the waters), and Mot, death, in order to secure his ranking in the Ugaritic pantheon. The deities each play a role in ordering the cosmos while they play out their political intrigue. The excerpt below describes Baal's conflict with Yamm. On Yahweh and Baal pitted against each other in their roles as storm gods see, for instance, 1 Kings 18.

. . .

Baal set his face towards El
At the intersection of the Two Rivers,
In the middle of the streams of the Deeps.
He entered the house of El,
He came to the abode of the King, Father of Shunem,
At the feet of El he bowed and fell,
Prostrated himself and honored him.

. . .

[Yamm sends messengers as well],
"Say to Tôr, his father, El!
Declare to the Assembled Pantheon,
The message of Yamm, your lord,
Of Judge River, your master:
'Give up, O gods, the one you harbor (Baal),
The one the multitudes harbor!
Give up Baal and his supporters,
Dagân's son, so that I will inherit his territory.'"
The messengers departed and returned.
Then they set their faces
Toward the mountain of Lalu,
Toward the Assembled Pantheon.
The gods had sat down,
The deities, to dine.

Baal was standing before El.
As soon as the gods saw them,
Saw the messengers of Yamm,
The emissaries of Judge River,
The gods bowed their heads to their knees
Upon their lofty thrones.
Baal rebuked them:
"Why, O gods, have you bowed
Your heads to your knees
Upon your lofty thrones?
May some of the gods read
The tablets of the messengers of Yamm,
Of the emissaries of Judge River!
Gods, lift up your heads
From your knees,
From your lofty thrones,
And I will answer
The messengers of Yamm,
The emissaries of Judge River."
The gods lifted their heads
From their knees,
From their lofty thrones.
. . .
They said to Ṭôr, his father, El:
"The message of Yamm, your lord,
Of your master, Judge River:
Give up, O gods, the one that you harbor
The one whom the multitudes harbor!
Give up Baal and his supporters,
Dagân's Son, so that I will inherit his territory!"
And Ṭôr, his father, El replied:
"Baal is your slave, O Yamm!
Dagân's Son is your captive!
He will bring you a tribute like the gods . . ."
Prince Baal was enraged;
He took a knife in his hand,   .
A dagger in his right hand.
To strike the messengers.
Anat seized his right hand,
Astarte seized his left hand:
"How can you strike the messengers of Yamm,
The emissaries of Judge River?
. . ."

Baal was enraged . . .
"I will bring them out,
I will drive them out
Into the sea,
To the earth let the mighty one fall
To the dust, the strong one."
From his mouth the word went out,
From his lips, his utterance,
And as his voice went forth,
Yamm fell at the throne.
And Kotaru declared:
"Did I not tell you, O Prince Baal,
Did I not declare, O Rider of Clouds?
Your enemies, Baal,
Your enemies you will strike,
You will vanquish your foes,
You will take the kingdom forever,
Your everlasting sovereignty!"
Kotaru brings down two clubs
And declares their names.
"Your name is Expeller!
Expeller, expel Yamm,
Expel Yamm from his throne,
River from the seat of his sovereignty!
Thou will fly in the hands of Baal
Like an eagle in his fingers!
Strike the back of Prince Yamm,
Cleave the hands of Judge River!"
The club flew in the hands of Baal,
Like an eagle in his fingers.
It struck the back of prince Sea
Cleaved the hands of Judge River.
But Judge River was strong;
Yamm was not vanquished
His joints did not fail
His body did not collapse.
Kotaru brought down two sticks
And declared their names.
"Your name is Driver!
Driver, drive Yamm
Drive Yamm from his throne,
River from the seat of his sovereignty!
You shall fly in the hands of Baal,

Like an eagle in his fingers!
Strike the head of Prince Yamm
Cleave the eyes of Judge River!
Let Yamm sink
And fall to the ground!"
The stick flew in the hands of Baal,
Like an eagle in his fingers.
It struck the head of Prince Yamm,
Cleaved the eyes of Judge River.
Yamm sunk,
Fell to the earth.
His joints failed,
His body collapsed.

. . .

Astarte rebuked him:
"Shame on you Aliyn Baal,
Shame, O Rider of Clouds!
Prince Yamm was our captor,
Judge River was our captor."
From there Baal went out,
Very ashamed was Aliyn Baal.
Yamm was dead,
So let Baal reign!

. . .

SOURCE: Translation by Katherine E. Smith.

E. INSCRIPTIONS AND LETTERS

W hen extrabiblical writings are discovered with information relating to the biblical texts, those writings can often provide insight into the biblical world. At times, they confirm the events discussed in the Hebrew Bible, or provide more information than the biblical text and help to give a more complete picture of Israel's history and society, or, at other times, provide an alternative interpretation of historical events. The texts presented in this section fall into one of those categories. The inscriptions and letters from Mari, Egypt, Moab, Assyria, northern Israel, and Judea date from the eighteenth to the sixth century BCE.

27

MARI LETTERS

A collection of tablets was discovered at the site of ancient Mari (Tell Hariri) in southern Mesopotamia dating from the reign of its last king, Zimri-Lim (eighteenth century BCE). The tablets found at Mari consist of administrative tablets, calendars, letters from the king to his wives, and letters to and from the servants of Zimri-Lim. These letters provide some information related to the early tribal history of Israel and its surrounding areas. The first letter excerpt below refers to the Benjaminites (Yaminites) in conflict with Mari and the second to the tribal systems in place that Zimri-Lim conquered, similar to the tribal system described in Joshua and Judges. The third letter excerpt discusses the practice of omen taking and divination by the servants of Zimri-Lim, similar to the divination at times practiced and at others prohibited in the Hebrew Bible (see, for example, Gen 30:27; Num 22:7; 23:23; 24:1; Deut 18:10; 1 Sam 15:23; and 2 Kgs 17:17).

Bannum to Zimri-Lim

I left Mari yesterday and on my way spent a night at Zurubban. All the Yaminites [Benjaminites] have lifted torches. From Samanum to Ilum-muluk and from Ilum-muluk to Mišlan, in response all the Yaminite towns in the Terqa district lifted torches. I have not yet figured out (the reason for) these torches, but I plan to do so now. I will then write my lord this or that (explanation). The guard-posts of the city Mari must be strengthened. My lord must not exit his door.

Yaḫuduri-Lim

Yaḫuduri-Lim, son of Yaggid-Lim; king of Mari, Tuttul, and the Tribal (ḫana) Land, the powerful king who controls the Bank of the Euphrates.

Dagan proclaimed my kingship and, handing me a powerful weapon, "Destroyer of Kings Hostile to Me," I defeated seven kings—tribal chiefs—who successively challenged me, annexing their territory. I removed the *hostile forces* from the Bank of the Euphrates, giving peace to my land. I opened canals, thus removing the (need for) drawing well water. I built Mari's ramparts and dug its moat; I built Terqa's ramparts and dug its moat. And in a wasteland—an arid spot—where not one king since days of yore founded a town, indeed I, having wished it, founded a town, dug its moat and called it "Dur Yaḫdullim." I then opened a canal for it and called it "Išim Yaḫdullim." I, therefore, enlarged my country and strengthened the structure of Mari and of my land, establishing my reputation for eternity. . . .

Omen Taking

. . . when a couple of times in the omens that are the lot of a diviner there occurred a (negative) portent . . . he told me, "The civilians of the city are continuously coming out." This is what the diviner told me. I have just had the matter reconsidered and have had omens taken for the people of the city, clan by clan. The omens he took for Ḫurran were unfavorable. For this reason, I spoke to him saying, "Are you having the civilians of my own lord, the people of the town, continuously coming out?" This is what I told him in front of witnesses. As I was sending him to my lord, this man got anxious and said, "I fear that in the future someone will disseminate my word, adding, 'In this way, he has *overlooked* Ḫurran . . .'"

SOURCE: Jack Sasson, *From the Mari Archives: An Anthology of Old Babylonian Letters* (Winona Lake, Ind.: Eisenbrauns, 2015), 32, 207–8, 277. Used by permission of the publisher.

28

MERNEPTAH STELE

The following is an excerpt from a much longer monumental text that celebrates the victories of the Egyptian king Merneptah (both real and imagined) in the ancient Near East in the thirteenth century BCE. This text contains the only ancient Egyptian reference to Israel, hence it is often referred to as the "Israel Stele."

. . .

The Princes are prostrate saying: "Shalom!"
Not one of the Nine Bows lifts his head:
Tjehenu is vanquished, Khatti at peace,
Canaan is captive with all woe.
Ashkelon is conquered, Gezer seized,
Yanoam made nonexistent;
Israel is laid waste, bare of seed.

SOURCE: Miriam Lichtheim, *Ancient Egyptian Literature: The New Kingdom*, vol. 2 (Berkeley: University of California Press, 1973), 77. Used by permission of the publisher.

29

MESHA STELE

The Mesha Stele is a ninth-century BCE commemoration of the exploits of Mesha, king of Moab (see 2 Kgs 3). The stone was discovered in the Moabite city of Dibon (modern day Dhiban, Jordan) and celebrates Mesha's victory over Israel. Previously, Moab had been under the subjugation of the house of Omri (on Omri, see 1 Kgs 16), mentioned in the inscription.

I am Mesha of Dibon, king of Moab, son of Chemosh. My father reigned thirty years over Moab and I succeeded him, and I erected this sanctuary of Chemosh in Khorkhah in commemoration of my victory over hostile kings, because Chemosh gave me victory and vengeance over all my enemies.

When Chemosh was angry with his land, Omri, king of Israel, held Moab in subjection for many years; and his son succeeded him, and he also purposed to subdue Moab. This was in my days. But I avenged myself upon him and upon his house, and Israel finally lost all power over Moab.

Omri annexed the land of Medeba, and for forty years, his reign and half his son's reign, it was occupied by Israel, but Chemosh restored it to Moab in my days.

I extended and fortified Baal-meon, where I made the reservoir, and Kirjathaim. From of old the Gadites occupied the land of Ataroth; and the king of Israel fortified Ataroth, but I besieged and took it, and massacred all the population to gratify Chemosh and Moab. I removed thence the altar-hearth of Dawdoh and transferred it to the temple of Chemosh at Kerioth; and I settled in Ataroth the men of Sharon and the men of Makharath.

Chemosh said to me, "Go and take Nebo from Israel," and I went by night, and assaulted it from daybreak till noon, and I took it, and massacred all the inhabitants, seven thousand men and boys, and women and girls and slave girls, because I had vowed to destroy it utterly in honor of Ashtor-Chemosh. And I took thence the altar-hearths of Yahweh and transferred them to the temple of Chemosh.

Then the king of Israel fortified Jahaz, and made it his headquarters while he fought against me; but Chemosh drove him out before me. I took the fighting men of the two hundred clans of Moab, and led them against Jahaz and took it, to annex it to the territory of Dibon. I extended and fortified Khorkhah, providing it with walls and gates and towers, and a palace, and, in the midst of the city, reservoirs. There were no cisterns in Khorkhah, and I bade every householder provide a cistern in his own house. I used the Israelite prisoners as navies for my public works at Khorkhah. . . .

SOURCE: W. H. Bennett, *The Moabite Stone* (Edinburgh: T&T Clark, 1911), 2–5, with modifications.

30

TEL DAN INSCRIPTION

The following inscription was discovered at Tel Dan (Tell el-Qadi), identified with the biblical town of Dan in northern Israel (see, for instance, Jdg 18). The text was once likely part of a larger monumental inscription, and although extremely fragmented, the ninth-century BCE inscription is important because it refers to the king of Judah as the "king of the House of David."

> . . . my father went up . . .
> . . . and my father died, he went to [his fate . . . Is-]
> rael formerly in my father's land . . .
> I [fought against Israel?] and Hadad went in front of me . . .
> . . . my king. And I slew of [them X footmen, Y cha-]
> riots and two thousand horsemen . . .
> the king of Israel. And [I] slew [. . . the kin-]
> g of the House of David. And I put . . .
> their land . .
> other . . . [. . . ru-]
> led over Is[rael . . .]
> siege upon . . .
> . . .

SOURCE: Avraham Biran and Joseph Naveh, "An Aramaic Stele Fragment from Tel Dan," *Israel Exploration Journal* 43 (1993): 81–98, translation 90. Used by permission of the publisher.

31

DEIR ʿALLA INSCRIPTION

Two plaster texts were found at Tell Deir ʿAlla in modern-day Jordan. The texts were likely part of the wall of a sanctuary that was destroyed by an earthquake. The texts date to the eighth century BCE and are written in a Semitic language other than Hebrew. The first text, an excerpt from which is given below, describes a vision of Balaam, son of Beor, who also appears in the biblical text in Numbers 22–24.

The warning of the Book of [Balaam, son of Beo]r, who was a seer of the gods.

The gods came to him at night [and spoke to] him according to the ora[-cle] of El. They said to Ba[la]am, son of Beor, "Thus will [. . .] do hereafter. No one [has seen . . .] . . ."

When Balaam arose on the morrow, (his) hand [was slack], (his) right hand [hung] low. [He fasted continually] in his chamber, he could not [sleep], and he wept continually. Then his people came up to him and [they said] to

Balaam, son of Beor: "Why do you fast [and w]hy do you weep?" He said to them: "Sit down and I shall tell you what the Shadda[yin have done]; come, see the acts of the gods! The gods gathered together; the Shaddayin took their places in the assembly. And they said . . . : 'May you break the bolts of heaven, with your raincloud bringing about darkness and not light, eeriness and not your brightness. May you bring terror [through the] dark [rainclo]ud. May you never again be aglow. For the *ss'gr*(-birds) taunts the eagle and the voice of the vultures resounds. . . . the young of the *nhṣ*(-bird) and one rips the young of cormorants. . . .' "

SOURCE: C. L. Seow, "Deir 'Alla Plaster Texts," in M. Nissinen, *Prophets and Prophecy in the Ancient Near East*, Writings from the Ancient World 12 (Atlanta: Society of Biblical Literature, 2003), 207–12, translation 210–11. Used by permission of the publisher.

32

SILOAM TUNNEL INSCRIPTION

Second Kings 20:20 states that Hezekiah of Judah (late eighth–early seventh century BCE) made a pool and a tunnel by which he brought water into Jerusalem as part of his plan to defend Jerusalem from the Assyrians (see also 2 Chron 32). A tunnel is still present under Jerusalem and connects the Gihon Spring to the Siloam Pool. An inscription in the pool describes how workmen dug from north to south and met in the middle of the tunnel, although it does not mention Hezekiah by name.

The day of the breach. This is the record of how the tunnel was breached. While the excavators were wielding their pickaxes, each man toward his coworker, and while there were yet three cubits for the breach, a voice was heard each man calling to his coworker; because there was a cavity in the rock (extending) from the south to the north. So on the day of the breach, the excavators struck, each man to meet his coworker, pickaxe against pickaxe. Then the water flowed from the spring to the pool, a distance of one thousand and two hundred cubits. One hundred cubits was the height of the rock above the heads of the excavators.

SOURCE: K. Lawson Younger Jr., *The Context of Scripture*, vol. 2, ed. William W. Hallo and K. Lawson Younger Jr. (Leiden: Brill, 2003), 145–46. Used by permission of the translator.

33

SENNACHERIB'S PRISM

Sennacherib's Prism (the Taylor Prism) is an Assyrian monument displaying a list of the military campaigns of the Assyrian king Sennacherib and dates to 691 BCE. Of particular note in the following excerpt is the account of Sennacherib's campaign against Judah. It states that Sennacherib shut king Hezekiah of Judah up in Jerusalem like a caged bird and plundered the Judean cities outside of Jerusalem (cp. 2 Kgs 18–19).

The kings of Amurru, all of them, brought their heavy tribute before me in the neighborhood of the city of Ushû, and Sidkâ, king of Ashkelon, who had not submitted to my yoke, the gods of his father's house, himself, together with [his] family, I tore up and carried away to Assyria. Sharru-lu-dâri, son of Rukibti, their [former] king, I placed [over the people of] Ashkelon, and imposed my royal tribute upon him.

In the course of my campaign I captured his cities, which had not submitted at my feet, I carried off their spoil. The governors and people of Amkaruna (Ekron), who had thrown into iron fetters Padî, their king, who was bound by oath to Assyria, and had given him to Hezekiah, the Jew, he kept him in confinement; they became afraid, and appealed (for aid) to the Egyptian kings, the bowmen, the chariots and horses of the king of Meluhha, a countless host. In the plain of Altakuh (Eltekeh) I fought with them, I defeated them. The charioteers and Egyptian princes, together with the charioteers of the king of Meluhha, I captured alive with my (own) hand.

I drew near to Amkaruna. The governors who had rebelled (committed sin) I slew with the sword. The citizens who had rebelled (sinned) I counted as spoil. The rest of them, who were guiltless, I pardoned. Padî, their king, I brought out of Jerusalem and placed on the throne over them. My royal tribute I imposed upon him. As for Hezekiah, the Jew, who had not submitted to my yoke, forty-six of his strong, walled cities and the cities of their environs, which were numberless, I besieged, I captured, I plundered, as booty I counted them. Him, like a caged bird, in Jerusalem, his royal city, I shut up. Earthworks I threw up about it. His cities which I plundered, I cut off from his land and gave to the kings of Ashdod, Ashkelon, Ekron, and Gaza; I diminished his land. To the former tribute, I imposed the payment of yearly gifts by them, as tax, and laid it upon him. That Hezekiah, the terrifying splendor of my royalty overcame him, and the Arabs and his picked troops whom he had brought into Jerusalem, his royal city, ran away (took leave). With thirty talents of gold, eight hundred talents of silver and all kinds of treasure from his palace, he sent his daughters, his palace women, his male and female singers, to Nineveh, and he dispatched his messengers to pay the tribute.

SOURCE: Daniel David Luckenbill, *Ancient Records of Assyria and Babylonia*, vol. 2: *Historical Records of Assyria from Sargon to the End* (Chicago: University of Chicago Press, 1927), 142–43.

34

HEBREW LETTERS

The following letters are from the end of the Judean monarchy and discuss, among other things, events surrounding the fall of Judah. The letters from Arad (in ancient Judea) date to around 597 BCE, and those from Lachish (in ancient Judea) to around 589 BCE. The letters help to document the chaotic years between the fall of Assyria and the siege of Jerusalem by Babylon. The letters also document some social elements of Judean society including names with Yahwistic elements as well as relationships between Judah and surrounding nations like Egypt and Edom.

Arad Ostraca

Arad 18

To my lord Elyashib:
    May YHWH bless you.
    Issue Shemaryahu half a donkey-load of flour(?). And give the Qerosite a full donkey-load.
    As for the matter about which you gave me orders—all is well. He is staying in the temple of YHWH.

Arad 40

Your son Gemar[yahu] and Nehemyahu send [greetings] to Maliyah.
    I bless [you by YHWH].

Your servant has applied himself to what you ordered. [I am] writing to my lord [everything that] the man wanted.

[Eshyahu has] come from you, but [he has not given] them any men. You know [the reports from] Edom. I sent them to [my] lord [before] evening. Eshyahu is staying [in my house]. He tried to obtain the report, [but I would not give it to him].

The king of Judah should be told [that] we [are unable] to send [. . .], [This is] the evil which the Edomites [have done].

Lachish Ostraca

Lachish 2

To my lord Yaush.

May YHWH send you good news this very day!

I am nothing but a dog, why should you should think of me? May YHWH help you find out what you need to know!

Lachish 3

A report from your servant Hoshayahu to my lord Yaush.

May YHWH send you good news and prosperity!

Now then, would you please explain to me what you meant by the letter you sent me last night? I've been in a state of shock ever since I got it. "Don't you know how to read a letter?" you said. By God, nobody ever had to read *me* a letter! And when I get a letter, once I've read it, I can recite it back verbatim, word for word!

I have just received word that Commander Konayahu son of Elnatan has moved south to enter Egypt. He has sent to have Hodawyahu son of Ahiyahu and his men transferred from here.

I am sending a letter confiscated by Tobyahu, the royal administrator. It was sent to Shallum son of Yada from the prophet, saying, "Beware!"

Lachish 4

May YHWH send you good news this very day!

I have carried out all of your orders and have kept a written record of them. On the matter you spoke of regarding Beth-*hrpd*: there is no one there. Regarding Semakyahu: Shemayahu has arrested him and had him taken up to the city. I cannot send the witness there today.

If you could be here during the morning watch, you would understand that we are tending the signal fire of Lachish according to the code you gave us, for we cannot see Azekah.

SOURCE: James M. Lindenberger, *Ancient Aramaic and Hebrew Letters*, ed. Kent Harold Richards, Writings from the Ancient World 4 (Atlanta: Scholars Press, 1994), 103–4, 106–7, 110–13. Used by permission of the publisher.

❀

35

CYRUS CYLINDER

The Cyrus Cylinder is an inscription on a cylindrical tablet that commemorates the defeat of Babylon by Cyrus of Persia in 539 BCE. It states that the gods, angry with Babylon, picked Cyrus as their chosen one to be king of the world. Cyrus claims that he brought peace to Babylon as the one who freed the enslaved population of Babylon. Towards the end of the excerpt below, Cyrus states that he allowed the captive people to return to their settlements and rebuild their destroyed sanctuaries (cp. Ezra 1).

───────────

. . . a low person was put in charge of his country, but he set [a . . . counter]feit over them. He ma[d]e a counterfeit of Esagil [and . . .] . . . for Ur and the rest of the cult cities. Rites inappropriate to them, [impure] fo[od offerings . . .] disrespectful . . . were daily gabbled, and, intolerably, he brought the daily offerings to a halt; he inter[fered with the rites and] instituted . . . within the sanctuaries. In his mind, reverential fear of Marduk, king of the gods, came to an end. He did yet more evil to his city every day; . . . his [people . . .], he brought ruin on them all by a yoke without relief. Enlil-of-the-gods became extremely angry at their complaints, and . . . their territory. The gods who lived within them left their shrines, angry that he had made them enter into Babylon (Shuanna). Ex[alted Marduk, Enlil-of-the-go]ds, relented. He changed his mind about all the settlements whose sanctuaries were in ruins and the population of the land of Sumer and Akkad who had become like corpses, and took pity on them. He inspected and checked all the countries, seeking for the upright king of his choice.

He took under his hand Cyrus, king of the city of Anshan, and called him by his name, proclaiming him aloud for the kingship over all of everything. He made the land of the Qutu and all the Medean troops prostrate themselves at his feet, while he looked out in justice and righteousness for the black-headed people whom he had put under his care. Marduk, the great lord, who nurtures his people, saw with pleasure his fine deeds and true heart and ordered that he should go to Babylon he had him take the road to Tintir, and, like a friend and companion, he walked at his side. His vast troops whose number, like the water in a river, could not be counted, marched fully armed at his side. He had him enter without fighting or battle right into Shuanna; he saved his city Babylon from hardship. He handed over to him Nabonidus, the king who did not fear him. All the people of Tintir, of all Sumer and Akkad, nobles and governors, bowed down before him and kissed his feet, rejoicing over his kingship and their faces shone. The lord through whose trust all were rescued from death and who saved them all from distress and hardship, they blessed him sweetly and praised his name.

I am Cyrus, king of the universe, the great king, the powerful king, king of Babylon, king of Sumer and Akkad, king of the four quarters of the world, son of Cambyses, the great king, king of the city of Anshan, grandson of Cyrus, the great king, ki[ng of the ci]ty of Anshan, descendant of Teispes, the great king, king of Anshan, the perpetual seed of kingship, whose reign Bel and Nabu love, and with whose kingship, to their joy, they concern themselves.

When I went as harbinger of peace i[nt]o Babylon I founded my sovereign residence within the palace amid celebration and rejoicing. Marduk, the great lord, bestowed on me as my destiny the great magnanimity of one who loves Babylon, and I every day sought him out in awe. My vast troops marched peaceably in Babylon, and the whole of [Sumer] and Akkad had nothing to fear. I sought the welfare of the city of Babylon and all its sanctuaries. As for the population of Babylon [. . . , w]ho as if without div[ine intention] had endured a yoke not decreed for them, I soothed their weariness, I freed them from their bonds(?). Marduk, the great lord, rejoiced at [my good] deeds, and he pronounced a sweet blessing over me, Cyrus, the king who fears him, and over Cambyses, the son [my] issue, [and over] all my troops, that we might proceed further at his exalted command. All kings who sit on thrones, from every quarter, from the Upper Sea to the Lower Sea, those who inhabit [remote distric]ts (and) the kings of the land of Amurru who live in tents, all of them, brought their weighty tribute into Shuanna, and kissed my feet. From [Shuanna] I sent back to their places to the city of Ashur and Susa, Akkad, the land of Eshnunna, the city of Zamban, the city of Meturnu, Der, as far as the border of the land of Qutu—the sanctuaries across the river Tigris—whose shrines had earlier become dilapidated, the gods who lived therein, and made permanent sanctuaries for them. I collected together all of their people and returned them to their settlements, and the gods of the land of Sumer and Akkad which Nabonidus—to the fury of the lord of the gods—had brought into Shuanna, at the command of Marduk, the great lord, I returned them unharmed to their cells, in the sanctuaries that make them happy. May all the gods that I returned to their sanctuaries, every day before Marduk and Nabu, ask for a long life for me, and mention my good deeds, and say to Marduk, my lord, this: "Cyrus, the king who fears you, and Cambyses his son, may their . . .". The population of Babylon call blessings on my kingship, and I have enabled all the lands to live in peace. Every day I copiously supplied [. . . ge]ese, two ducks, and ten pigeons more than the geese, ducks, and pigeons . . . I sought out to strengthen the guard on the wall Imgur-Enlil, the great wall of Babylon, and . . . the quay of baked brick on the bank of the moat which an earlier king had bu[ilt but not com]pleted, . . . its work. [. . . which did not surround the city] outside, which no earlier king had built, his troops, the levee from his land, into Shuanna. . . . with bitumen and baked brick I built anew, and completed its work. . . . great [doors of cedarwood] with copper cladding. I installed all their doors, threshold slabs, and door fittings with copper parts.

SOURCE: Irving Finkel, "Cyrus Cylinder," http://www.britishmuseum.org/research/collection_online/collection_object_details.aspx?objectId=327188&partId=1. © The Trustees of the British Museum, 2018.

F. HYMNS AND PRAYERS

The biblical book of Psalms is not the only place in the corpus of ancient Eastern Mediterranean literature to find hymns and prayers. The texts below are examples of hymns and prayers to gods from Greece, Babylon, and Assyria dating from the third millennium BCE forward. The poems involve themes found in biblical poetry, such as suffering, confession, divine justice, and care of the poor.

36

BABYLONIAN HYMN TO MARDUK

The following Babylonian hymn praises Marduk, the chief god of the Babylonian pantheon in the latter part of the second millennium BCE. The hymn contains parallels to the book of Job in that the speaker claims his innocence despite his suffering. Likewise, it has parallels to the psalms of confession (see, for example, Pss 6; 38; 51).

> O warrior Marduk, whose anger is the deluge,
> Whose relenting is that of a merciful father,
> I am left anxious by speech unheeded,
> My hopes are deceived by outcry unanswered,
> Such as has sapped my courage,
> And hunched me over like an aged man.
> O great lord Marduk, merciful lord!
> Men, by whatever name,
> What can they understand of their own sin?
> Who has not been negligent, which one has committed no sin?
> Who can understand a god's behavior?
> I would fain be obedient and incur no sin,
> Yes, I would frequent the haunts of health!

Men are commanded by the gods to act under curse,
Divine affliction is for mankind to bear.
I am surely responsible for some neglect of you,
I have surely trespassed the limits set by the god.
Forget what I did in my youth, whatever it was,
Let your heart not well up against me!
Absolve my guilt, remit my punishment,
Clear me of confusion, free me of uncertainty,
Let no guilt of my father, my grandfather, my mother,
my grandmother, my brother, my sister, my family, kith, or kin
Approach my own self, but let it be gone!
If my god has commanded (it) for me, purify me as with medicaments.
Commend me into the hands of my (personal) god
and my (personal) goddess for well-being and life,
Let me stand before you always in prayer, supplication, and entreaty,
Let the fruitful peoples of a well-ordered land praise you.
Absolve my guilt, remit my guilt!
O warrior Marduk, absolve my guilt, remit my guilt!
O great lady Erua-Sarpanitu, absolve my guilt,
O Nabu of the good name, absolve my guilt,
O great lady, Tashmetu, absolve my guilt,
O warrior Nergal, absolve my guilt,
O gods who dwell <in> Anu's <heaven>, absolve my guilt!
The monstrous guilt that I have built up from my youth,
Scatter it hence, absolve it sevenfold.
Like my real father and my real mother,
Let your heart be reconciled to me.
O warrior Marduk, let me sound your praises!

SOURCE: Benjamin R. Foster, *From Distant Days: Myths, Tales, and Poetry of Ancient Mesopotamia* (Bethesda, Md.: CDL Press, 1995), 247–48. Used by permission of the publisher.

37

PRAYER TO THE MOON GOD

The following text is from the library of Ashurbanipal of Assyria (668–633 BCE). The prayer, like many of the biblical hymns, is a request for forgiveness and justice. It was likely part of a festival for the Assyrian moon god.

O Sin, O Nannar, glorified one . . . ,
Sin, unique one, who makes bright . . . ,
Who furnishes light for the people . . . ,
To guide the dark-headed people aright . . . ,
Bright is thy light in heaven. . . .
Brilliant is thy torch like fire. . . .
Thy brightness has filled the broad land.
The people are radiant; they take courage at seeing thee.
O Anu of heaven whose designs no one can conceive,
Surpassing is thy light like Shamash thy firstborn.
Bowed down in thy presence are the great gods; the decisions of the land are
    laid before thee;
When the great gods inquire of thee thou dost give counsel.
They sit (in) their assembly (and) debate under thee;
O Sin, shining one of Ekur, when they ask thee thou dost give the oracle
    of the gods.
On account of the evil of an eclipse of the moon which took place in such
    and such a month, on such and such a day,
On account of the evil of bad and unfavorable portents and signs which have
    happened in my palace and in my country,
In the dark of the moon, the time of thy oracle, the mystery of the
    great gods,
On the thirtieth day, thy festival, the day of delight of thy divinity,
O Namrasit, unequaled in power, whose designs no one can conceive,
I have spread out for thee a pure incense offering of the night; I have poured
    out for thee the best sweet drink.
I am kneeling; I tarry (thus); I seek after thee.
Bring upon me wishes for well-being and justice.
May my god and my goddess, who for many days have been angry with me,
In truth and justice be favorable to me; may my road be propitious; may my
    path be straight.
After he has sent Zaqar, the god of dreams,
During the night may I hear the undoing of my sins; let my guilt be
    poured out;
(And) forever let me devotedly serve thee.

SOURCE: Ferris J. Stephens, "Sumero-Akkadian Hymns and Prayers," in *Ancient Near Eastern Texts Relating to the Old Testament*, ed. James B. Pritchard, 3rd edition with supplement (Princeton: Princeton University Press: 1969), 386. © 1950, 1955, 1969 by Princeton University Press. Renewed 1978 by Princeton University Press. Used by permission of the publisher.

38

NANSHE HYMN

The Nanshe hymn describes the goddess Nanshe's relationship with her city, the exact name of which is unclear in the poem, though it may refer to her close association with Nina in the Lagash region of ancient Mesopotamia (modern-day Surghul, Iraq). The hymn, which dates to the late third millennium BCE, describes Nanshe as the protector of the poor, particularly the widow and the orphan, and provides an outline of the New Year celebration. Compare the texts in the Hebrew Bible in which the LORD is described as the protector of the poor (see for example Pss 68; 72; 146; Jer 22; Isa 3:14-15; 10:1-2; 11:4; 25:4; 41:17).

> Is it not the city, is it not the city, is its *me* not proclaimed?
> Is it not . . . , the city, is its *me* not proclaimed?
> Is it not the pure city, the city, is its *me* not proclaimed?
> Is it not the mountain risen from the water, the city, is its *me* not
>   proclaimed?
> Does not its light shine over the good house, is its destiny not decided?
> Does not propriety shine brightly over the city?
> Are the rites of mother Nanshe not performed?
> Does not its lady, the child born in Eridu,
> Nanshe, the lady of the precious *me*, return?
> . . .
> She knows the orphan, she knows the widow.
> She knows that man oppresses man, (is) a mother for the orphan.
> Nanshe, watching over the widow,
> finding a way for houses in debt,
> the lady, she shelters the fugitive in her lap.
> She seeks out a place for the weak.
> She swells his . . . basket for him.
> She makes his . . . vat profitable for him.
> For the righteous maid who has seized her feet,
> Nanshe chooses a young man of good means.
> Over the widow, the person who has no spouse,
> Nanshe raises the good house like a roof.
> Does not propriety shine brightly in the presence of the lady?
> . . .
> the regular offerings, the daily goods of the house, come straight from
>   the Bursag.

For these rites the grain does not suffice.
The vessels are empty, do not pour water.
After the (appointed) person started overseeing the regular offerings, he did
      not receive extra.
What was distributed besides food, what was distributed besides drink,
what was left over from the regular offerings and was not used by the house,
what was expended in heads of taxed fish,
the extending of one-acre reed marsh to each of its (the temple's) servants,
what was received in nuts and green plants from within the garden
has it (the occasion for the distribution of any of these items)
passed, then no utterance shall touch (upon it).
When a person comes for a gift of prime beer, he shall not (even) receive
      cool water.
Its (the temple's) established first fruit offerings shall be performed
      unceasingly.
May there be a fat carrier who passes fat on to the house.
May there be a milk carrier who passes milk on to the house.
May there be a fish courier, a person of daily assignment.
When that which the firewood carrier has brought from the steppe
has passed on to the house of his lady
—may it stand in a corner, or stand at the side—
—and (whatever) may be the intention, firm word, or disagreement:
what enters the house of Nanshe from the outside shall not go out from
      the inside.
The supervisor of the house of Nanshe, the child born to Utu,
lord Hendursaga enforces these matters.
The king knows the good deed, he knows the evil deed.
. . .
On year's end, the day of rites,
the lady pours water in the holy *bar*.
On the day when the bowls of food allotments are inspected
Nanshe inspects the reviewing of the servants.
Her chief scribe Nisaba
places the precious tablets on the knees.
She takes the golden stylus in the hand.
She arranges for Nanshe the servants in single file.
One leather-clad enters before her according to his leather.
One linen-clad passes before her according to his linen.
Another leather-clad does not enter before her according to his leather.
Another linen-clad does not pass before her according to his linen.
Its (the temple's) registered person and the person who is hired by
      the sanctuary
whom eye or ear witnesses,
witnesses to his having run away from the house, have mentioned,

shall be terminated in his office (at) the first (stroke) of the harp.
The king who supervises the good servant, Haja, the man of the tablet,
puts down on clay the good servant of his lady who has been mentioned.
He takes off the clay the maid of his lady who has not been mentioned.
Should vessels pour no water, the affairs (of the temple) not be in order,
the trough for the dough not be clean,
the fire in the house by night be permitted to go out,
the incantations in the house by day be stifled,
Her Shita'aba who serves his term
shall be terminated in his office.
When to a Susbu who serves his term (administering) food allotments
    against whom a complaint has been lodged,
and to a Sanga who while living in the house
did not let the holy song and her (Nanshe's) thoughts shine,
when to him—he may acknowledge it, he may not acknowledge it—further
    rations are denied,
then mother Nanshe's rules are made to shine brightly.
Nothing further shall be placed beside these rules.
Nothing shall be added on to these rites.
No one shall impose other *me* upon these *me*.
. . .
Then Nanshe will not let that person eat upon threat
From bread of fat and white eggs.
She will not further the affairs of a violent person who has eaten from it.
. . .
the wealthy person with a reed hut on the street,
the married person who gave away his wife for a widow,
one day (such a person) laughs in his rage,
another day he makes fun of his calamity.
To the lady he cannot raise his . . . word.
The lady who watches over the countries,
Innin, mother Nanshe, has (her) eyes on the hidden.
Making the orphan of best repute, valuing the widow as a jewel,
surrendering the waif to a wealthy person,
surrendering the wealthy person to a poor person,
a mother who shouts at her child,
a child who talks obstinately to his mother,
a younger brother who talks arrogantly to his elder brother, talks back at
    his father—
the lady before whom one lies on the hands in the storeroom,
Nanshe before whom one holds up the hands in the storeroom,
on the inside of the land she, Nanshe, has (her) eyes as if it were a split reed.
. . .
the king, lord Hendursaga, brings with him

these commands out of the house of Nanshe.
Like heavy smoke they settle on the ground.
This word spreads along the sky, a moving thundercloud.
(With) the needle of matrimony he joins together,
the king, lord Hendursaga, twists it apart.
The just he places among the just.
The evil he turns over to an evil place.
He decides the right of the orphan.
He enforces the right of the widow.
He executes the right of mother and child.

. . .

Source: W. Heimpel, "The Nanshe Hymn," *Journal of Cuneiform Studies* 33 (1981): 65–139, translation 83–95. Used by permission of the publisher.

39

HOMERIC HYMN TO ARES

The so-called Homeric Hymns are a collection of thirty-four ancient Greek poems once attributed to Homer, though they are from different times and authors. The collection includes several hymns to major Greek gods, including the one below, written to Ares. The poems were likely meant to be read publicly and contain a variety of material. As seen below, like the biblical psalms, these hymns often praise the prowess of the god and request help and well-being.

Ares, exceeding in strength, chariot rider, golden-helmed,
Doughty in heart, shield bearer, Savior of cities, harnessed in bronze,
Strong of arm, unwearying, mighty with the spear, O defense of Olympus,
Father of warlike Victory, ally of Themis,
Stern governor of the rebellious, leader of righteous men,
Sceptered King of manliness, who whirl your fiery sphere among
The planets in their sevenfold courses through the aether
Wherein your blazing steeds ever bear you above the third firmament
    of heaven;
Hear me, helper of men, giver of dauntless youth!
Shed down a kindly ray from above upon my life,
And strength of war, that I may be able
To drive away bitter cowardice from my
Head and crush down the deceitful impulses of my soul.

Restrain also the keen fury of my heart which provokes me
To tread the ways of bloodcurdling strife. Rather, O blessed one,
Give me boldness to abide within the harmless laws of peace,
Avoiding strife and hatred and the violent fiends of death.

SOURCE: Hugh Evelyn-White, *Hesiod, Homeric Hymns, Epic Cycle, Homerica*, Loeb Classical Library 57 (Cambridge, Mass.: Harvard University Press, 1914), 433–35. Loeb Classical Library® is a registered trademark of the President and Fellows of Harvard College.

G. WISDOM LITERATURE

There is a significant amount of literature in the Hebrew Bible that falls into the genre of wisdom. Wisdom is a broad umbrella category encompassing collections of proverbs (Proverbs), lengthy theological debates (Job), and personal reflections (Ecclesiastes). These various works are connected by common themes, such as questions of divine justice, the meaning of life, how to live a good life, and the nature of good and evil. The Hebrew writers were not the only ones interested in those questions. The selections below show that multiple societies in the ancient Near East were interested in the nature of life and divine justice as well.

40

INSTRUCTION OF AMENEMOPET

The Egyptian wisdom book the *Instruction of Amenemopet* contains parables that are nearly word-for-word parallels with the biblical book of Proverbs (particularly 22:17–24:22). The extant text comes from Thebes and dates somewhere between the tenth and sixth centuries BCE.

> Beginning of the meditations on good living,
>   the guide to health and happiness,
> The various regulations for gaining entrée to officials,
>   and the customs of the courtiers;
> To know how to reply to one who speaks to you,
>   to bring back a report to one who sends you;
> To help you enter upon the Way of Life,
>   to keep you safely while on earth,
> To help your mind withdraw into its chapel —
>   which can provide an oar to steer through evil;

To rescue you from the mouths of the crowd,
    one praised in the speech of good people.
Composed by the Minister of Agriculture, wise in office,
    scribe of the seed-corn of Ta-Mery,

. . .

Amenemopet, son of Kanakht,
    vindicated in This.
This for his son, the youngest of his offspring,
    smallest of his associates . . .
Give ear to hear my words,
    and give your mind to searching into them.
Great benefit is yours if you will place them in your heart,
    while failure follows the neglect of them.
Let them rest within the strongbox of your body,
    let them provide a lock upon your heart—
Sea-lost is he who is a storm of words—
    let these provide an anchor for your tongue.
If you will live your life with all this in your heart,
    you shall find in it the means to be successful;
You will find my words a treasure house for living,
    And you yourself shall prosper upon earth.
Avoid demeaning the already miserable
    by any show of strength against the weak.
Do not raise your hand against the aging
    nor criticize the conversations of the great.
Do not formulate your messages in an abrasive manner
    nor envy one who does.
Do not raise a cry against the man who injures you,
    and do not you yourself reply.
One who does evil—the deep canal will get him;
    and its moving waters, they will bear him off!
The Northwind, it descends, darkening his hour,
    dragging him into the howling storm;
The clouds pile high, the crocodiles are restless,
    and this fevered man of yours—how does he fare?
It is his voice up there crying before the Highest,
    and the Moon above shall specify his crimes.
"Ply the oars that the evil one may cross to Us,
    We have not seen his like before."
—Raise him up, give him your hand,
    hurl him into the arms of God;
Fill him with bread at your table
    so that he be satisfied and be ashamed.

This too is a thing dear to the heart of God—
    let a man go slow before speaking.
Do not start a quarrel with the hot-mouthed man
    nor be a disdainful toward him in your speech;
Be deliberate before an adversary, bow to a foe,
    and sleep on what you think before you speak.
A stormwind moving like a flame in straw—
    that is the hothead in his hour!
Yield before him, leave the bellicose man
    to the god who knows how to mend him.
If you spend your days with these things in your heart,
    your offspring shall live to see them.
A man of the temple who is intemperate
    is like a tree which grows indoors.
In a short moment its leaves and blossoming are finished
    so that its journey ends on the rubbish heap;
It floats to its final destination
    and its burial is fire.
But the truly thoughtful man, though he keeps himself aside,
    is like a tree growing in sunlight;
It greens and flourishes, it doubles its harvest,
    standing before the face of its Lord;
Its fruit is sweet, its shade is pleasant,
    and it ends its days in the garden.
Do not hold back the portions meant for the temple—
    do not be greedy as the way to wealth;
Do not defraud God's servant
    merely to profit someone else.
And do not say, "Alas, today is like tomorrow!"
    —How can you arrive at this?
Come tomorrow, today is in the past—
    look, floodwaters brim the well mouths,
The crocodiles are loose, hippos rest in the shadows,
    the fish are leaping,
Small beasts are filled, birds are ecstatic,
    full nets are drawn ashore.
And all the thoughtful men of the temple
    say, "Great is the gift of Rê!"
Consider the thoughtful man that you may discover Life,
    and you yourself will flourish upon earth.
Do not move the markers at the edges of the fields
    nor alter findings of the measuring cord;
Do not be greedy in distributing the holdings
    nor violate the boundaries of the widow.

The furrows of the plough are cultivated for a lifetime—
    and the swindler covets them;
But should he get them, lyingly and falsely,
    surely he will fall at last to the Moon's justice.
Keep watch on one who does this while on earth—
    he is a despoiler of defenseless people,
He is a foe, wreaking havoc on your very body,
    and malice dwells in his eye.
His household is declared a public enemy
    and his granaries are leveled to the ground;
They seize his goods out of his children's hands,
    and the little that he had is given to another.

. . .

SOURCE: John L. Foster, *Ancient Egyptian Literature, An Anthology* (Austin: University of Texas Press, 2001), 207–11. © 2001. Used by permission of the author and the University of Texas Press.

41

INSTRUCTION OF PTAH-HOTEP

The *Instruction of Ptah-hotep* is an Egyptian collection of wise sayings compiled by Ptah-hotep, vizier of King Izezi of Egypt (around 2450 BCE). The book is stylized as wisdom passed on from father to son (cp. Proverbs) and offers instruction on how to be successful.

The Instruction of the Governor of his City, the Vizier, Ptah-hotep, in the Reign of the King of Upper and Lower Egypt, Isôsi, living forever, to the end of time.

The Governor of his City, the Vizier, Ptah-hotep, he said: "O Prince, my Lord, the end of life is at hand; old age descends upon me; feebleness comes, and childishness is renewed. He that is old lies down in misery every day. The eyes are small; the ears are deaf. Energy is diminished, the heart has no rest. The mouth is silent, and he speaks no word; the heart stops, and he remembers not yesterday. The bones are painful throughout the body; good turns to evil. All taste departs. These things do old age for mankind, being evil in all things. The nose is stopped, and he breathes not for weakness, whether standing or sitting. . . ."

Here begin the proverbs of fair speech, spoken by the Hereditary Chief, the Holy Father, Beloved of the God, the Eldest Son of the King, of his body, the Governor of his City, the Vizier, Ptah-hotep, when instructing the ignorant in the knowledge of exactness in fair-speaking; the glory of him that obeys, the shame of him that transgresses them.

He said to his son:

Be not proud because you are learned; but discourse with the ignorant man, as with the sage. For no limit can be set to skill, neither is there any craftsman that possesses full advantages. Fair speech is rarer than the emerald that is found by slave maidens on the pebbles. If you find an arguer talking, one that is well disposed and wiser than you, let your arms fall, bend your back, do not be angry with him if he does not agree with you. Refrain from speaking evilly; oppose him not at any time when he speaks. If he addresses you as one ignorant of the matter, your humbleness shall bear away his contentions. . . .

If you are a leader, as one directing the conduct of the multitude, endeavor always to be gracious, that your own conduct be without defect. Great is Truth, appointing a straight path; never has it been overthrown since the reign of Osiris. One that oversteps the laws shall be punished. Overstepping is by the covetous man; but degradations bear off his riches, for the season of his evildoing does not cease. For he says, "I will obtain by myself for myself," and says not, "I will obtain because I am allowed." But the limits of justice are steadfast; it is that which a man repeats from his father.

Cause not fear among men; for this the God punishes likewise. For there is a man that says, "Therein is life"; and he is bereft of the bread of his mouth. There is a man that says, "Power is therein"; and he says, "I seize for myself that which I perceive." Thus a man speaks, and he is smitten down. It is another that attains by giving to him that has not; not he that causes men dread. For it happens that what the God has commanded, even that thing comes to pass. Live, therefore, in the house of kindliness, and men shall come and give gifts of themselves.

If you are among the guests of a man that is greater than you, accept that which he gives you, putting it to your lips. If you look at him that is before you (your host), pierce him not with many glances. It is abhorred of the soul to stare at him. Speak not till he address you; one knows not what may be evil in his opinion. Speak when he questions you; so shall your speech be good in his opinion. The noble who sits before food divides it as his soul moves him; he gives to him that he would favor—it is the custom of the evening meal. It is his soul that guides his hand. It is the noble that bestows, not the underling that attains. Thus the eating of bread is under the providence of the God; he is an ignorant man that disputes it.

If you are an emissary sent from one noble to another, be exact after the manner of him that sent you, give his message even as he has said it. Beware of making enmity by your words, setting one noble against the other by perverting truth. Overstep it not, neither repeat that which any man, be he prince or peasant, says in opening the heart; it is abhorrent to the soul.

If you have ploughed, gather your harvest in the field, and the God shall make it great under your hand. Fill not your mouth at your neighbors' table . . . If a crafty man is the possessor of wealth, he steals like a crocodile from the priests.

Let not a man be envious that has no children; let him be neither downcast nor quarrelsome on account of it. For a father, though great, may be grieved; as to the mother of children, she has less peace than another. Truly, each man is created to his destiny by the God, who is the chief of a tribe, trustful in following him.

If you are lowly, serve a wise man, that all your actions may be good before the God. If you have known a man of no account that has been advanced in rank, do not be haughty toward him on account of that which you know concerning him; but honor him that has been advanced, according to that which he hath become.

Behold, riches come not of themselves; it is their rule for him that desires them. If he bestir him and collect them himself, the God will make him prosperous; but he will punish him, if he is slothful.

SOURCE: Battiscombe George Gunn, *The Instruction of Ptah-hotep and The Instruction of Ke'gemni: The Oldest Books in the World* (London: John Murray, 1912), 41–46, with modifications.

42

INSTRUCTION OF VIZIER KE'GEMNI

The *Instruction of Vizier Ke'gemni* is an Egyptian wisdom text attributed to Kagemni, a high-ranking official in Egypt in the third millennium BCE, but the authorship is debatable given that the oldest copies of the text date to the second millennium BCE. The epilogue of the text has not survived. The extant text consists of a collection of short wisdom sayings (cp. Proverbs) that champion a path of moderation.

The cautious man flourishes, the exact one is praised; the innermost chamber opens to the man of silence. Wide is the seat of the man gentle of speech; but knives are prepared against one that forces a path, that he advances not, save in due season.

If you sit with a company of people, desire not the bread that you like: short is the time of restraining the heart, and gluttony is an abomination; therein is the quality of a beast. A cup of water quenches the thirst, and a mouthful of melon supports the heart. A good thing stands for goodness, but some small thing stands for plenty. A base man is he that is governed by his belly; he departs only when he is no longer able to fill full his belly in men's houses.

If you sit with a glutton, eat with him, then depart.

If you drink with a drunkard, accept drink, and his heart shall be satisfied.

Refuse not meat when with a greedy man. Take what he gives you; set it not on one side, thinking that it will be a courteous thing.

If a man lacks in good fellowship, no speech has any influence over him. He is sour of face toward the gladhearted that are kind to him; he is a grief to his mother and his friends; and all men cry, "Let your name be known; you are silent in your mouth when you are addressed!"

Do not be haughty because of your might in the midst of your young soldiers. Beware of making strife, for one knows not the things that the God will do when He punishes.

The Vizier caused his sons and daughters to be summoned, when he had finished the rules of the conduct of men. And they marveled when they came to him. Then he said to them, "Hearken unto everything that is in writing in this book, even as I have said it in adding to profitable sayings." And they cast themselves on their bellies, and they read it, even as it was in writing. And it was better in their opinion than anything in this land to its limits.

Now they were living when His Majesty, the King of Upper and Lower Egypt, Heuni, departed, and His Majesty, the King of Upper and Lower Egypt, Senforu, was enthroned as a gracious king over the whole of this land.

Then was Ke'gemni made Governor of his City and Vizier.

It is finished.

Source: Battiscombe George Gunn, *The Instruction of Ptah-hotep and The Instruction of Ke'gemni: The Oldest Books in the World* (London: John Murray, 1912), 62–64, with modifications.

43

DIALOGUE BETWEEN A MAN
AND HIS GOD

"Dialogue between a Man and his God" is an Akkadian (Semitic-speaking region of northern Mesopotamia; modern-day central Iraq) wisdom text from the seventeenth century BCE. It is a prose account, setting it apart from other similar Mesopotamian texts, and it consists of a conversation between an afflicted young man who addresses his god as he would a friend and claims his innocence (cp. Job). A messenger of the god comes and heals the young man and lets him know that the god had planned the healing all along. After the healing, the messenger instructs the young man to use his newly found health and strength to feed the hungry and give water to the thirsty.

A young man was imploring his god as a friend,
He was constantly supplicating, he was [praying to?] him.
His heart was seared, he was sickened with his burden,
His feelings were somber from misery.
He weakened, fell to the ground, prostrated himself.
His burden had grown too heavy for him,
    he drew near to weep.
He was moaning like a donkey foal separated
    (from its mother),
He cried out before his god, his master.
His mouth a wild bull, his clamor two mourners,
[His] lips bear a lament to his lord.
He recounts the burdens he suffered to his lord,
The young man expounds the misery he is suffering:
"My Lord, I have debated with myself, and in my feelings
[. . .] of heart: the wrong I did I do not know!
Have I [. . .] a vile forbidden act?
Brother does not de[sp]ise his brother,
Friend is not calumniator of his friend!
The [. . .] does not [. . .]
   . . .
[From] when I was a child until I grew up,
    (the days?) have been long, when . . . [. . .]?
How much have you been kind to me, how much

I have blasphemed you, I have not forgotten.
In[stead?] of good you have revealed evil, O my Lord,
    you made [. . .] glow . . .
My bad repute had grown excessive, it . . . to (my) feet.
It [rains] blows on my skull(?).
Its [. . .] turned my mouth . . . to gall."
. . .
[. . .] brought him to earth,
[. . .] he has anointed him with medicinal oil,
[. . .] food, and covered his blotch,
He attended him and gladdened his heart,
He ordered the restoration of his good health to him:
"Your disease is under control,
    let your heart not be despondent!
The years and days you were filled with misery are over.
Were you not ordained to live,
How could you have lasted the whole
    of this grievous illness?
You have seen distress, . . . is (now) held back.
You have borne its massive load to the end.
I flung wide your access(?), the way is open to you,
The path is straight for you, mercy is granted you.
You must never, till the end of time, forget [your] god
Your creator, now that you are favored.
I am your god, your creator, your trust,
My guardians are strong and alert on your behalf.
The field will open [to you] its refuge.
I will see to it that you have long life.
So, without qualms, do you anoint the parched,
Feed the hungry, water the thirsty,
But he who sits there with burning e[yes],
Let him look upon your food, melt, flow down,
    and dis[solve].
The gate of life and well-being is open to you!
Going away(?), drawing near, coming in, going out:
    may you be well!"
Make straight his way, open his path:
    May your servant's supplication reach your heart!

SOURCE: Benjamin R. Foster, *From Distant Days: Myths, Tales, and Poetry of Ancient Mesopotamia* (Bethesda, Md.: CDL Press, 1995), 295–97. Used by permission of the publisher.

❦

44

POEM OF THE RIGHTEOUS SUFFERER

The "Poem of the Righteous Sufferer," also known by its opening line, "I Will Praise the Lord of Wisdom" (*Ludlul bēl nēmeqi*), recounts the suffering of a man who proclaims his innocence (cp. Job). The monologue claims that Marduk, the chief god of Babylon, has caused the man's suffering for no apparent reason. The text is Akkadian (Semitic-speaking region of northern Mesopotamia; modern-day central Iraq) and dates to the third century BCE.

> I will praise the lord of Wisdom, solicitous god,
> [Fur]ious in the night, calming in the daylight;
> Marduk! lord of wisdom, solicitous god,
> [Fur]ious in the night, claiming in the daylight;
> Whose anger engulfs(?) like a tempest,
> Whose breeze is sweet as the breath of morn,
> In his fury not to be withstood, his rage the deluge,
> Merciful in his feelings, his emotions relenting.
> The skies cannot sustain the weight of his hand,
> His gentle palm rescues the moribund.
> Marduk! The skies cannot sustain the weight of his hand,
> His gentle palm rescues the moribund.
> When he is angry, graves are dug,
> His mercy raised the fallen from disaster.
> When he glowers, protective spirits take flight,
> He has regard for and turns to the one whose god has forsaken him.
> Harsh is his punishments, he . . . in battles (?),
> When moved to mercy, he quickly feels pain like a mother in labor.
> He is bull-headed in love of mercy,
> Like a cow with a calf, he keeps turning around watchfully.
> His scourge is barbed and punctures the body,
> His bandages are soothing, they heal the doomed.
> He speaks and makes one incur many sins,
> On the day of his justice sin and guilt are dispelled.
> He is the one who makes shivering and trembling,
> Through his sacral spell chills and shivering are relieved.
> Who raises the flood of Adad, the blow of Erra,
> Who reconciles the wrathful god [and god]dess,

The Lord divines the gods' inmost th[oughts],
(But) no [god] understands his behavior,
Marduk divines the gods' inmost thoughts
(But) no god understands his behavior!
As heavy his hand, so compassionate his heart,
As brutal his weapons, so life-sustaining his feelings,
Without his consent, who could cure his blow?
Against his will, who could sin and [escape]?
I will proclaim his anger, which [runs deep(?)], like a fish,
He punished(?) me abruptly, then gran[ted(?)] life.
I will teach the people, [I will instruct the land] to [fear],
To be mindful of him is propitious for . . .
After the Lord [changed] day [into night],
And the warrior Marduk [became furious with me],
My own god threw me over(?) and disap[peared],
My goddess broke rank and vanis[hed].
He cut off the benevolent angel who (walked) beside [me],
My protecting spirit was frightened off, to seek out someone else.
My vigor was taken away, my manly appearance became gloomy,
My dignity flew off, my cover leaped away.
Terrifying signs beset me:
I was forced out of my house, I wandered outside,
My omens were confused, they were abnormal(?) every day,
The prognostication of diviner and dream interpreter could not explain what
    I was undergoing.
What was said in the street portended ill for me,
When I lay down at nights, my dream was terrifying.
The king, incarnation of the gods, sun of his peoples,
His heart was enraged with me and appeasing him was impossible.
Courtiers were plotting hostile against me,
They gathered themselves to instigate base deeds:
If the first "I will make him end his life,"
Says the second "I ousted (him) from his command,"
So likewise the third "I will get my hands on his post!"
"I will force his house!" vows the fourth
As the fifth pants (to speak),
Sixth and seventh follow in his train!
The clique of seven have massed their forces,
Merciless as fiends, equal to demons.
So one is their body, united in purpose,
Their hearts fulminate against me, ablaze like fire.
Slander and lies they try to lend credence against me
My mouth once proud was muzzled like a . . . ,
My lips, which used to discourse, became those of a dead man.

My resounding call struck dumb,
My proud head bent earthward,
My stout heart turned feeble for terror,
My broad breast brushed aside by a novice,
My far-reaching arms pinned by (flimsy) matting(?),
I, who walked proudly, learned slinking,
I, so grand, became servile.
To my vast family, I became a loner,
As I went through the streets, ears(?) were pricked up(?) at me,
I would enter the palace, eyes would squint at me,
My city was glowering at me like an enemy,
Belligerent and hostile would seem my land!
My brother became my foe,
My friend became a malignant demon,
My comrade would denounce me savagely,
My colleague was constantly keeping the taint to this weapons,
My best friend would pinch off my life.
My slave cursed me openly in the assembly (of gentlefolk),
My slave girl defamed me before the rabble.
An acquaintance would see me and make himself scarce,
My family disowned me,
A pit awaited anyone speaking well of me,
While he who was uttering defamation of me forged ahead.
One who relayed base things about me had a god for his help,
For the one who said "What a pity about him!" death came early,
The one of no help, his life became charmed,
I had no one to go at my side, nor saw I a champion.
They parceled my possessions among the riffraff,
The sources of my watercourses they blocked with muck,
They chased the harvest song from my fields,
They left my community deathly still, like that of a (ravaged) foe.
They let another assume my duties,
They appointed an outsider to my prerogatives.
By day sighing, by night lamentation,
Monthly, trepidation, despair the year,
I moaned like a dove all my days,
I let out groans as my song.
My eyes are forced to look(?) through constant crying,
My eyelids are smarting(?) through [. . .] of tears.
My face is darkened from the apprehensions of my heart,
Terror and pain have jaundiced my face.
[The . . . of] my heart is quaking in ceaseless apprehension.
[. . .] like a burning fire,
Like the bursting of a flame falsehood beset me,

[. . .] lamentation, my imploring!
[The speech of] my lips was senseless, like a moron's,
When I tried to talk, my conversation was gibberish.
I watch, that in daylight good will come upon me!
The moon will change, the sun will shine!
One whole year to the next! The (normal) time passed.
As I turned around, it was more and more terrible,
My ill luck was on the increase, I could find no good fortune.
I called to my god, he did not show his face,
I prayed to my goddess, she did not raise her head.
The diviner with his inspection did not get the bottom of it,
Nor did the dream interpreter with his incense clear up my case.
I beseeched a dream spirit, but it did not enlighten me,
The exorcist with his ritual did not appease divine wrath.
What bizarre actions everywhere!
I looked behind: persecution, harassment!
Like one who had not made libations to his god,
Nor invoked his goddess with a food offering,
Who was not wont to prostrate, nor seen to bow down,
From whose mouth supplication and prayer were wanting,
Who skipped holy days, despised festivals,
Who was neglectful, omitted the gods' rites,
Who had not taught his people reverence and worship,
Who did not invoke his god, but ate his food offering,
Who snubbed his goddess, brought (her) no flour offering,
Like one possessed(?), who forgot his lord,
Who casually swore a solemn oath by his god: I indeed seemed (such a one)!
I, for my part, was mindful of supplication and prayer,
Prayer to me was the natural recourse, sacrifice my rule.
The day for reverencing the gods was a source of satisfaction to me,
The goddess' procession day was my profit and return.
Praying for the king, that was my joy,
His sennet was as if for (my own) good omen.
I instructed my land to observe the god's rites,
The goddess' name did I drill my people to esteem.
I made my praises of the king like a god's,
And taught the populace reverence for the palace.
I wish I knew that these things were pleasing to a god!
What seems good to one's self could be an offense to a god,
What in one's own heart seems abominable, could be good to one's god!
Who could learn the reasoning of the gods in heaven?
Who could grasp the intentions of the gods of the depths?
Where might human beings have learned the ways of a god?
He who lived by (his) brawn died in confinement.

Suddenly one is downcast, in a trice full of cheer,
One moment he sings in exaltation,
In a trice he groans like a professional mourner.
People's motivations change in a twinkling!
Starving, they become like corpses,
Full, they would rival their gods.
In good times, they speak of scaling heaven,
When it goes badly, they complain of going down to hell.
I have ponde[red] these things; I have made no sense of them.
But as for me, in despair a whirlwind is driving(?) me!
Debilitating disease is let loose upon me:
An evil vapor has blown against me [from the] ends of the earth,
Head pain has surged upon me from the breast of hell,
A malignant specter has come forth from its hidden depth,
A relentless [ghost] came out of its dwelling place.
[A she-demon came] down from the mountain,
Ague set forth [with the] flood [and sea(?)],
Debility broke through the ground with the plants.
[They assembled] their host, together they came upon me:
[They struck my he]ad, they closed around my pate,
[My features] were gloomy, my eyes ran a flood,
They wrenched my muscles, made my neck limp,
They thwacked [my chest], pounded(?) my breast,
They affected my flesh, threw (me) into convulsion,
They kindled a fire in my epigastrium,
They churned up my bowels, they tw[isted] my entrails(?),
Coughing and hacking infected my lungs,
They infected(?) my limbs, made my flesh pasty,
My lofty stature they toppled like a wall,
My robust figure they flattened like a bulrush,
I was dropped like a dried fig, I was tossed on my face.
A demon has clothed himself in my body for a garment,
Drowsiness smothers me like a net,
My eyes stare, they cannot see,
My ears prick up, they cannot hear.
Numbness has spread over my whole body,
Paralysis has fallen upon my flesh.
Stiffness has seized my arms,
Debility has fallen upon my loins,
My feet forgot how to move.
[A stroke] has overcome me, I choke like one fallen,
Signs of death have shrouded my face!
[If someone th]inks of me, I can't respond to the enquirer,

"[Ala]s" they weep, I have lost consciousness.
A snare is laid on my mouth,
And a bolt bars my lips.
My way in is barred, my point of slaking blocked,
My hunger is chronic, my gullet constricted.
If it be of grain, I choke it down like stinkweed,
Beer, the sustenance of mankind, is sickening to me.
Indeed, the malady drags on!
For lack of food my features are unrecognizable,
My flesh is waste, my blood has run dry,
My bones are loose, covered (only) with skin,
My tissues are inflamed, afflicted with gangrene(?).
I took to bed, confined, going out was exhaustion,
My house turned into my prison.
My flesh was a shackle, my arms being useless,
My person was a fetter, my feet having given way.
My afflictions were grievous, the blow was severe!
A scourge full of barbs thrashed me,
A crop lacerated me, cruel with thorns.
All day long tormentor would torment [me],
Nor a night would he let me breathe freely a moment,
From writhing, my joints were separated,
My limbs were splayed and thrust apart.
I spent the night in my dung like an ox,
I wallowed in my excrement like a sheep.
The exorcist recoiled from my symptoms,
While my omens have perplexed the diviner.
The exorcist did not clarify the nature of my complaint,
While the diviner put no time limit on my illness.
No god came to the rescue, nor lent me a hand,
No goddess took pity on me, nor went at my side.
My grave was open, my funerary gods ready,
Before I had died, lamentation for me was done.
All my country said, "How wretched he was!"
When my ill-wisher heard, his face lit up,
When the tidings reached her, my ill-wisher, her mood became radiant.
The day grew dim for my whole family,
For those who knew me, their sun grew dark.
. . .
A second time [I saw a dream].
In the dream I saw [at night],
A remarkable purifier . . .
Holding in his hand a tamarisk rod of purification.

"Laluralimma, resident of Nippur,
He sent me to cleanse you."
He was carrying water, he p[oured it] over me,
He pronounced the resuscitating incantation, he massaged [my] bo[dy].
A third time I saw a dream.
In my dream I saw at night:
A remarkable young woman in shining countenance,
Clothed like a person(?), being li[ke] a god,
A queen among peoples . . .
She entered upon me and [sat down] . . .
She ordered my deliverance . . .

. . .

She ordered my deliverance, "Most wre[tched] indeed is he,
Whoever he might be, the one who saw the vision at night."
In the dream (was) Ur-Nindinugga, a Babylonian(?) . . .
A bearded young man wearing a tiara,
He was an exorcist, carrying a tablet,
"Marduk has sent me!
To Shubshi-meshre-Sakkan I have brought a sw[athe],
From his pure hands I have brought a sw[athe]."
He has entru[sted] me into the hands of my ministrant.
In waking hours he sent a message,
He reve[aled] his favorable sign to my people.
I was awake in my sickness, a (healing) serpent slithered by.
My illness was quickly over, my fetters were broken.
After my lord's heart had quiet[ed],
(And) the feelings of merciful Marduk were ap[peased],
[And he had] accepted my prayers . . .

. . .

[He applied] to me his spell which binds [debilitating disease],
[He drove] back the evil vapor to the ends of the earth,
He bore off [the head pain] to the breast of hell,
[He sent] down the malignant specter to its hidden depth,
The relentless ghost he returned [to] its dwelling,
He overthrew the she-demon, sending her off to a mountain,
He replaced the ague in flood and sea.
He eradicated debility like a plant,
Uneasy sleep, excessive drowsiness,
He dissipated like smoke filling the sky.

. . .

SOURCE: Benjamin R. Foster, *Before the Muses: An Anthology of Akkadian Literature*, vol. 1 (Bethesda, Md.: CDL Press, 1993), 310–19. Used by permission of the publisher.

45

THE BABYLONIAN THEODICY

The "Babylonian Theodicy" is an acrostic poem framed as a dialogue between a sufferer questioning justice and order and a friend attempting to uphold the popular understanding of justice (cp. Job). The oldest copies are from the Ashurbanipal library (seventh century BCE), but the poem itself likely dates to around 1000 BCE.

Sufferer

O sage, [. . .], come, [let] me speak to you,
. . .
[I . . .], who have suffered greatly, let me always praise you,
Where is one whose reflective capacity is as great as yours?
Who is he whose knowledge could rival yours?
Wh[ere] is the counselor to whom I can tell of woe?
I am without recourse, heartache has come upon me.
I was the youngest child when fate claimed (my) father,
My mother who bore me departed to the land of no return,
My father and mother left me, and with no one my guardian!

Friend

Considerate friend, what you tell is a sorrowful tale,
My dear friend, you have let your mind harbor ill.
You make your estimable discretion feeble-minded,
You alter your bright expression to a scowl.
Of course our fathers pay passage to go death's way,
I too will cross the river of the dead, as is commanded from of old.
When you survey teeming mankind all together,
The poor man's son advanced, someone helped him get rich,
Who did favors for the sleek and wealthy?
He who looks to his god has a protector,
The humble man who reveres his goddess will garner wealth.

Sufferer

My friend, your mind is a wellspring of depth unplumbed,
The upsurging swell of the ocean that brooks no inadequacy.
To you, then, let me pose a question, learn [what I would say].

Hearken to me but for a moment, hear my declaration.
My body is shrouded, craving wears me do[wn],
My assets have vanished, my res[ources(?)] dwindled.
My energies have turned feeble, my prosperity is at a standstill,
Moaning and woe have clouded [my] features.
The grain of my mead is nowhere near satisfying [me],
Beer, the sustenance of mankind, is far from being enough.
Can a happy life be a certainty? I wish I knew how that might come about!

Friend

My well-thought-out speech is the ulti[mate] in good advice,
But you [make?] your well-ordered insight [sound] like babble.
You force [your . . .] to be [sca]tterbrained, irrational,
You render your choicest offerings without conviction.
As to your [ever]lasting, unremitting desire . . .
The [fore]most protection [lies] in prayer:
The reconciled goddess returns to . . .
The re[conciled gods] will take pity on the fool(?), the wrongdoer.
. . .

Sufferer

I bow down before you, my [comrade], I apprehend your w[isdom],
. . . what you say.
Come, let me [tell you],
The on[ager], the wild ass, that had its fill of [wild grass(?)],
Did it carefully ca[rry out(?)] a god's intentions?
The savage lion that devoured the choicest meat,
Did it bring its offerings to appease a goddess' anger?
The parvenu who multiplies his wealth,
Did he weigh out precious gold to the mother goddess for a family?
[Have I] withheld my offerings? I prayed to my god,
[I] said the blessing over the regular sacrifice to my goddess, my speech . . .

Friend

O date palm, wealth-giving tree, my precious brother,
Perfect in all wisdom, O gem of wis[dom],
You are a mere child, the purpose of the gods is remote as the netherworld.
Consider that magnificent wild ass on the [plain],
An arrow will gash that headstrong trampler of the leas!
Come, look at that lion you called to mind, the enemy of livestock,
For the atrocity that lion committed, a pit yawns for him.
The well-heeled parvenu who treasured up possessions,

A king will put him to the flames before his time.
Would you wish to go the way these have gone?
Seek after the lasting reward of (your) god.

Sufferer

Your reasoning is a cool breeze, a breath of fresh air for mankind,
Most particular friend, your advice is e[xcellent].
Let me [put] but one matter before you:
Those who seek not after a god can go the road of favor,
Those who pray to a goddess have grown poor and destitute.
Indeed, in my youth I tried to find out the will of (my) god,
With prayer and supplication I besought my goddess.
I bore a yoke of profitless servitude:
(My) god decreed (for me) poverty instead of wealth.
A cripple rises above me, a fool is ahead of me,
Rogues are in the ascendant, I am demoted.

Friend

O just, knowledgeable one, your logic is perverse,
You have cast off justice, you have scorned divine design.
In your emotional state you have an urge to disregard divine ordinances
. . . the sound rules of your goddess.
The strategy of a god is [as remote as] innermost heaven,
The command of a goddess cannot be dr[awn out].
Teeming humanity well understands trouble.
. . .

Friend

As for the rascal whose good will you wanted,
The . . . of his feet will soon disappear.
The godless swindler who acquires wealth,
A deadly weapon is in pursuit of him.
Unless you serve the will of a god, what will be your profit?
He who bears a god's yoke shall never want for food, though it may
    be meager.
Seek after the favorable breeze of the gods,
What you lost for a year you will recoup in a moment.

Sufferer

I have looked around in society, indications are the contrary:
God does not block the progress of a demon.

A father hauls a boat up a channel,
While his firstborn sprawls in bed.
The eldest son makes his way like a lion,
The second son is content to drive a donkey.
The heir struts the street like a peddler,
The younger son makes provision for the destitute.
What has it profited me that I knelt before my god?
It is I who must (now) bow before my inferior!
The riffraff despise me as much as the rich and proud.

Friend

Adept scholar, master of erudition,
You blaspheme in the anguish of your thoughts.
Divine purpose is as remote as innermost heaven,
It is too difficult to understand, people cannot understand it.
Among all creatures the birth goddess formed,
Why should offspring be completely unmatched(?)?
The cow's first calf is inferior,
Her subsequent offspring is twice as big.
The first child is born a weakling,
The second is called a capable warrior.
Even if one (tries to) apprehend divine intention, people cannot
    understand it.

Sufferer

Pay attention, my friend, learn my (next) parry,
Consider the well-chosen diction of my speech.
They extol the words of an important man who is accomplished in murder,
They denigrate the powerless who has committed no crime.
They esteem truthful the wicked to whom tr[uth] is abhorrent,
They reject the truthful man who he[eds] the will of god.
They fill the oppressor's st[rongroom] with refined gold,
They empty the beggar's larder of [his] provisions.
They shore up the tyrant whose all is crime,
They ruin the weak, they oppress the powerless.
And as for me, without means, a parvenu harasses me.

Friend

Enlil, king of the gods, who created teeming mankind,
Majestic Ea, who pinched off their clay,
The queen who fashioned them, mistress Mami,
Gave twisted words to the human race,

They endowed them in perpetuity with lies and falsehood.
Solemnly they speak well of a rich man,
"He's the king," they say, "he has much wealth."
They malign a poor man as a thief,
They lavish mischief upon him, they conspire to kill him.
They make him suffer every evil because he has no wherewithal(?).
They bring him to a horrible end, they snuff him out like an ember.

Sufferer

You are sympathetic, my friend, be considerate of (my) misfortune.
Help me, see (my) distress, you should be cognizant of it.
Though I am humble, learned, supplicant,
I have not seen help or succor for an instant.
I would pass unobtrusively through the streets of my city,
My voice was not raised, I kept my speaking low.
I did not hold my head high, I would look at the ground.
I was not given to servile praise among my associates.
May the god who has cast me off grant help,
May the goddess who has [forsaken me] take pity,
The shepherd Shamash will past[ure] people as a god should.

SOURCE: Benjamin R. Foster, *From Distant Days: Myths, Tales, and Poetry of Ancient Mesopotamia* (Bethesda, Md.: CDL Press, 1995), 316–23. Used by permission of the publisher.

46

DEBATE BETWEEN A MAN TIRED OF LIFE AND HIS SOUL

The Egyptian "Debate Between a Man Tired of Life and His Soul" dates to the latter part of the third millennium BCE. The text is framed as a debate between a man who wants to take his own life out of despair and his own soul, who fears the consequences of suicide and despair.

"The tongues of the gods, they do not speak amiss,
    they make no special cases."
*I opened my mouth to my soul
    that I might answer what it had said:*
"This is more than I can bear just now!
    —my soul could find no time for me!

It is beyond belief
    —as if I should hesitate to do the deed!
Let my soul not disappear like this, not flutter off,
    but let it take its stand beside me!—
Or never shall it have the chance
    to wrap my person in its stifling bonds;
And for all its twitter, never
    shall it escape the Day of Reckoning.
O all you gods,
    see how my soul defames me!
I will not listen to it ever
    as I drag my way toward dissolution;
For it will not help me do the death by fire—
    myself the victim, who shall no more suffer.
Let I be near me on the Day of Reckoning!
    Let it stand tall on that side yonder
        as one who shares my joy!
Yet this the very soul that rushes off, it vanishes,
    to separate itself from death.
My foolish soul is going to ease the pains of living, is it?
    Keep me from death until I come to it by nature?
No! make the West sweet for me now!
    Is there not pain and suffering enough?
—That is the stuff of life: a troubled journey, a circuit of the sun;
    even the trees decay and fall.
O tread you down upon injustice,
    end my helplessness!
Judge me, O Thoth, you who can soothe the gods;
    defend, O Khonsu, me, a teller of the truth;
Hear, O Rê, my speaking, you who command the skyship;
    defend me, O Anubis, in the holy hall of judgment—
Because my need is heavy in the scale,
    and it has raised the pan of sweetness out of reach.
        Preserve, O gods, the quiet center of my being!"
What my soul said to me:
"You are no man at all!
    Are you even alive?
How full you are of your complaints of life
    like a man of means preaching to passersby!
Things sink down to ruin. Well! save yourself by getting up!"

. . .

Then my soul opened its mouth to me
    that it might answer what I had said:

"Your graveyard thoughts bring sadness to the heart,
 and tears, feeding our misery;
That is what shovels a man into his house
 dug in the rock on the high hill:
—There, there is no more coming forth for you
 to see the sunny days,
Or workmen crafting their buildings in granite,
 putting last touches on pyramids,
Or the beauties of the monuments,
 or where builders fashion altars for the gods:
—You are emptied and drear, like those without motion
 dead on the riverbank, no one caring:
Water laps at their backs,
 the sun does its work,
  and, lips in the current, fish whisper to them.
Now listen to me—
 pay some attention to what people say:
  Spend your days happily! Forget your troubles!
There was a man, and he farmed his plot of land;
 and he was loading his harvest into a ship
  for the voyage to his accounting, which drew near.
And he saw coming a night of wind and weather
 so that he was watchful of the ship, waiting for day,
While he dreamed of life with his wife and children
 who had perished on the Lake of Death
  on a dark night, with crocodiles.
And after he was pondering there some time,
 he shaped the silence into words, saying,
'I have not wept for that mother yonder—
 for her there is no returning from the West,
  no more than any who have lived on earth.
But let me mourn the children, killed in her womb,
 who saw the face of Death ere ever they were born.'
There was another man, and he wanted his evening meat;
 and there was his wife, who said,
  'There will be bread.'
And he went outdoors to fume awhile
 and then go back inside
Behaving like a better person
 (his wife was wise to his ways).
Yet he never really listened to her,
 so the death demons came and carried him off."

I opened my mouth to my soul
that I might answer what it had said:
"How my name stinks because of you
    more than the stink of bird dung on a summer's day
        under a burning sky.
How my name stinks because of you
    more than the catch of fish on a good angling day
        under a burning sky.
How my name stinks because of you
    more than the stench of marsh birds on the hummocks
        filthy with waterfowl.
How my name stinks because of you
    more than the fishermen's smell at runnels of swamps
        after they have been fishing.
How my name stinks because of you
    more than the reek of crocodiles sunning on sandbanks
        alive with their crocodile kind.
How my name stinks because of you
    more than the wife about whom lies
        are told to her wedded husband.
How my name stinks because of you
    more than the able youth of whom they falsely say
        that he is prisoner of everything he should despise.
How my name stinks because of you
    more than the crocodile's cove, where the fool taunts him
        careful his back is turned."

  . . .

SOURCE: John L. Foster, *Ancient Egyptian Literature, An Anthology* (Austin: University of Texas Press, 2001), 56–61. © 2001. Used by permission of the author and the University of Texas Press.

H. LOVE SONGS

Several love songs emerged from Egypt in the second millennium BCE. The following selections are two such poems, likely meant to be accompanied by music and sung for public entertainment. The first selection below is from a collection of love songs from Cairo in which the singer refers to his love as his "sister." The second is the first stanza from "My Love is One and Only." The poem moves back and forth between the voice of the male partner and the female partner. The first stanza is the voice of the male partner. The Egyptian love poems bear similarities to the love poetry of the Song of Solomon.

47

THE CAIRO LOVE SONGS

My god, my [lover . . .],
it is pleasant to go to the [canal]
. . .
and to bathe in your presence.
I shall let [you see . . .] my perfection
in a garment of royal linen, wet [and clinging].
Then I'll go into the water at your bidding,
and I'll come out to you with a red fish
who will be happy in my fingers . . .
So come and look me over.
    The love of my sister lies on yonder side,
    and the river is between [us];
    a crocodile waits on the sandbank.
    Yet I'll go down to the water,
    I'll head into the waves;
    my heart is brave on the water,

and the waves like land to my legs
It is love of her which strengthens me,
as if for me she made a water spell.
I'll watch the lady love return.
My heart rejoices and my arms spread out to clasp her,
my heart is giddy in its seat,
as if this were [not] fated forever.
Do not keep away, but come to me, my lady.
    I embrace her,
    and her arms open wide,
    I am like a man in Punt,
    like someone overwhelmed with drugs.
    I kiss her,
    her lips open,
    and I am drunk
    without a beer.
What is the last thing for preparing her bed?
I tell you, boy,
set fine linen between her limbs,
draw not the covers with royal sheets,
but care [for her] with simple white stuffs,
sprinkled with fine scented oils.
    I wish I were her Negro maid
    who follows at her feet;
    then the skin of all her limbs
    would be [revealed] to me.
    I wish I were her washerman,
    if only for a single month,
    then I would be [entranced],
    washing out the Moringa oils
    in her diaphanous garments . . .
    I wish I were the seal ring,
    the guardian of her [fingers],
    . . .

Source: William Kelly Simpson, *The Literature of Ancient Egypt: An Anthology of Stories, Instructions, and Poetry* (New Haven, Conn.: Yale University Press, 1972), 309–11. © 1972 Yale University Press. Used by permission of the publisher.

48

MY LOVE IS ONE AND ONLY

My love is one and only, without peer,
    lovely above all Egypt's lovely girls.
On the horizon of my seeing,
    see her, rising,
Glistening goddess of the sunrise star
    bright in the forehead of a lucky year.
So there she stands, epitome
    of shining, shedding light,
Her eyebrows, gleaming darkly, marking
    eyes which dance and wander.
Sweet are those lips, which chatter
(but never a word too much),
And the line of the long neck lovely, dropping
    (since song's notes slide that way)
To young breasts firm in the bouncing light
    which shimmers that blueshadowed sidefall of hair.
And slim are those arms, overtoned with gold,
    those fingers which touch like a brush of lotus.
And (ah) how the curve of her back slips gently
    by a whisper of waist to god's plenty below.
(Such thighs as hers pass knowledge
    of loveliness known in the old days.)
Dressed in the perfect flesh of woman
    (heart would run captive to such slim arms),
        she ladies it over the earth,
Schooling the neck of each schoolboy male
    to swing on a swivel to see her move.
(He who could hold that body tight
    would know at last
        perfection of delight—
Best of the bullyboys,
    first among lovers.)
Look you, all men, at that golden going,
    like Our Lady of Love,
        without peer.

Source: John L. Foster, *Love Songs of the New Kingdom* (Austin: University of Texas Press, 2001), 21–22. © 1969, 1970, 1971, 1972, 1973, 1974 by John L. Foster. Used by permission of the University of Texas Press.

I. LAMENTS

The first of the following texts, "Lament for a City," is from a fragment of an Akkadian (Semitic-speaking region in northern Mesopotamia; modern-day Iraq) text in which a goddess laments the destruction of her favored city. There are several Mesopotamian laments that compare to the biblical Lamentations, but texts like this are rare in Akkadian. This lament dates to sometime in the third–second millennium BCE. The second, "Lament over the Destruction of Ur," mourns the destruction of the Sumerian city-state Ur (southern Mesopotamia; modern-day southern Iraq) and dates to sometime in the first half of the second millennium BCE after the fall of the Third Dynasty of Ur. As in the biblical Lamentations, the city is personified, and the poem captures the grief of the people, the gods, and the city itself.

49

LAMENT FOR A CITY

Who stood where I stand to cry out,
To cry out like a helpless one on her bed?
Among the established cities,
    my city has been smashed,
Among the established populace,
    my man has gone away!
Among the gods(?) residing there,
    I too have surely fled!
My ewe cries out in the land of the enemy,
    my lamb is bleating,
My ewe and her lamb they have taken away!

140

When my ewe crossed the river,
She abandoned(?) her lamb on the bank
My birds . . .
Without knowing it they are cutting off their wings!
Where is my house that I used to dwell in?

SOURCE: Benjamin R. Foster, *Before the Muses: An Anthology of Akkadian Literature*, vol. 1 (Bethesda, Md.: CDL Press, 1993), 91. Used by permission of the publisher.

50

LAMENTATION OVER THE DESTRUCTION OF UR

. . .
His [righteous city] which has been destroyed—bitter is its lament;
His Ur which has been destroyed—bitter is its lament;
Its antiphon.
Together with the lord, whose house has been attacked, his city was given
  over to tears;
Together with Nanna, whose land had perished,
Ur joined (its) lament.
The righteous woman, because of his city to grieve the lord,
Ningal, because of his [*land*] to give no rest to [*the lord*]
Unto h[im] for the sake of his city approached—bitterly she weeps,
Unto the lord for the sake of his house which had been attacked
  approached—bitterly she weeps;
[*For the sake*] of his [*city which had been attacked*] she approached him—
  bitterly she weeps.
[*For the sake*] of his [*house*] which had been attacked she approached him—
  its bitter lament *she sets before him.*
The woman, *after her . . . had set the lamentation down upon the ground,*
Herself utters *softly* the wail of *the smitten house.*
"The storm ever breaking forth—its wail has filled me full.
Raging about because of the storm,
Me, a woman, the storm *ever breaking forth*—its wail has filled me full.
The storm *ever breaking forth*—its wail has filled me full.
During the day a bitter *storm* having been raised unto me,
I, *although,* for that day I tremble,
Fled not before that day's violence.

Because of its affliction I saw not one good day during my rule, one good day
    during my rule.
At night a bitter lament having been *raised unto me,*
I, *although,* for that night I tremble,
Fled not before that night's violence.
The storm's cyclone-like destruction—verily its terror has filled me full.
Because of its [affliction] in my nightly sleeping place, in my nightly sleeping
    place verily there is no *peace* for me;
Nor, verily, *because of its affliction,* has the quiet of my sleeping place, the
    quiet of my sleeping place been allowed me.
Although, because in my land there was bitter [distress],
I, like a cow for (its) calf, *trudge the earth,*
My land was not *delivered of fear.*
Although, because in my city there was bitter [distress],
I, like a bird of heaven, flap (my) wings,
(And) to my city I fly,
My city on its foundation verily was destroyed;
Ur where it lay verily perishes.
Although because the *hand of the storm appeared above,*
I screamed and cried to it, 'Return, O storm, to the plain,'
The storm's breast verily rose not to depart,
Me, the woman, in the Enunkug, my house of ladyship,
For whose rule long days had not been granted me,
Verily weeping and lamentation follow.
As for the house which used to be the place where was soothed the spirit of
    the black-headed people,
Instead of its feasts wrath (and) distress verily *multiply.*
Because of its affliction, in my house, the favorable place,
My attacked righteous house upon which no eye *had* been cast,
With heavy spirit, laments that are bitter,
Laments that are bitter, have been brought.
My house founded by the righteous,
Like a garden hut, verily on its side has caved in.
The Ekishnugal, my royal house,
The righteous house, my house which has been given over to tears,
Whose building, falsely, *whose* perishing, truly,
Had been set for me *as* its lot and share,
Like a tent, the house where the crops have been . . . ,
Like the house where the crops have been . . . , to wind and rain verily has
    been exposed.
Ur, my *all-surpassing chamber,*
My *smitten* house (and) city which have been *torn down,*
Like the sheepfold of a shepherd verily has been torn down;

My possessions which had accumulated in the city verily have been
   dissipated."

   . . .

SOURCE: S. N. Kramer, "Sumerian Lamentations," in *Ancient Near Eastern Texts Relating to the Old Testament*, ed. James B. Pritchard, 3rd ed. with supplement (Princeton: Princeton University Press: 1969), 457. © 1950, 1955, 1969 by Princeton University Press. Renewed 1978 by Princeton University Press. Used by permission of the publisher.

J. APOCRYPHA

The Apocrypha is a collection of works related to biblical literature written during the intertestamental period (largely fifth to first centuries BCE). The apocryphal books are not considered canon in Protestant and Jewish traditions, are deuterocanonical ("second canon") in the Catholic tradition, and considered canonical by Eastern Orthodox churches. There are Persian and Greek influences on the apocryphal works, which include mix of apocalyptic writings, wisdom books, historical fiction, hymns and prayers, additions to the biblical books, idealized history, and short fiction. The following selections are from 1 Maccabees and Judith.

51

FIRST MACCABEES

The anonymous apocryphal book of 1 Maccabees discusses Jewish legendary history, covering the period from the reign of Alexander the Great through the rule of the high priest John Hyrcanus (134 CE–104 CE), and likely dates to shortly after Hyrcanus' rule. First Maccabees describes the period when Judea was under the control of the Greek Seleucids, the successors of Alexander, during which there was a divide between the ruling class in Judea that had embraced Hellenistic culture and the rural Jewish population. Complicating matters, the Seleucid ruler, Antiochus IV, effectively outlawed the Jewish religion and defiled the temple in Jerusalem as described in the excerpt below. In response to Hellenization and Antiochus' persecution of the Jewish people, the priest Mattathias and his sons revolted against Antiochus and eventually purified the temple (a tradition later commemorated by the celebration of Hanukkah).

1 Maccabees 1–4

After Alexander son of Philip, the Macedonian, who came from the land of Kittim, had defeated King Darius of the Persians and the Medes, he succeeded him as king. (He had previously become king of Greece.) . . . He gathered a very strong army and ruled over countries, nations, and princes, and they became tributary to him.

After this he fell sick and perceived that he was dying. So he summoned his most honored officers, who had been brought up with him from youth, and divided his kingdom among them while he was still alive. And after Alexander had reigned twelve years, he died. Then his officers began to rule, each in his own place. They all put on crowns after his death, and so did their descendants after them for many years; and they caused many evils on the earth. From them came forth a sinful root, Antiochus Epiphanes, son of King Antiochus; he had been a hostage in Rome. He began to reign in the one hundred thirty-seventh year of the kingdom of the Greeks.

In those days certain renegades came out from Israel and misled many, saying, "Let us go and make a covenant with the Gentiles around us, for since we separated from them many disasters have come upon us." This proposal pleased them, and some of the people eagerly went to the king, who authorized them to observe the ordinances of the Gentiles. So they built a gymnasium in Jerusalem, according to Gentile custom, and removed the marks of circumcision, and abandoned the holy covenant. They joined with the Gentiles and sold themselves to do evil.

. . .

After subduing Egypt, Antiochus returned in the one hundred forty-third year. He went up against Israel and came to Jerusalem with a strong force. He arrogantly entered the sanctuary and took the golden altar, the lampstand for the light, and all its utensils. He took also the table for the bread of the Presence, the cups for drink offerings, the bowls, the golden censers, the curtain, the crowns, and the gold decoration on the front of the temple; he stripped it all off. He took the silver and the gold, and the costly vessels; he took also the hidden treasures that he found. . . .

Two years later the king sent to the cities of Judah a chief collector of tribute, and he came to Jerusalem with a large force. Deceitfully he spoke peaceable words to them, and they believed him; but he suddenly fell upon the city, dealt it a severe blow, and destroyed many people of Israel. He plundered the city, burned it with fire, and tore down its houses and its surrounding walls. They took captive the women and children, and seized the livestock.

Then they fortified the city of David with a great strong wall and strong towers, and it became their citadel. . . .

Then the king wrote to his whole kingdom that all should be one people, and that all should give up their particular customs. All the Gentiles accepted the command of the king. Many even from Israel gladly adopted his religion; they sacrificed to idols and profaned the Sabbath. And the king sent letters by messengers to Jerusalem and the towns of Judah; he directed them to follow customs strange to the land, to forbid burnt offerings and sacrifices and drink offerings in the sanctuary, to profane sabbaths and festivals, to defile the sanctuary and the priests, to build altars and sacred precincts and shrines for idols, to sacrifice swine and other unclean animals, and to leave their sons uncircumcised. They were to make themselves abominable by everything unclean and profane, so that they would forget the law and change all the ordinances. He added, "And whoever does not obey the command of the king shall die." In such words he wrote to his whole kingdom. He appointed inspectors over all the people and commanded the towns of Judah to offer sacrifice, town by town. Many of the people, everyone who forsook the law, joined them, and they did evil in the land; they drove Israel into hiding in every place of refuge they had.

Now on the fifteenth day of Chislev, in the one hundred forty-fifth year, they erected a desolating sacrilege on the altar of burnt offering. They also built altars in the surrounding towns of Judah, and offered incense at the doors of the houses and in the streets. The books of the law that they found they tore to pieces and burned with fire. Anyone found possessing the book of the covenant, or anyone who adhered to the law, was condemned to death by decree of the king. They kept using violence against Israel, against those who were found month after month in the towns. On the twenty-fifth day of the month they offered sacrifice on the altar that was on top of the altar of burnt offering. According to the decree, they put to death the women who had their children circumcised, and their families and those who circumcised them; and they hung the infants from their mother's necks. But many in Israel stood firm and were resolved in their hearts not to eat unclean food. They chose to die rather than to be defiled by food or to profane the holy covenant; and they did die. Very great wrath came upon Israel.

In those days Mattathias son of John son of Simeon, a priest of the family of Joarib, moved from Jerusalem and settled in Modein. He had five sons, John surnamed Gaddi, Simon called Thassi, Judas called Maccabeus, Eleazar called Avaran, and Jonathan called Apphus. . . . The king's officers who were enforcing the apostasy came to the town of Modein to make them offer sacrifice. Many from Israel came to them; and Mattathias and his sons were assembled. . . . Mattathias answered (the king's officers) and said in a loud voice: "Even if all the nations that live under the rule of the king obey him, and have chosen to obey his commandments, every one of them abandoning the religion of their ancestors, I and my sons and my brothers will continue to live by the covenant of our ancestors. Far be it from us to desert the law and the ordinances. We will not obey the king's words by turning aside from our religion to the right hand or to the left."

. . .

Then Mattathias cried out in the town with a loud voice, saying: "Let everyone who is zealous for the law and supports the covenant come out with me!" Then he and his sons fled to the hills and left all that they had in the town. . . .

Then there united with them a company of Hasideans, mighty warriors of Israel, all who offered themselves willingly for the law. And all who became fugitives to escape their troubles joined them and reinforced them. They organized an army, and struck down sinners in their anger and renegades in their wrath; the survivors fled to the Gentiles for safety. And Mattathias and his friends went around and tore down the altars; they forcibly circumcised all the uncircumcised boys that they found within the borders of Israel. They hunted down the arrogant, and the work prospered in their hands. They rescued the law out of the hands of the Gentiles and kings, and they never let the sinner gain the upper hand.

. . .

Then he (Mattathias) blessed them (his sons), and was gathered to his ancestors. He died in the one hundred forty-sixth year and was buried in the tomb of his ancestors at Modein. And all Israel mourned for him with great lamentation. Then his son Judas, who was called Maccabeus, took command in his place. All his brothers and all who had joined his father helped him; they gladly fought for Israel.

. . .

Apollonius now gathered together Gentiles and a large force from Samaria to fight against Israel. When Judas learned of it, he went out to meet him, and he defeated and killed him. Many were wounded and fell, and the rest fled. Then they seized their spoils; and Judas took the sword of Apollonius, and used it in battle the rest of his life.

When Seron, the commander of the Syrian army, heard that Judas had gathered a large company, including a body of faithful soldiers who stayed with him and went out to battle, he said, "I will make a name for myself and win honor in the kingdom. I will make war on Judas and his companions, who scorn the king's command." Once again a strong army of godless men went up with him to help him, to take vengeance on the Israelites.

When he approached the ascent of Beth-horon, Judas went out to meet him with a small company. But when they saw the army coming to meet them, they said to Judas, "How can we, few as we are, fight against so great and so strong a multitude? And we are faint, for we have eaten nothing today." Judas replied, "It is easy for many to be hemmed in by few, for in the sight of Heaven there is no difference between saving by many or by few. It is not on the size of the army that victory in battle depends, but strength comes from Heaven. They come against us in great insolence and lawlessness to destroy us and our wives and our children, and to despoil us; but we fight for our lives and our laws. He himself will crush them before us; as for you, do not be afraid of them."

When he finished speaking, he rushed suddenly against Seron and his army, and they were crushed before him. They pursued them down the descent of Beth-horon to the plain; eight hundred of them fell, and the rest fled into the land of the Philistines. Then Judas and his brothers began to be feared, and terror fell on the Gentiles all around them. His fame reached the king, and the Gentiles talked of the battles of Judas.

When King Antiochus heard of these reports, he was greatly angered; and he sent and gathered all the forces of his kingdom, a very strong army. He opened his coffers and gave a year's pay to his forces, and ordered them to be ready for any need. Then he saw that the money in the treasury was exhausted, and that the revenues from the country were small because of the dissension and disaster that he had caused in the land by abolishing the laws that had existed from the earliest days. He feared that he might not have such funds as he had existed from the earliest days. He feared that he might not have such funds as he had before for his expenses and for the gifts that he used to give more lavishly than preceding kings. He was greatly perplexed in mind; then he determined to go to Persia and collect the revenues from those regions and raise a large fund.

He left Lysias, a distinguished man of royal lineage, in charge of the king's affairs from the river Euphrates to the borders of Egypt. Lysias was also to take care of his son Antiochus until he returned. And he turned over to Lysias half of his forces and the elephants, and gave him orders about all that he wanted done. As for the residents of Judea and Jerusalem, Lysias was to send a force against them to wipe out and destroy the strength of Israel and the remnant of Jerusalem; he was to banish the memory of them from the place, settle aliens in all their territory, and distribute their land by lot. Then the king took the remaining half of his forces and left Antioch his capital in the one hundred and forty-seventh year. He crossed the Euphrates river and went through the upper provinces.

Lysias chose Ptolemy son of Dorymenes, and Nicanor and Gorgias, able men among the friends of the king, and sent with them forty thousand infantry and seven thousand cavalry to go into the land of Judah and destroy it, as the king had commanded. So they set out with their entire force, and when they arrived they encamped near Emmaus in the plain. When the traders of the region heard what was said to them, they took silver and gold in immense amounts, and fetters, and went to the camp to get the Israelites for slaves. And forces from Syria and the land of the Philistines joined with them.

Now Judas and his brothers saw that misfortunes had increased and that the forces were encamped in their territory. They also learned what the king had commanded to do to the people to cause their final destruction. But they said to one another, "Let us restore the ruins of our people, and fight for our people and the sanctuary." So the congregation assembled to be ready for battle, and to pray and ask for mercy and compassion.

. . .

Then they gathered together and went to Mizpah, opposite Jerusalem, because Israel formerly had a place of prayer in Mizpah. They fasted that day, put on sackcloth and sprinkled ashes on their heads, and tore their clothes. And they opened the book of the law to inquire into those matters about which the Gentiles consulted the likenesses of their gods. They also brought the vestments of the priesthood and the firstfruits and the tithes, and they stirred up the nazirites who had completed their days; and they cried aloud to Heaven . . .

Then they sounded the trumpets and gave a loud shout. After this Judas appointed leaders of the people, in charge of thousands and hundreds and fifties and tens. Those who were buildings houses, or were about to be married, or were planting a vineyard, or were fainthearted, he told to go home again, according to the law. Then the army marched out and encamped to the south of Emmaus.

And Judas said, "Arm yourselves and be courageous. Be ready early in the morning to fight with these Gentiles who have assembled against us to destroy us and our sanctuary. It is better for us to die in battle than to see the misfortunes of our nation and of the sanctuary. But as his will in heaven may be, so shall he do."

Now Gorgias took five thousand infantry and one thousand picked cavalry, and this division moved out by night to fall upon the camp of the Jews and attack them suddenly. Men from the citadel were his guides. But Judas heard of it, and he and his warriors moved out to attack the king's force in Emmaus while the division was still absent from the camp. When Gorgias entered the camp of Judas by night, he found no one there, so he looked for them in the hills, because he said, "These men are running away from us."

At daybreak Judas appeared in the plain with three thousand men, but they did not have armor and swords such as they desired. And they saw the camp of the Gentiles, strong and fortified, with cavalry all around it; and these men were trained in war. But Judas said to those who were with him, "Do not fear their numbers or be afraid when they charge. Remember how our ancestors were saved at the Red Sea, when Pharaoh with his forces pursued them. And now, let us cry to Heaven, to see whether he will favor us and remember his covenant with our ancestors and crush this army before us today. Then all the Gentiles will know that there is one who redeems and saves Israel."

When the foreigners looked up and saw them coming against them, they went out from their camp to battle. Then the men with Judas blew their trumpets and engaged in battle. The Gentiles were crushed, and fled into the plain, and all those in the rear fell by the sword. They pursued them to Gazara, and to the plains of Idumea, and to Azotus and Jamnia; and three thousand of them fell. Then Judas and his force turned back from pursuing them, and he said to the people, "Do not be greedy for plunder, for there is a battle before us; Gorgias and his force are near us in the hills. But stand now against our enemies and fight them, and afterward seize the plunder boldly."

Just as Judas was finishing this speech, a detachment appeared, coming out of the hills. They saw that their army had been put to flight, and that the Jews were burning the camp, for the smoke that was seen showed what had happened. When they perceived this, they were greatly frightened, and when they also saw the army of Judas drawn up in the plain for battle, they all fled into the land of the Philistines. Then Judas returned to plunder the camp, and they seized a great amount of gold and silver, and cloth dyed blue and sea purple, and great riches. On their return they sang hymns and praises to Heaven—"For he is good, for his mercy endures forever." Thus Israel had a great deliverance that day.

Those of the foreigners who escaped went and reported to Lysias all that had happened. When he heard it, he was perplexed and discouraged, for things had not happened to Israel as he had intended, nor had they turned out as the king had ordered. But the next year he mustered sixty thousand picked infantry and five thousand cavalry to subdue them. They came into Idumea and encamped at Beth-zur, and Judas met them with ten thousand men.

When he saw that their army was strong, he prayed, saying, "Blessed are you, O Savior of Israel, who crushed the attack of the mighty warrior by the hand of your servant David, and gave the camp of the Philistines into the hands of Jonathan son of Saul, and of the man who carried his armor. Hem in this army by the hand of your people Israel, and let them be ashamed of their troops and their cavalry. Fill them with cowardice; melt the boldness of their strength; let them tremble in their destruction. Strike them down with the sword of those who love you, and let all who know your name praise you with hymns."

Then both sides attacked, and there fell of the army of Lysias five thousand men; they fell in action. When Lysias saw the rout of his troops and observed the boldness that inspired those of Judas, and how ready they were either to live or to die nobly, he withdrew to Antioch and enlisted mercenaries in order to invade Judea again with an even larger army.

Then Judas and his brothers said, "See, our enemies are crushed; let us go up to cleanse the sanctuary and dedicate it." So all the army assembled and went up to Mount Zion. There they saw the sanctuary desolate, the altar profaned, and the gates burned. In the courts they saw bushes sprung up as in a thicket, or as on one of the mountains. They saw also the chambers of the priests in ruins. Then they tore their clothes and mourned with great lamentation; they sprinkled themselves with ashes and fell face down on the ground. And when the signal was given with the trumpets, they cried out to Heaven.

Then Judas detailed men to fight against those in the citadel until he had cleansed the sanctuary. He chose blameless priests devoted to the law, and they cleansed the sanctuary and removed the defiled stones to an unclean place. They deliberated what to do about the altar of burnt offering, which had been profaned. And they thought it best to tear it down, so that it would not be a lasting shame to them that the Gentiles had defiled it. So they tore down the altar, and stored the stones in a convenient place on the temple hill until a prophet should come to tell what to do with them. Then they took unhewn stones, as the law directs, and built a new altar like the former one. They also rebuilt the sanctuary and the interior of the temple, and consecrated the courts. They made new holy vessels, and brought the lampstand, the altar of incense, and the table into the temple. Then they offered incense on the altar and lit the lamps on the lampstand, and these gave light in the temple. They placed the bread on the table and hung up the curtains. Thus they finished all the work they had undertaken.

Early in the morning on the twenty-fifth day of the ninth month, which is the month of Chislev, in the one hundred forty-eighth year, they rose and offered sacrifice, as the law directs, on the new altar of burnt offering that they had built. At the very season and on the very day that the Gentiles had profaned it, it was dedicated with songs and harps and lutes and cymbals. All the people fell on their faces and worshiped and blessed Heaven, who had prospered them. So they celebrated the dedication of the altar for eight days, and joyfully offered burnt offerings; they offered a sacrifice of well-being and a thanksgiving offering. They decorated the front of the temple with golden crowns and small shields; they restored the gates and the chambers for the priests, and fitted them with doors. There was very great joy among the people, and the disgrace brought by the Gentiles was removed.

Then Judas and his brothers and all the assembly of Israel determined that every year at that season the days of dedication of the altar should be observed with joy and gladness for eight days, beginning with the twenty-fifth day of the month of Chislev.

Source: NRSV.

52

JUDITH

The apocryphal book of Judith relates the story of the titular character, Judith, a Jewish widow. The story is set in the time of Nebuchadnezzar, king of Assyria, although historically Nebuchadnezzar was king of Babylon. The novella is a work of historical fiction in which Judith singlehandedly takes out the general of the Assyrian army, Holofernes, in a fashion reminiscent of Jael's defeat of the Canaanite general Sisera in Judges 4–5.

Judith 1–15

. . . Nebuchadnezzar, king of the Assyrians, sent messengers to all who lived in Persia and to all who lived in the west, those who lived in Cilicia and Damascus, Lebanon and Antilebanon, and all who lived along the seacoast, and those among the nations of Carmel and Gilead, and Upper

Galilee and the great plain of Esdraelon, and all who were in Samaria and its towns, and beyond the Jordan as far as Jerusalem and Bethany and Chelous and Kadesh and the river of Egypt and Tahpanhes and Raamses and the whole land of Goshen, even beyond Tanis and Memphis, and all who lived in Egypt as far as the borders of Ethiopia. But all who lived in the whole region disregarded the summons of Nebuchadnezzar, king of the Assyrians, and refused to join him in the war; for they were not afraid of him, but regarded him as only one man. So they sent back his messengers empty-handed and in disgrace.

Then Nebuchadnezzar became very angry with this whole region, and swore by his throne and kingdom that he would take revenge on the whole territory of Cilicia and Damascus and Syria, that he would kill with his sword also all the inhabitants of the land of Moab, and the people of Ammon, and all Judea, and everyone in Egypt, as far as the coasts of the two seas.

. . .

In the eighteenth year, on the twenty-second day of the first month, there was talk in the palace of Nebuchadnezzar, king of the Assyrians, about carrying out his revenge on the whole region, just as he had said. He summoned all his ministers and all his nobles and set before them his secret plan and recounted fully, with his own lips, all the wickedness of the region. They decided that everyone who had not obeyed his command should be destroyed.

When he had completed his plan, Nebuchadnezzar, king of the Assyrians, called Holofernes, the chief general of his army, second only to himself, and said to him, "Thus says the Great King, the lord of the whole earth: Leave my presence and take with you men confident in their strength, one hundred twenty thousand foot soldiers and twelve thousand cavalry. March out against all the land to the west, because they disobeyed my orders. Tell them to prepare earth and water, for I am coming against them in my anger, and will cover the whole face of the earth with the feet of my troops, to whom I will hand them over to be plundered. . . . For as I live, and by the power of my kingdom, what I have spoken I will accomplish by my own hand. And you—take care not to transgress any of your lord's commands, but carry them out exactly as I have ordered you; do it without delay."

. . .

. . . Holofernes took his whole army, the infantry, cavalry, and chariots, and went up into the hill country. He ravaged Put and Lud, and plundered all the Rassisites and the Ishmaelites on the border of the desert, south of the country of the Chelleans. Then he followed the Euphrates and passed through Mesopotamia and destroyed all the fortified towns along the brook

Abron, as far as the sea. . . . Then he went down into the plain of Damascus during the wheat harvest, and burned all their fields and destroyed their flocks and herds and sacked their towns and ravaged their lands and put all their young men to the sword.

So fear and dread of him fell upon all the people who lived along the seacoast, at Sidon and Tyre, and those who lived in Sur and Ocina and all who lived in Jamnia. Those who lived in Azotus and Ascalon feared him greatly. They therefore sent messengers to him to sue for peace in these words: "We, the servants of Nebuchadnezzar, the Great King, lie prostrate before you. Do with us whatever you will. See, our buildings and all our land and all our wheat fields and our flocks and herds and all our encampments lie before you; do with them as you please. Our towns and their inhabitants are also your slaves; come and deal with them as you see fit."

The men came to Holofernes and told him all this. Then he went down to the seacoast with his army and stationed garrisons in the fortified towns and took picked men from them as auxiliaries. These people and all in the countryside welcomed him with garlands and dances and tambourines. Yet he demolished all their shrines and cut down their sacred groves; for he had been commissioned to destroy all the gods of the land, so that all nations should worship Nebuchadnezzar alone, and that all their dialects and tribes should call upon him as a god. Then he came toward Esdraelon, near Dothan, facing the great ridge of Judea; he camped between Geba and Scythopolis, and remained for a whole month in order to collect all the supplies for his army.

When the Israelites living in Judea heard of everything that Holofernes, the general of Nebuchadnezzar, the king of the Assyrians, had done to the nations, and how he had plundered and destroyed all their temples, they were therefore greatly terrified at his approach; they were alarmed both for Jerusalem and for the temple of the Lord their God. . . .

. . .

Then Achior, the leader of all the Ammonites, said to him (Holofernes) . . . "So now, my master and lord, if there is any oversight in this people and they sin against their God and we find out their offense, then we can go up and defeat them. But if they are not a guilty nation, then let my lord pass them by; for their Lord and God will defend them, and we shall become the laughingstock of the whole world." . . . Holofernes, the commander of the Assyrian army, said to Achior in the presence of all the foreign contingents: . . . "As for you, Achior, you Ammonite mercenary, you have said these words in a moment of perversity; you shall not see my face again from this day until I take revenge on this race that came out of Egypt." . . . Then Holofernes ordered his slaves, who waited on him in his tent, to seize Achior and take him away to Bethulia and hand him over to the Israelites. . . .

Then the Israelites came down from their town and found him; they untied him and brought him into Bethulia and placed him before the magistrates of their town, who in those days were Uzziah son of Micah, of the tribe of Simeon, and Chabris son of Gothoniel, and Charmis son of Melchiel. They called together all the elders of the town, and all their young men and women ran to the assembly. They set Achior in the midst of all their people, and Uzziah questioned him about what had happened. He answered and told them what had taken place at the council of Holofernes, and all that he had said in the presence of the Assyrian leaders, and all that Holofernes had boasted he would do against the house of Israel. Then the people fell down and worshiped God, and cried out:

"O Lord God of heaven, see their arrogance, and have pity on our people in their humiliation, and look kindly today on the faces of those who are consecrated to you." Then they reassured Achior, and praised him highly. Uzziah took him from the assembly to his own house and gave a banquet for the elders; and all that night they called on the God of Israel for help.

. . .

The Israelites then cried out to the Lord their God, for their courage failed, because all their enemies had surrounded them, and there was no way of escape from them. The whole Assyrian army, their infantry, chariots, and cavalry, surrounded them for thirty-four days, until all the water containers of every inhabitant of Bethulia were empty; their cisterns were going dry, and on no day did they have enough water to drink, for their drinking water was rationed. Their children were listless, and the women and young men fainted from thirst and were collapsing in the streets of the town and in the gateways; they no longer had any strength.

Then all the people, the young men, the women, and the children, gathered around Uzziah and the rulers of the town and cried out with a loud voice, and said before all the elders, "Let God judge between you and us! You have done us a great injury in not making peace with the Assyrians. For now we have no one to help us; God has sold us into their hands, to be strewn before them in thirst and exhaustion. Now summon them and surrender the whole town as booty to the army of Holofernes and to all his forces. For it would be better for us to be captured by them. We shall indeed become slaves, but our lives will be spared, and we shall not witness our little ones dying before our eyes and our wives and children drawing their last breath. We call to witness against you heaven and earth and our God, the Lord of our ancestors, who punishes us for our sins and the sins of our ancestors; do today the things that we have described!" . . . But Uzziah said to them, "Courage, my brothers and sisters! Let us hold out for five days more; by that time the Lord our God will turn his mercy to us again, for he will not forsake us utterly. But if these days pass by, and no help comes for us, I will do as you say."

. . .

Now in those days Judith heard about these things: she was the daughter of Merari son of Ox son of Joseph son of Oziel son of Elkiah son of Ananias son of Gideon son of Raphain son of Ahitub son of Elijah son of Hilkiah son of Eliab son of Nathanael son of Salamiel son of Sarasadai son of Israel. Her husband Manasseh, who belonged to her tribe and family, had died during the barley harvest. . . . She was beautiful in appearance, and was very lovely to behold. Her husband Manasseh had left her gold and silver, men and women slaves, livestock, and fields; and she maintained this estate. No one spoke ill of her, for she feared God with great devotion.

When Judith heard the harsh words spoken by the people against the ruler, because they were faint for lack of water, and when she heard all that Uzziah said to them, and how he promised them under oath to surrender the town to the Assyrians after five days, she sent her maid, who was in charge of all she possessed, to summon Uzziah and Chabris and Charmis, the elders of their town. They came to her, and she said to them: . . . "Listen to me. I am about to do something that will go down through all generations of our descendants. Stand at the town gate tonight so that I may go out with my maid; and within the days after which you have promised to surrender the town to our enemies, the Lord will deliver Israel by my hand. Only, do not try to find out what I am doing; for I will not tell you until I have finished what I am about to do."

. . .

When Judith had stopped crying out to the God of Israel, and had ended all these words, she rose from where she lay prostrate. She called her maid and went down into the house where she lived on sabbaths and on her festal days. She removed the sackcloth she had been wearing, took off her widow's garments, bathed her body with water, and anointed herself with precious ointment. She combed her hair, put on a tiara, and dressed herself in the festive attire that she used to wear while her husband Manasseh was living. She put sandals on her feet, and put on her anklets, bracelets, rings, earrings, and all her other jewelry. Thus she made herself very beautiful, to entice the eyes of all the men who might see her. She gave her maid a skin of wine and a flask of oil and filled a bag with roasted grain, dried fig cakes, and fine bread; then she wrapped up all her dishes and gave them to her to carry.

. . .

Then the guards of Holofernes and all his servants came out and led her into the tent. Holofernes was resting on his bed under a canopy that was woven with purple and gold, emeralds and other precious stones. When they told him of her, he came to the front of the tent, with silver lamps carried before him. When Judith came into the presence of Holofernes and his servants, they all marveled at the beauty of her face. She prostrated herself and did obeisance to him, but his slaves raised her up. . . . Judith (said to) him, "Accept the words of your slave, and let your servant speak in your presence. I will say nothing false to my lord this night. If you follow out the words of your servant, God will accomplish something through you, and my lord will not fail to achieve his purposes. By the life of Nebuchadnezzar, king of the whole earth, and by the power of him who has sent you to direct every living being! Not only do human beings serve him because of you, but also the animals of the field and the cattle and the birds of the air will live because of your power, under Nebuchadnezzar and all his house. For we have heard of your wisdom and skill, and it is reported throughout the whole world that you alone are the best in the whole kingdom, the most informed and the most astounding in military strategy. . . . God has sent me to accomplish with you things that will astonish the whole world wherever people shall hear about them. Your servant is indeed God-fearing and serves the God of heaven night and day. So, my lord, I will remain with you; but every night your servant will go out into the valley and pray to God. He will tell me when they have committed their sins. Then I will come and tell you, so that you may go out with your whole army, and not one of them will be able to withstand you. Then I will lead you through Judea, until you come to Jerusalem; there I will set your throne. You will drive them like sheep that have no shepherd, and no dog will so much as growl at you. For this was told me to give me foreknowledge; it was announced to me, and I was sent to tell you."

Her words pleased Holofernes and all his servants. They marveled at her wisdom and said, "No other woman from one end of the earth to the other looks so beautiful or speaks so wisely!" Then Holofernes said to her, "God has done well to send you ahead of the people, to strengthen our hands and bring destruction on those who have despised my lord. You are not only beautiful in appearance, but wise in speech. If you do as you have said, your god shall be my God, and you shall live in the palace of King Nebuchadnezzar and be renowned throughout the whole world."

Then he commanded them to bring her in where his silver dinnerware was kept, and ordered them to set a table for her with some of his own delicacies, and with some of his own wine to drink. But Judith said, "I cannot partake of them, or it will be an offense; but I will have enough with the things I brought with me. . . . As surely as you live, my lord, your servant will not use up the supplies I have with me before the Lord carries out by my hand what he has determined."

. . .

On the fourth day Holofernes held a banquet for his personal attendants only, and did not invite any of his officers. He said to Bagoas, the eunuch who had charge of his personal affairs, "Go and persuade the Hebrew woman who is in your care to join us and to eat and drink with us. For it would be a disgrace if we let such a woman go without having intercourse with her. If we do not seduce her, she will laugh at us."

So Bagoas left the presence of Holofernes, and approached her and said, "Let this pretty girl not hesitate to come to my lord to be honored in his presence, and to enjoy drinking wine with us, and to become today like one of the Assyrian women who serve in the palace of Nebuchadnezzar." Judith replied, "Who am I to refuse my lord? Whatever pleases him I will do at once, and it will be a joy to me until the day of my death." So she proceeded to dress herself in all her woman's finery. Her maid went ahead and spread for her on the ground before Holofernes the lambskins she had received from Bagoas for her daily use in reclining.

Then Judith came in and lay down. Holofernes' heart was ravished with her and his passion was aroused, for he had been waiting for an opportunity to seduce her from the day he first saw her. So Holofernes said to her, "Have a drink and be merry with us!" Judith said, "I will gladly drink, my lord, because today is the greatest day in my whole life." Then she took what her maid had prepared and ate and drank before him. Holofernes was greatly pleased with her, and drank a great quantity of wine, much more than he had ever drunk in any one day since he was born.

When evening came, his slaves quickly withdrew. Bagoas closed the tent from outside and shut out the attendants from his master's presence. They went to bed, for they all were weary because the banquet had lasted so long. But Judith was left alone in the tent, with Holofernes stretched out on his bed, for he was dead drunk.

Now Judith had told her maid to stand outside the bedchamber and to wait for her to come out, as she did on the other days; for she said she would be going out for her prayers. She had said the same thing to Bagoas. So everyone went out, and no one, either small or great, was left in the bedchamber. Then Judith, standing beside his bed, said in her heart, "O Lord God of all might, look in this hour on the work of my hands for the exaltation of Jerusalem. Now indeed is the time to help your heritage and to carry out my design to destroy the enemies who have risen up against us."

She went up to the bedpost near Holofernes' head, and took down his sword that hung there. She came close to his bed, took hold of the hair of his head, and said, "Give me strength today, O Lord God of Israel!" Then she struck his neck twice with all her might, and cut off his head. Next she rolled his body off the bed and pulled down the canopy from the posts. Soon afterward she went out and gave Holofernes' head to her maid who placed it in her food bag. Then the two of them went out together, as they were accustomed to do for prayer. They passed through the camp, circled around the valley, and went up to the mountain to Bethulia, and came to its gates. From a distance Judith called out to the sentries at the gates, "Open, open the gate! God, our God, is with us, still showing his power in Israel and his strength against our enemies, as he has done today!" . . . Then she pulled the head out of the bag and showed it to them, and said, "See here, the head of Holofernes, the commander of the Assyrian army, and here is the canopy beneath which he lay in his drunken stupor. The Lord has struck him down by the hand of a woman. As the Lord lives, who has protected me in the way I went, I swear that it was my face that seduced him to his destruction, and that he committed no sin with me, to defile and shame me."

. . .

As soon as it was dawn they hung the head of Holofernes on the wall. Then they all took their weapons, and they went out in companies to the mountain passes. When the Assyrians saw them they sent word to their commanders, who then went to the generals and the captains and to all their other officers. They came to Holofernes' tent and said to the steward in charge of all his personal affairs, "Wake up our lord, for the slaves have been so bold as to come down against us to give battle, to their utter destruction."

So Bagoas went in and knocked at the entry of the tent, for he supposed that he was sleeping with Judith. But when no one answered, he opened it and went into the bedchamber and found him sprawled on the floor dead, with his head missing. He cried out with a loud voice and wept and groaned and shouted, and tore his clothes. Then he went to the tent where Judith had stayed, and when he did not find her, he rushed out to the people and shouted, "The slaves have tricked us! One Hebrew woman has brought disgrace on the house of King Nebuchadnezzar. Look, Holofernes is lying on the ground, and his head is missing!"

When the leaders of the Assyrian army heard this, they tore their tunics and were greatly dismayed, and their loud cries and shouts rose up throughout the camp. When the men in the tents heard it, they were amazed at what had happened. Overcome with fear and trembling, they did not wait for one another, but with one impulse all rushed out and fled by every path across the plain and through the hill country. Those who had camped in the hills around Bethulia also took to flight. Then the Israelites, everyone that was a soldier, rushed out upon them. Uzziah sent men to Betomasthaim and Choba and Kola, and to all the frontiers of Israel, to tell what had taken place and to urge all to rush out upon the enemy to destroy them. When the Israelites heard it with one accord they fell upon the enemy, and cut them down as far as Choba. . . . And the Israelites, when they returned from the slaughter, took passion of what remained. . . .

SOURCE: NRSV.

K. REWRITTEN HEBREW BIBLE

Communities in the intertestamental period and beyond not only copied the texts of the Hebrew Bible but continued to write their own material as well. For instance, both biblical and nonbiblical texts were found in the large cache of scrolls found at Qumran near the Dead Sea. Among these texts are letters, apocalyptic texts, wisdom literature, rules for the community, and texts that retell or expand upon biblical texts. The selections from the Qumran texts are parabiblical texts that rewrite or expound on the texts of the Hebrew Bible. Later writers also rewrote texts of the Hebrew Bible, one of the most well known of which is the first-century CE writer Flavius Josephus, who expanded on the writings of the Hebrew Bible to tell the story of Jewish history. An excerpt from Josephus below, from his account of Moses, is included below.

53

QUMRAN TEXTS

A large collection of scrolls known as the Dead Sea Scrolls was found in several caves near the ancient site of Qumran near the Dead Sea. The hundreds of scrolls and fragments date from the first century BCE to the first century CE and consist of copies of books from the Hebrew Bible as well as nonbiblical religious writings from the Qumran community. The examples below are excerpts from nonbiblical writings, though they are closely related to the biblical texts. The first, 1Q22 (1QWords of Moses) embellishes the final words of Moses to the Israelites (cp. Deuteronomy). The second, 4Q216 (4QJubilees[a]), is a retelling of Genesis that describes the divisions of creation (cp. Gen 1). 4Q400 (4QSongs of Sabbath Sacrifice[a]), also referred to as the Angelic Liturgy, contains songs for the yearly Sabbaths, as well as references to angelic prayers and celebrations in the heavenly throne room. Lastly, the excerpt from the Isaiah pesher consists of quotes from Isaiah 10:20-22; 11:1-5 and the community's interpretation of the text.

Words of Moses (1Q22)

[And God spoke] to Moses in the year [forty] of the depart[ure of the children of I]sra[el from the land of E]gypt, in the eleventh mo[nth,] the first day of the [mo]nth, saying: "[Muster] all the con[gre]gation, climb [Mount Nebo] and stay [there,] you and Elea[zar,] Aar[on's s]on. Inter[pret for the heads of fam]ilies, for the Levites and for all the [priests] and decree to the sons of Israe[l the wo]rds of the Law which [I] commanded [you] on Mount S[i]nai to decree to th[em. Proclaim] in the[ir] ears everything accura[tely,] for I will [requi]re it from them. [Take the] heavens and [the earth as witnesses against] them, [f]or they will not [lo]ve wha[t] I have commanded [them,] th[ey] and [their] sons, [all] the days they [live upon the ea]rth. [However] I announce that they will desert [me and ch]oose the [sins of the] peo[ples,] their [abo]minations [and] their [disre]putable acts [and will serve] ido[l]s who will become a tr[ap and] a snare. They will vio[late all the ho]ly [assemblies], the sabbath of the covenant, [the festivals] which I command you today [to k]eep. [This is why I will stri]ke them with a great [blow] in the midst of [the] land [for] [the con]quest of whi[ch th]ey are going to cross [the Jo]rdan there. And [w]hen all the curse[s] happen t[o] them and overtake them un[til] they die and until they are de[stroyed], then they will know [that] the truth has been ca[rried out] on them." . . . And Moses called Eleazar, son of [Aaron] and Joshu[a, son of Nun, and said to] them: "Speak [all the words of the Law, without] leaving any [out. Be silent,]" . . .

Jubilees (4Q216)

[And the angel of the Presence told Moses at God's command: "Write all the wo]rds of the creation: h[ow] [on the sixth day YHWH God finished all his works and all that he had created] and rested on the [seventh] day [and made it holy for all the centuries and placed it as a sign for all] his works" . . . [For on the first day he created the] upper [heaven]s, the ear[th,] [the waters and all the spirits who serve before him: the angels of] the presence, the angels of ho[liness,] the an[gels of the spirits of fire, the angels of the spirits of the current]s [and] the angels of the spirits of the [clouds] . . . of thunder[s] and the angels of the [storm] winds . . . creatures [which he made in the heavens and which he made in the ear]th and in everything, the aby[sses,] darkness, dawn, [light, the dusk which he prepared with] his [know]ledge. Then we saw his deeds and [blessed him] on account of all his [d]eeds and [we praised him in his presence because] he ma[de seven] great works [on the first day.] And on the [second] da[y he made the vault in the midd]le of the [water]s, [and the waters were separated on that day. Half] went up on top of the vault and half went down below the vault which was in its midst . . .

[On the] sixth [da]y [he made] all the anim[als of the earth and all the cattle and everything that creeps over the earth. After all these] he made man, male and fem[ale he made them, and gave them control over everything there is on the earth and in the seas and over everything that flies] over the animas and over all the creeping animals that [creep over the earth, and the cattle and over all the earth. Over all these he gave them control.] He made these [four] kinds on [the sixth day. And in all there were twenty-two kinds. And he finished all his works on the sixth day: everything] . . . in the light and in the darkness and in everything. And he gave us a huge sign, the day of] the Sabbath on which he rested [from doing all the works which he had created over the six days . . . they were made in six days. . . .] . . . and we observe the sabbath on the sev[enth] day [(refraining) from all work. For we, all the angels of the presence and all the angels of holiness—these] two kinds—he comman[ded us to observe the sabbath with him in the heavens and on the earth. And he said to us: "I am going to isolate for myself] a nation among my nations. . . . They will be my people and I will be their God."] And he chose the descendants of Jacob among [all those I saw. And I registered them for me as the firstborn son and consecrated them to me] for ever and ever. . . .

Songs of the Sabbath Sacrifice (4Q400)

[Of the Instructor. Song for the sacrifice] of the first [Sabba]th, the fourth of the first month. Praise [the God of . . .] you, gods of all the most holy ones; and in {his} the divinity [of his kingdom, rejoice. Because he has established] the most holy ones among the eternal holy ones, so that for him they can be priests [of the inner sanctum in the temple of his kingship,] the servants of the Presence in his glorious sanctuary. In the assembly of all the divinities [of knowledge, and in the council of all the spirits] of God, he has engraved his ordinances for all spiritual creatures, and [his] [glorious] precepts [for those who establish] knowledge, the people of the intelligence of his divine glory, for those who are close to knowledge . . . eternal. And from the holy source of the [most] holy sanctuaries . . . prie[sts] of the inner sanctum, servants of the Presence of the [most] holy king . . . And by each regulation they become stronger for the seven [eternal counsels. Because he] established them [for] himself to be [most] h[oly ones, servants in the ho]ly of holies . . . among them according to the council . . . [. . . Th]ey are princes of . . . in the temples of the king. . . . They do not tolerate anyone whose path is de[praved.] There is n[o] impurity in their holy offerings. For them he has engraved [ho]ly [precepts], by them all the holy ones sanctify themselves perpetually; and he purifies the pure [shining ones, so that they dea]l with all those of depraved path. And they shall appease his will, in favor of all those converted from sin.

Isaiah Pesher (4Q161)

["On that day, the remnant of Israel, the survivors of Jacob, will cease to lean] [on their assailant but will lean loyally on YHWH, the Holy One of Israel. (Isa 10:20)] [A remnant will return, a remnant of J]a[cob to] G[od the warrior" (Isa 10:21). . . .] [Its interpretation: the remnant of I]srael is [the assembly of his chosen one . . .] . . .

["Even if your people, Israel were like the sand of the sea, only a remnant will return; extermination is decreed,] [but justice will overflow. For it is decided and decreed: the Lord, YHWH of Hosts, will execute it in the midst of the whole earth" (Isa 10:22-23)] [Its interpretation concerns . . .] . . . the sons of . . . his people. [And a]s for what he says: "Even if [your people, Israel were like the sand of the sea,] [only a remnant will return;] ex[termination is decr]eed, but just[ice] will overflow." [Its interpretation concerns] . . . "This is why the Lo[rd YHWH of Hosts] says: [Do not fear, my people] [who liv]e in Zio[n, of Assyria: it will hit you with a st]ick [and lift its rod against you in the fashion of Egypt;] [for] very shortly [my anger will end and my wrath will destroy] them. [YHWH of Hosts] will la[sh against them] [the flail as in the destruction of Midian, on the rock of Ho]reb, and he will lift his rod [against the sea] [in the fashion of Egypt. And on that day it will happen] that [his] loa[d] will be removed [from your shoulder, and his yoke] [from your neck]" (Isa 10:24-27) . . .

"[A shoot will issue from the stu]mp of Jesse and [a bud] will sprout from [its] ro[ots.] Upon him [will be placed] the spi[rit of] [YHWH; the spirit] of discretion and wisdom, the spirit of ad[vice and courage,] the spirit of knowl[edge] [and of respect for YHWH and his delight will be in respecting] YHWH. [He will not judge] by appearances [or give verdi]cts [on hearsay alone;] he will judge [the poor with justice and decide] [with honesty for the humble of the earth. He will destroy the land with the rod of his mouth and with the breath of his lips] [he will execute the evil. Justice will be the belt of] his [l]oins and lo[yalty the belt of his hips" (Isa 11:1-5)] . . . which will sprout in the fi[nal days, since] [with the breath of his lips he will execute] his [ene]my and God will support him with [the spirit of c]ourage . . . [. . . thro]ne of glory, h[oly] crown and multicolor[ed] vestments . . . his sword will judge [al]l the peoples. And as for what he says: "He will not [judge by appearances] or give verdicts on hearsay," its interpretation: which . . . and according to what they teach him, he will judge, and upon their authority . . . with him will go out one of the priests of renown, holding in his hand clothes . . .

SOURCE: Florentino García Martínez and Eibert J. C. Tigchelaar, *The Dead Sea Scrolls Study Edition*, 2 vols. (Grand Rapids: Eerdmans, 2000), 1:59–61, 1:313–17, 1:461–63, 2:807–9. Used by permission of the publisher.

54

MOSES

Among the works of the Jewish writer Flavius Josephus (first century CE) is *Jewish Antiquities*, which gives a history of the Jewish people from creation to the period slightly before the beginning of the Jewish revolt against Rome in 66 CE. The first part of *Antiquities* describes the major events of the Hebrew Bible, although, as can be seen below, Josephus elaborates at times and adds his own flourish to the biblical accounts. The following excerpt elaborates on Moses' birth and his time as part of the household of Pharaoh in which he serves as a brilliant military strategist who leads the Egyptian army to victory against the Ethiopians.

Josephus, *Jewish Antiquities* 2.201–258

Now it happened that the Egyptians grew delicate and lazy, as to pains-taking, and gave themselves up to other pleasures, and in particular to the love of gain. They also became very disaffected towards the Hebrews, having envy at their prosperity. For when they saw how the nation of the Israelites flourished, and had become distinguished already by plenty of wealth, which they had acquired by their virtue and natural love of labor, they thought their increase was to their own detriment. And having, by the passing of time, forgotten the benefits they had received from Joseph, particularly with the kingship being now come to another family, they became very abusive to the Israelites and contrived many ways of afflicting them. They ordered them to cut a great number of channels for the river, and to build walls for their cities and ramparts, that they might restrain the river, and hinder its waters from stagnating, when it flooded over its own banks. They set them also to build pyramids, and by all this wore them out. They also forced them to learn all sorts of mechanical arts and to familiarize themselves to hard labor. And four hundred years they spent under these afflictions. These two nations strove against one another for who should get the mastery; the Egyptians desiring to destroy the Israelites by these labors, and the Israelites desiring to hold out to the end under them.

While the affairs of the Hebrews were in this condition, there was an event that came about to the Egyptians that made them more intent to the extinction of our nation. One of those sacred scribes, who was very learned in foretelling future events accurately, told the king that about this time there would a child be born to the Israelites, who, if he were reared, would bring the Egyptian dominion low, and would raise the Israelites; that he would excel all men in virtue, and obtain a glory that would be remembered through all ages. This prophecy was so feared by the king that, according to this man's opinion, he commanded that they should cast every male child, which was born to the Israelites, into the river and destroy it. And besides this, the Egyptian midwives should watch the labors of the Hebrew women, and observe what is born, for those were the women who were charged to do the office of midwives to them; and by reason of their relation to the king, would not transgress his commands. He enjoined also, that if any parents should disobey him and venture to save their male children alive, they and their families should be destroyed. This was a severe affliction indeed to those that suffered it, not only as they were deprived of their sons, and while they were the parents themselves, they were obliged to be subservient to the destruction of their own children, but as it was to be supposed to tend to the extermination of their nation, while upon the destruction of their children, and their own gradual dissolution, the calamity would become very hard and inconsolable to them. And this was the ill state they were in. But no one can be too hard for the purpose of God, though he contrive ten thousand subtle devices for that end; for this child, whom the sacred scribe foretold, was brought up and concealed from the observers appointed by the king; and the one who foretold about the child was not mistaken in the consequences of his preservation, which were brought to pass in the following manner.

A man whose name was Amram, one of the nobler sort of the Hebrews, was afraid for his whole nation, that it would cease to be because of the lack of young men to be brought up hereafter. He was also very uneasy about it, because his wife was with child, and he did not know what to do. Because of this, he decided to pray to God and entreat him to have compassion on those who had in no way transgressed the laws of his worship, and to give them deliverance from the miseries they at that time endured, and to render unsuccessful their enemies' hopes of the destruction of their nation. Accordingly God had mercy on him, and was moved by his supplication. God stood by him in his sleep, and exhorted him not to despair of his future. He said further that he did not forget their piety towards him, and would always reward them for it, as he had formerly granted his favor to their forefathers, and made them increase from a few to so great a multitude. . . . "Know therefore that I will provide for you all in common what is for your good, and particularly for yourself what will make you renown; for that child, out of dread of whose birth the Egyptians have doomed the Israelite children to destruction, will be your child, and he will be concealed from those who watch to destroy him. And when he is brought up in a surprising way, he will deliver the Hebrew nation from the distress they are under from the Egyptians. His memory will be celebrated as long as the world lasts; and this will not only be among the Hebrews, but by foreigners also. And all this will be because of my favor to you and to your posterity. He will also have such a brother, that he will himself obtain my priesthood, and his posterity will have it after him to the end of the world."

When the vision had informed him of these things, Amram woke up and told it to Jochebed, his wife. And now the distress increased upon them on account of the prediction in Amram's dream; for they were under concern, not only for the child, but on account of the great happiness that was to come to him also. However, the mother's labor was a confirmation to what was foretold by God, for it was not known to those that watched her—her labor was easy, and the pains of her delivery did not fall upon her with intensity. They then nourished the child at home privately for three months. But after that time, Amram feared that he would be discovered, and, by falling under the king's displeasure, both he and his child would perish, making the promise of God of no effect. So he determined to trust the safety and care of the child to God instead of his own concealment of him, which he looked upon as a thing uncertain, and whereby both the child, so privately to be nourished, and himself should be in imminent danger. But he believed that God would some way for certain procure the safety of the child, in order to secure the truth of his own predictions. When they had thus determined this, they made an ark of bulrushes in the manner of a cradle and sufficiently large for an infant to be laid in without being too straitened. They then smeared it over with paste, which would naturally keep out the water from entering between the bulrushes, and put the infant into it. And setting it afloat upon the river, they left its preservation to God. So the river received the child, and carried him along. But Miriam, the child's sister, passed along upon the bank opposite him, as her mother had instructed her, to see where the ark would be carried, in what way God demonstrated that human wisdom was nothing, but that the Supreme Being is able to do whatsoever he pleases: that those who, in order to ensure their own security, condemn others to destruction, and use great endeavors about it, fail of their purpose; but that others are in a surprising manner preserved, and obtain a prosperous condition almost from the very midst of their calamities; those, I mean, whose dangers arise by the appointment of God. And, indeed, such a providence was exercised in the case of this child, as showed the power of God.

. . .

Moses, therefore, when he was born, and brought up in the foregoing manner, and came to the age of maturity, made his virtue manifest to the Egyptians; and showed that he was born for bringing them down, and raising the Israelites. And the occasion he laid hold of was this: the Ethiopians, who are next neighbors to the Egyptians, made an inroad into their country, which they seized upon, and carried off the effects of the Egyptians, who, in their rage, fought against them, and revenged the affronts they had received from them; but being overcome in battle, some of them were slain, and the rest ran away in a shameful manner, and by that means saved themselves; whereupon the Ethiopians followed after them in the pursuit, and thinking that it would be a mark of cowardice if they did not subdue all Egypt, they went on to subdue the rest with greater vehemence; and when they had tasted the sweets of the country, they never left off the prosecution of the war: and as the nearest parts had not courage enough at first to fight with them, they proceeded as far as Memphis, and the sea itself, while not one of the cities was able to oppose them. The Egyptians, under this sad oppression, betook themselves to their oracles and prophecies; and when God had given them this counsel, to make use of Moses the Hebrew, and take his assistance, the king commanded his daughter to produce him that he might be the general of their army. Upon which, when she had made him swear he would do him no harm, she delivered him to the king, and supposed his assistance would be of great advantage to them. She reproached the priest, who, when they had before admonished the Egyptians to kill him, was not ashamed now to own their want of his help.

So Moses, at the persuasion both of Thermuthis (Pharaoh's daughter) and the king himself, cheerfully undertook the business: and the sacred scribes of both nations were glad; those of the Egyptians, that they should at once overcome their enemies by his valor, and that by the same piece of management Moses would be slain; but those of the Hebrews, that they should escape from the Egyptians, because Moses was to be their general. But Moses prevented the enemies, and took and led his army before those enemies were apprised of his attacking them; for he did not march by the river, but by land, where he gave a wonderful demonstration of his sagacity; for when the ground was difficult to be passed over, because of the multitude of serpents (which it produces in vast numbers, and, indeed, is singular in some of those productions, which other countries do not breed, and yet such as are worse than others in power and mischief, and an unusual fierceness of sight, some of which ascend out of the ground unseen, and also fly in the air, and so come upon men at unawares, and do them a mischief). Moses invented a wonderful stratagem to preserve the army safe, and without hurt; for he made baskets, like unto arks, of sedge, and filled them with ibis, and carried them along with them; which animal is the greatest enemy to serpents imaginable, for they fly from them when they come near them; and as they fly they are caught and devoured by them, as if it were done by the harts; but the ibis are tame creatures, and only enemies to the serpentine kind: but about these ibis I say no more at present, since the Greeks themselves are not unacquainted with this sort of bird. As soon, therefore, as Moses was come to the land which was the breeder of these serpents, he let loose the ibis, and by their means repelled the serpentine kind, and used them for his assistants before the army came upon that ground. When he had therefore proceeded thus on his journey, he came upon the Ethiopians before they expected him; and, joining battle with them, he beat them, and deprived them of the hopes they had of success against the Egyptians, and went on in overthrowing their cities, and indeed made a great slaughter of these Ethiopians. Now when the Egyptian army had once tasted of this prosperous success, by the means of Moses, they did not slacken their diligence, insomuch that the Ethiopians were in danger of being reduced to slavery, and all sorts of destruction; and at length they retired to Saba, which was a royal city of Ethiopia, which Cambyses afterwards named Mero, after the name of his own sister. The place was to be besieged with very great difficulty, since it was both encompassed by the Nile quite round, and the other rivers, Astapus and Astaboras, made it a very difficult thing for such as attempted to pass over them; for the city was situated in a retired place, and was inhabited after the manner of an island, being encompassed with a strong wall, and having the rivers to guard them from their enemies, and having great ramparts between the wall and the rivers, insomuch, that when the waters come with the greatest violence, it can never be drowned; which ramparts make it next to impossible for even such as are gotten over the rivers to take the city. However, while Moses was uneasy at the army's lying idle (for the enemies dared not come to a battle) this accident happened: Tharbis was the daughter of the king of the Ethiopians: she happened to see Moses as he led the army near the walls, and fought with great courage; and admiring the subtlety of his undertakings, and believing him to be the author of the Egyptians' success, when they had before despaired of recovering their liberty, and to be the occasion of the great danger the Ethiopians were in, when they had before boasted of their great achievements, she fell deeply in love with him; and upon the prevalence of that passion, sent to him the most faithful of all her servants to discourse with him about their marriage. He thereupon accepted the offer, on condition she would procure the delivering up of the city; and gave her the assurance of an oath to take her to his wife; and that when he had once taken possession of the city, he would not break his oath to her. No sooner was the agreement made, but it took effect immediately; and when Moses had cut off the Ethiopians, he gave thanks to God, and consummated his marriage, and led the Egyptians back to their own land.

SOURCE: William Whiston, *The Works of Flavius Josephus* (Philadelphia: John E. Potter, 1895), 67–70, with modifications.

PART II

The New Testament Background

L. FIRST-CENTURY JEWISH GROUPS

Judaism during the first centuries BCE and CE consisted of a variety of groups. Though most Jewish people of that time did not belong to a particular group, the various Jewish sects demonstrate a remarkable, dynamic diversity of first-century Judaism. The following selections from the Jewish writer Josephus (writing in the late first century CE) and the Dead Sea Scrolls (see introduction to "Qumran Texts," p. 161) provide descriptions of some of these groups.

55

PHARISEES AND SADDUCEES

Outside the New Testament, Josephus is our only source of the Pharisees and Sadducees (rabbinic literature is complex for reconstructing first century Pharisees). Compare Mark 7:1-4; 12:18-27; Acts 23:6-8.

Josephus, *Jewish War* 2.162–166

As to the other two groups first mentioned, the Pharisees are those who are considered to interpret the laws strictly and to be the leading sect. They attribute everything to fate and to God, and yet allow that to act rightly or to the contrary is principally in the power of men, although fate does cooperate in every action. They say that every soul is incorruptible, but that only the soul of the good passes into another body, while the souls of the bad suffer eternal punishment. The Sadducees are those that compose the second group. They do away with fate entirely, and place God outside the doing, or even observing, of evil. They say that both good and evil is presented before men as a choice, and that it belongs to each one whether he accepts the one or the other. They also reject the belief of the continuation of the soul after death and the idea of punishments and rewards in the afterlife. Moreover, the Pharisees are friendly to one another and strive for harmony for the public. However, the behavior of the Sadducees towards one another is in some degree vicious, and their interactions with those that are of their own party are as rude as if they were strangers to them.

Josephus, *Jewish Antiquities* 18.12–17

Now, for the Pharisees, they live in moderation and despise delicacies in diet. They follow the conduct of reason, and what that prescribes to them as good for them they do. They think they ought earnestly to strive to observe reason's dictates for practice. They also honor the traditions of those before them, and are not so bold as to contradict them in anything which they have introduced. Even though they determine that all things are done by fate, they do not take away the freedom from men of acting as they think fit. Their notion is, that it has pleased God to make a temperament in which what he wills is done, but also so that the will of man can act virtuously or viciously. They also believe that souls have an immortal rigor in them, and that under the earth there will be rewards or punishments, according as they have lived virtuously or viciously in this life. The latter are to be detained in an everlasting prison, but the former will have power to revive and live again. Because of these doctrines they are able greatly to persuade the body of the people; and whatever they do about divine worship, prayers, and sacrifices, they perform them according to their direction. The cities give great attestations to them on account of their entire virtuous conduct, both in the actions of their lives and their discourses also. But the doctrine of the Sadducees is this. Souls die with the bodies. They do not observe anything besides what the law directs them, and they think it an instance of virtue to dispute with those teachers of philosophy whom they frequent. But this doctrine is received but by a few, yet by those still of the greatest dignity. But they are able to do almost nothing of themselves, for when they become magistrates, as they are unwillingly and by force sometimes obliged to be, they follow the notions of the Pharisees, because the multitude would not otherwise bear them.

SOURCE: William Whiston, *The Works of Flavius Josephus* (Philadelphia: John E. Potter, 1895), 617–18, 484, with modifications.

56

ESSENES

The Essenes are not mentioned in the New Testament, but their existence and practices were well known (see also Philo, *Every Good Man is Free* 75–89; *On the Contemplative Life* 21–23; Pliny the Elder, *Natural History* 5.72).

Josephus, *Jewish War* 2.119–144

There are three philosophical sects among the Jews. The followers of the first are the Pharisees; of the second, the Sadducees; and the third sect, which has the reputation of practicing solemnity, are called Essenes. These last are Jews by birth, and seem to have a greater affection for one another than the other sects have. These Essenes reject pleasures as a vice, but regard temperance and control over passions to be virtue. They neglect marriage, but adopt other people's children while they are pliable and fit for learning, and regard them as their own kin and form them according to their own ways. They do not in principle deny marriage and the propagation of mankind thereby continued; but they guard against the lascivious behavior of women, and are convinced that none of them preserve their fidelity to one man.

They despise riches, and their sharing of goods is most admirable. Nor is there anyone among them who has more than another; for it is a law among them that those who join them must let what they have be common to the whole order, so that among them there is no appearance of poverty or excess of riches, but everyone's possessions are intermingled with everyone else's possessions; and so there is, as it were, one estate shared by all the brothers. . . .

They are not in one particular city, but many of them dwell in every city. If any of their sect come from other places, what they have is available to them, just as if it were their own. And they arrive to these who they never knew before, as if they had been long acquaintances with them. For this reason they carry nothing with them when they travel into remote parts, except they still take their weapons with them for fear of thieves. Accordingly, there is in every city where they live one appointed to take care of strangers and to provide garments and other necessities for them. . . .

And as for their piety towards God, it is very extraordinary; for before sunrise they do not speak a word about common matters, but offer up certain prayers that they have received from their forefathers, as if they made a supplication for its rising. After this each one is sent away by those in charge to do some of those trades wherein they are skilled, in which they labor with great diligence till the fifth hour. After which they assemble themselves together again into one place; and when they have clothed themselves in white garments, they then bathe their bodies in cold water. And after this purification, they meet together in a private apartment, where no outsider is permitted to enter. Having been purified they go into the dining room, like entering a certain holy temple, and quietly sit down. The baker then gives them loaves of bread in order; the cook also brings a single plate of one sort of food and sets it before each one. The priest prays over the food; it is unlawful for anyone to taste of the food before the prayer is said. The same priest, when he has dined, says a prayer again; so in the beginning and at the end they praise God as the One who bestows their food upon them. After this, they lay aside their white garments, and return to their labors again till the evening. They then return home to supper, and proceed in the same manner. If there are any traveling strangers there, they sit down with them. . . .

And truly, as for other things, they only act according to the commands of who have charge over them. There are only two things that they are allowed to do on their own accord: to give assistance and to show mercy. They are permitted of their own accord to give relief to those who deserve it and have need of it, and they can give food to those who are in distress. They cannot, however, give anything to their own without permission of those in charge. They vent their anger in a righteous manner and restrain their passion. They are noteworthy for trustworthiness, and are the servants of peace. Whatever they say is firmer than an oath, but swearing is avoided by them, thinking it is worse than perjury; for they say that he who cannot be believed without swearing by God is already condemned. . . .

Now if any one desires to join their sect, he is not immediately admitted. Instead, he is prescribed the same method of living as they do for a year, while he continues as a non-member . . . . And when he has given evidence during that time that he can observe their temperance, and when he approaches nearer to their way of living, he is made a partaker of the waters of purification. Yet even now he is not admitted to live with them, for after this demonstration of his fortitude, he is tested for two more years. If he then appears to be worthy, they admit him into their community. And before he is allowed to partake of their shared meal, he is required to take serious oaths. First, he will exercise piety towards God. Then he will observe justice towards men, and he will do no harm to anyone, either of his own accord or by the command of others.

He will always hate the wicked and aid the righteous. He will always be trustworthy to others, especially to those in authority because no one obtains the government without God's assistance. And that if he is in authority, he will never abuse his authority in any way, nor endeavor to outshine his subjects either in his garments or any other finery. He will always be a lover of truth, and be determined to reprove those who tell lies. He will keep his hands clear from theft and his soul from unlawful gains. He will neither keep secret anything from those of his own sect, nor make known any of their doctrines to others, even if someone should compel him to do so at the hazard of his life. . . . These are the oaths by which they secure their converts to themselves.

But for those that are caught in any heinous sins, they cast them out of their community. And he who is thus separated from them does often die after a miserable manner, for as he is bound by the oath he has taken and by the customs he been engaged in, he is not at liberty to partake of that food that he meets with elsewhere, but is forced to eat grass, and to famish his body with hunger till he perishes. For this reason they take back many of them again when they are at their last gasp out of compassion for them, thinking the miseries they have endured till they came to the very brink of death to be a sufficient punishment for the sins they had been guilty of.

Source: William Whiston, *The Works of Flavius Josephus* (Philadelphia: John E. Potter, 1895), 615–16, with modifications.

57

THE QUMRAN COMMUNITY

Scholars refer to the Jewish community that produced or preserved the Dead Sea Scrolls as the Qumran community, because of the discovery of community ruins at modern-day Khirbet Qumran, near the Dead Sea. The Qumran community was established sometime in the late second century or early first century BCE, separating themselves from mainstream society because of the corruption they perceived among the Jerusalem temple leadership. Their location in the wilderness was also dictated by their conviction, based on Isaiah 40:3, that God's end-time action would begin in the wilderness (cp. Mark 1:2–13//Matt 3:1–4:11//Luke 3:1–9, 15–17). Most scholars believe the Qumran community was a particular sect of the Essenes, but that theory continues to be debated. The following selection provides their own account of their history.

Damascus Document (CD)

1.2–2.1

And now, listen, all those who know justice, and understand the actions of God; for he has a dispute with all flesh and will carry out judgment on all those who spurn him. For when they were unfaithful in forsaking him, he hid his face from Israel and from his sanctuary and delivered them up to the sword. But when he remembered the covenant with his forefathers, he saved a remnant for Israel and did not deliver them up to destruction. And at the period of wrath, three hundred and ninety years after having delivered them up into the hand of Nebuchadnezzar, king of Babylon, he visited them and caused to sprout from Israel and from Aaron a shoot of the planting, in order to possess his land and to become fat with the good things of his soil. And they realized their iniquity and knew that they were guilty [men]; but they were like blind persons and like those who grope for a path over twenty years. And God appraised their deeds, because they sought him with an undivided heart, and raised up for them a Teacher of Righteousness, in order to direct them in the path of his heart. And he made known to the last generations what he had done for the last generation, the congregation of traitors. These are the ones who stray from the path. This is the time about which is has been written: "Like a stray heifer so has Israel strayed" (Hos 4:16), when "the scoffer" arose, who poured out over Israel waters of lies and made them stray into a wilderness without a path, causing the everlasting heights to sink down, diverging from tracks of justice and removing the boundary with which the forefathers had marked their inheritance, so that the curses of his covenant would adhere to them, to deliver them up to the sword carrying out the vengeance of the covenant. For they sought easy interpretations, chose illusions, scrutinized loopholes, chose the handsome neck, acquitted the guilty and sentenced the just, violated the covenant, broke the precept, banded together against the life of the just man, their soul abominated all those who walk in perfection, they hunted them down with the sword and provoked the dispute of the people. And kindled was the wrath of God against their congregation, laying waste all its great number, for their deeds were unclean in front of him. . . .

4.2–6.11

The priests are the converts of Israel who left the land of Judah; and the Levites are those who joined them; and the sons of Zadok are the chosen of Israel, the men of renown, who stand (to serve) at the end of days. . . .

[. . .] of holiness are the forefathers, for whom God atoned, and who are declared the righteous man as righteous, and declared the wicked as wicked, and all those who entered after them in order to act according to the exact interpretation of the law in which the forefathers were instructed until the period of these years is complete. According to the covenant which God established with the forefathers, in order to atone for their iniquities, so will God atone for them. But when the period corresponding to the number of these years is complete, there will no longer be any joining with the house of Judah but rather each one standing up on his watchtower. The wall is built, the boundary far away. And during all these years Belial [=Satan] will be set loose against Israel, as God said by means of the prophet Isaiah, son of Amaz, saying: "Panic, pit and net against you, earth-dwellers" (Isa 24:17). Its explanation: They are Belial's three nets about which Levi, son of Jacob spoke, by which he catches Israel and makes them appear before them like three types of justice. The first is fornication; the second, wealth; the third, defilement of the temple. He who eludes one is caught in another and he who is freed from that, is caught in another. The builders of the wall who go after "Precept"—"Precept" is the preacher of whom he said: "Assuredly they will preach" (Mic 2:6)—are caught twice in fornication: by taking two wives in their lives, even though the principle of creation is "male and female he created them" (Gen 1:27), and the ones who went into the ark "went in two by two into the ark." (Gen 7:9) . . . And they also defiled the temple, for they did not keep apart in accordance with the law, but instead lay with her who sees blood of her menstrual flow. And each man takes as a wife the daughter of his brother and the daughter of his sister. But Moses said: "Do not approach your mother's sister, she is a blood relation of your mother" (Lev 18:13). The law of prohibited marriages, written for males, applies equally to females, and therefore to the daughter of the brother who uncovers the nakedness of the brother of her father, for he is a blood relation. And also they defile their holy spirit, for with blasphemous tongue they have opened their mouth against the statutes of God's covenant, saying: "they are unfounded." They speak abomination against them. They are all igniters of fire, kindlers of blazes; webs of a spider are their webs, and their eggs are vipers' eggs. Whoever comes to them will not be unpunished; the more he does it, the guiltier he shall be, unless he has been compelled. . . .

But God remembered his covenant of the forefathers. And he raised from Aaron men of knowledge and from Israel wise men, and made them listen. And they dug the well: "A well which the princes dug, which the nobles of the people delved with the staff" (Num 21:18). The well is the law. And those who dug it are the converts of Israel, who left the land of Judah and lived in the land of Damascus, all of whom God called princes, for they sought him, and their renown has not been repudiated in anyone's mouth. And the staff is the interpreter of the law, of whom Isaiah said: "He produces a tool for this labor" (Isa 54:16). And the nobles of the people are those who came to dig the well with the staves that the scepter decreed, to walk in them throughout the whole age of wickedness, and without which they will not obtain it, until there arises he who teaches righteousness at the end of days.

Source: Florentino García Martínez and Eibert J. C. Tigchelaar, *The Dead Sea Scrolls Study Edition*, vol. 1 (Grand Rapids: Eerdmans, 2000), 551–53, 555–59. Used by permission of the publisher.

58
QUMRAN COMMUNITY, ON JUSTIFICATION

This selection articulates an understanding of justification rooted in God's righteousness and mercy (cp. Rom 1:16-17; 3:21-26; Gal 2:15-21). This belief was widespread in first-century Judaism. The idea that Judaism at this time was legalistic and promoted self-righteousness is a misleading caricature.

Community Rule (1QS) 11.2–17

As for me, to God belongs my justification; in his hand is the perfection of my behavior with the uprightness of my heart; and with his righteous acts he cancels my iniquities. For from the source of his knowledge he discloses his light, and my eyes have observed his wonders, and the light of my heart the mystery of existence. What always is, is support for my right hand, the path of my steps goes over firm rock, it does not waver before anything. For the truth of God is the rock of my steps, and his might the support of my right hand. From the spring of his righteousness is my justification and from the wonderful mystery is the light in my heart. My eyes have observed what always is, wisdom that has been hidden from mankind, knowledge and prudent understanding (hidden) from the sons of man, fount of righteousness and well of strength and spring of glory (hidden) from the assembly of flesh. To those whom God has selected he has given them as everlasting possession; and he has given them an inheritance in the lot of the holy ones. He unites their assembly to the sons of the heavens in order (to form) the council of the Community and a foundation of the building of holiness to be a firmly planted people throughout all future ages. However, I belong to evil human-kind, to the assembly of unfaithful flesh; my failings, my iniquities, my sins, {. . .} with the depravities of my heart, belong to the assembly of worms and those who walk in darkness. For to man (does not belong) his path, nor can human being steady his step, since justification belongs to God, and from his hand is the perfection of the path. By his knowledge everything shall come into being, and all that does exist he establishes with his calculations and nothing is done outside of him. As for me, if I stumble, the mercies of God shall be my salvation always; and if I fall in sin of the flesh, in the righteousness of God, which endures eternally, shall my justification be; if my distress commences, he will free my soul from the pit and make my steps steady on the path; he will draw me near his mercies, and by kindnesses set in motion my justification; he will judge me in the righteousness of his truth, and in his plentiful goodness always atone for my sins; in his righteousness he will cleanse me from the uncleanness of the human being and from the sin of the sons of man, so that I can give God thanks for his righteousness and The Highest for his majesty.

SOURCE: Florentino García Martínez and Eibert J. C. Tigchelaar, *The Dead Sea Scrolls Study Edition*, vol. 1. (Grand Rapids: Eerdmans, 2000), 97–99. Used by permission of the publisher.

M. FIRST-CENTURY PROPHETIC FIGURES

The Jewish writer Josephus recounts a number of occasions where individuals gathered a following based on the person's claim to be a prophet. Scholars have sometimes referred to these incidents as "messianic movements," but that designation is misleading; none of the individuals or their followers use the term "messiah" (at least in Josephus' descriptions). Though he is critical of these individuals, even sometimes calling them "pretenders," Josephus does use the term "prophet." (Note the number of times Jesus is identified as a prophet: Matt 16:14; 21:11, 46; Luke 7:16; 24:19; John 9:17.) Josephus also notes that several of these prophetic figures and their followings were located in the wilderness, which reflected a common expectation that God's end-time action would begin in the wilderness (cp. Mark 1:2-13// Matt 3:1–4:11//Luke 3:1-9, 15-17). For Theudas, compare Acts 5:36; for the Egyptian Jew, compare Acts 21:38; for Jesus, son of Ananas, compare Mark 11:15-18; 13:1-21; 14:55-59.

59

THE SAMARITAN (ca. 36 CE)

Josephus, *Jewish Antiquities* 18.85–87

Now the nation of the Samaritans did not escape without disturbances. The man who incited them was one who thought lying a thing of little consequence, and who contrived everything so that the masses might be pleased. So he told them to gather at Mount Gerizim, which is to them the most holy of all mountains, and assured them that when they had come there he would show them the sacred vessels that were buried there, where Moses had put them. So, persuaded by the man's words, they came to that place armed. Staying at a certain village, which was called Tirathaba, they gathered a multitude together intending to go up to the mountain. But (the Roman governor) Pilate prevented their going up by sending a large group of cavalry and infantry, and they seized upon those who had gathered in the village. When the soldiers encountered them, some were killed, some ran away, but most were captured. The leader, along with those who fled, Pilate ordered to be executed.

SOURCE: William Whiston, *The Works of Flavius Josephus* (Philadelphia: John E. Potter, 1895), 489, with modifications.

60

THEUDAS (ca. 44–46 CE)

Josephus, *Jewish Antiquities* 20.97–98

Now it came to pass, while Fadus was Roman governor of Judea, there was a certain pretender whose name was Theudas, who persuaded a great part of the people to take their possessions with them and follow him to the river Jordan. For he told them he was a prophet, and that he would by his own command divide the river and provide them an easy passage through it. And many were deceived by his words. However, Fadus did not permit them to make any advantage of his wild attempt, but sent a group of cavalry out against them. The cavalry came upon them unexpectedly, killing many and taking many alive. They also captured Theudas, cut off his head, and carried it to Jerusalem.

SOURCE: William Whiston, *The Works of Flavius Josephus* (Philadelphia: John E. Potter, 1895), 539, with modifications.

61

THE EGYPTIAN JEW (ca. 52–60 CE)

Josephus, *Jewish War* 2.261–263

There was an Egyptian false prophet who did more injury to the Jews than the former, for he was an imposter, pretending to be a prophet. He got together thirty thousand men who were deceived by him, and he led them from the wilderness to the mount which was called the Mount of Olives. He planned on breaking into Jerusalem by force from that place, intending to conquer the Roman garrison and to domineer over the people by the assistance of those guards of his that were to break into the city with him. But (the Roman governor) Felix prevented his attempt, and met him with his Roman soldiers, while all the people assisted him in his attack upon them, insomuch that when it came to a battle, the Egyptian ran away, with a few others, while the greatest part of those that were with him were either killed or taken alive, while the rest dispersed their own homes and hid themselves.

Josephus, *Jewish Antiquities* 20.167–170

And now certain impostors and deceivers persuaded the multitude to follow them into the wilderness, claiming that they would perform wonders and signs by the providence of God. And many, persuaded by them, suffered the punishments of their folly, for (the Roman governor) Felix brought them back and punished them. Moreover, about this time there came from Egypt to Jerusalem one that said he was a prophet. And he advised the multitude of the common people to go along with him to the Mount of Olives, as it was called, which lies opposite the city about two-thirds of a mile. He further stated that he would show them how, at his command, the walls of Jerusalem would fall down; and he promised them that he would secure for them an entrance into the city through those walls, when they were fallen down. Now when Felix was informed of these things, he ordered his soldiers to take their weapons, and came against them with a great number of cavalry and infantry from Jerusalem, and attacked the Egyptian and the people that were with him. He killed four hundred of them, and took two hundred alive. But the Egyptian himself escaped from the attack, but did not appear any more.

SOURCE: William Whiston, *The Works of Flavius Josephus* (Philadelphia: John E. Potter, 1895), 563, 492, with modifications.

62

AN ANONYMOUS "PRETENDER"
(ca. 60–62 CE)

Josephus, *Jewish Antiquities* 20.188

(The Roman governor) Festus sent both cavalry and infantry to attack those who had been deceived by a certain pretender, who promised them deliverance and freedom from the hardships they were under, if they would follow him into the wilderness. The forces that were sent destroyed both the pretender and those who had followed him.

SOURCE: William Whiston, *The Works of Flavius Josephus* (Philadelphia: John E. Potter, 1895), 493, with modifications.

63

JESUS, SON OF ANANUS (ca. 62 CE)

Josephus, *Jewish War* 6.300–309

There was a certain Jesus, son of Ananus, who was a common laborer who worked the land. Four years before the war began when the city was in very great peace and prosperity, during Pentecost feast where it is our custom for everyone to make tabernacles to God in the temple, he suddenly began to cry aloud, "A voice from the east, a voice from the west, a voice from the four winds, a voice against Jerusalem and the holy house, a voice against the bridegrooms and the brides [cp. Jer 7:34], and a voice against this whole people!" This was his cry, as he went about day and night in the streets of the city. However, certain of the most eminent among the people had great indignation at his dire cry, and they seized the man and whipped him severely. But he did not say anything on behalf of himself, nor did he say anything to those who punished him. He simply went on with the same words which he cried before. At this point, our rulers, thinking (as the case proved to be) that this was a sort of divine impulse in the man, brought him to the Roman governor, who had him flogged till his bones were laid bare. But he did not make any plea for himself, nor did he shed any tears; but at every stroke of the whip he answered in the most lamentable tone possible, "Woe, woe to Jerusalem!" And when Albinus (for he was then our governor) asked him who he was, where did he come from, and why he uttered such words, the man did not answer him in any way; he only continued his lament chant till Albinus took him to be a madman, and dismissed him. Now, during all the time that passed before the war began, this man did not go near any of the citizens, nor was seen by them while he said so; but he every day uttered these lamentable words, as if it were his premeditated vow, "Woe, woe to Jerusalem!" Nor did he give ill words to any of those that beat him every day, nor good words to those that gave him food; but this was his reply to all men, and indeed no other than simply this predicted doom of what was to come. This cry of his was the loudest at the festivals; and he continued this dirge for seven years and five months, without growing hoarse or growing tired, until the very time that he saw his prophecy fulfilled in our siege. As he was going around the wall, he cried out with his utmost force, "Woe, woe to the city again, and to the people, and to the holy house!" And just as he added at the last, "Woe, woe to myself also!" a stone from one of the catapults hit him and killed him immediately.

SOURCE: William Whiston, *The Works of Flavius Josephus* (Philadelphia: John E. Potter, 1895), 680–81, with modifications.

64

JONATHAN (ca. 70 CE)

Josephus, *Jewish War* 7.437–442

Now did the madness of the Sicarii, like a disease, reach as far as the cities of Cyrene. For one Jonathan, a wicked person and by trade a weaver, having escaped to that place, persuaded many of the poorer sort to follow him. He led them into the wilderness, promising them that he would show them signs and apparitions. And as for the other Jews of Cyrene, he concealed his mischief from them. But those of the greatest dignity among them informed Catullus, the (Roman) governor of the Libyan Pentapolis, of his trek into the wilderness and of the preparations he had made for it. So he sent both cavalry and infantry after him, and they easily overcame them because they were unarmed. Many were killed in the attack, but some were taken alive and brought to Catullus. As for Jonathan, the leader of this conspiracy, he escaped. But after great and very diligent search for him in all the country, he was finally taken and brought to Catullus.

Josephus, *Life* 424–425

For a certain Jew, whose name was Jonathan, created an uproar in Cyrene. He persuaded two thousand men of that country to join with him, and this became the occasion of their ruin. He was bound by the governor of that country and sent to the emperor, and he told the emperor that I had sent him both weapons and money. However, he could not conceal his being a liar from (the emperor) Vespasian, who condemned him to die; and handed over, he was put to death.

Source: William Whiston, *The Works of Flavius Josephus* (Philadelphia: John E. Potter, 1895), 706, 26, with modifications.

N. JOSEPHUS ON JOHN THE BAPTIST AND JESUS

The Jewish writer Josephus mentions both John the Baptist and Jesus in his *Jewish Antiquities*. Josephus' reference to Jesus has been amended by later Christians. The selection below has both the "Christianized" version and a reconstruction of what scholars think were Josephus' original comments. For John the Baptist, compare Mark 1:4-6; 6:17-29; Luke 3:1-20.

65

JOHN THE BAPTIST

Josephus, *Jewish Antiquities* 18.116–119

Now some of the Jews thought that the destruction of Herod's army came from God, and that it was certainly a just punishment for what he did against John, who was called the Baptist. For Herod had executed him, though he was a good man and urged the Jews to join in baptism—if they practiced virtue, righteousness towards one another, and piety towards God. For the baptism was acceptable to him (God), not in pardoning some sins they committed, but for the purification of the body, as though the soul was thoroughly purified beforehand by righteousness. Now when many others gathered—for they were very pleased by hearing his words—Herod, who feared that John's influence over the people might result in a rebellion (for they seemed ready to do anything he should advise), thought it best to put him to death, in order to prevent any trouble he might cause, and not bring himself into difficulties, by sparing a man who might make him think twice of it when it would be too late. Accordingly, because of Herod's suspicious temper, John was sent as a prisoner to Machaerus—the castle I previously mentioned—and was put to death there. Now it seemed to the Jews that the destruction of this army was sent as a punishment upon Herod, and a mark of God's displeasure with him.

SOURCE: William Whiston, *The Works of Flavius Josephus* (Philadelphia: John E. Potter, 1895), 445, with modifications.

66
JESUS

Josephus, *Jewish Antiquities* 18.63–64

Now there was about this time Jesus, a wise man, if indeed one ought to call him a man. For he was a doer of marvelous deeds and a teacher of such men as receive the truth with pleasure. He drew over to himself many of both the Jews and the Greeks. He was the Christ. And when Pilate, at the prompting of our leading men, had condemned him to the cross, those that loved him at the first did not forsake him; for he appeared to them alive again on the third day, as the divine prophets had foretold these and ten thousand other wonderful things concerning him. And the tribe of Christians, so named from him, are not extinct to this day.

Reconstructed Version

Now there was about this time Jesus, a wise man. For he was a doer of marvelous deeds and a teacher of such men as receive the truth with pleasure. He drew over to himself many of both the Jews and the Greeks. And when Pilate, at the prompting of our leading men, had condemned him to the cross, those that loved him at the first did not forsake him. And the tribe of Christians, so named from him, are not extinct to this day.

SOURCE: William Whiston, *The Works of Flavius Josephus* (Philadelphia: John E. Potter, 1895), 441–42, with modifications.

O. MESSIANISM

The term "messianism" is a modern term used to describe a variety of Jewish expectations of a figure (or figures) who would act on behalf of or in tandem with God's dramatic, mostly end-time action. Not all Jews had an expectation for such a figure, and for those who did the figure's mission or task varied. Also, the term "messiah" was not always used to denote this expected figure. The following selections represent the variety of expectations and use of "messiah." See also reading §109, "4 Ezra."

67

THE CONQUERING MESSIAH

Written in the late first century BCE, the Psalms of Solomon originated from a group of Jews who criticized the (Jewish) leadership of the Hasmoneans and loathed the newly Roman rule. This excerpt articulates a hope for the "Lord Messiah," who will overthrow and replace both the Hasmoneans and the Romans. Compare Revelation 19:11-21.

Psalms of Solomon 17:21-46

Behold, O Lord, and raise up for them their king, the son of David,
  At the time in which you see, O God, that he may reign over Israel
    your servant.
And gird him with strength, that he may shatter unrighteous rulers,
  And that he may purge Jerusalem from nations that trample (her) down
    to destruction.
He shall cast out sinners from your inheritance,
  He shall destroy the pride of the sinner as a potter's vessel.
With a rod of iron he shall break in pieces all their substance,
  He shall destroy the godless nations with the word of his mouth;

At his rebuke nations shall flee before him,
> And he shall reprove sinners for the thoughts of their heart.

And he shall gather together a holy people, whom he shall lead in righteousness,
> And he shall judge the tribes of the people that has been sanctified by the Lord his God.

And he shall not suffer unrighteousness to reside any more in their midst,
> Nor shall there dwell with them any man that knows wickedness,
> For he shall know them, that they are all sons of their God.

And he shall divide them according to their tribes upon the land,
> And neither sojourner nor alien shall sojourn with them anymore.

He shall judge peoples and nations in the wisdom of his righteousness. Selah.

And he shall have the heathen nations to serve him under his yoke;
> And they shall glorify the Lord in a place to be seen by all the earth;

And he shall purge Jerusalem, making it holy as of old:

So that nations shall come from the ends of the earth to see his glory,
> Bringing gifts to her sons who had fainted,
> And to see the glory of the Lord, wherewith God hath glorified her.

And he shall be a righteous king, taught by God, over them,

And there shall be no unrighteousness in his days in their midst,
> For all shall be holy
> And their king will be the Lord Messiah.

For he shall not put his trust in horse and rider and bow,
> Nor shall he multiply for himself gold and silver for war,
> Nor shall he have confidence in a multitude on the day of battle.

The Lord Himself is his king.
> His hope for might rests in his hope in God.

All nations shall be in fear before him.

For he will smite the earth with the word of his mouth forever.
> He will bless the people of the Lord with wisdom and gladness,

And he himself will be pure from sin, so that he may rule a great people.
> He will rebuke rulers, and remove sinners by the might of his word;

And relying upon his God, throughout his days he will not stumble;
> For God will make him mighty by means of (His) holy spirit,
> And wise by means of the spirit of understanding, with strength and righteousness.

And the blessing of the Lord will be with him;
> He will be strong and not stumble.

His hope will be in the Lord;
> Who then can prevail against him?

For he will be mighty in his works and strong in the fear of God,
> Shepherding the flock of the Lord faithfully and righteously,

And allowing none among them to stumble in their pasture.
He will lead them all aright,
And there will be no pride among them that any among them should be oppressed.
This will be the majesty of the king of Israel whom God knows;
He will raise him up over the house of Israel to correct him.
His words shall be more refined than costly gold, the choicest;
In the assemblies he will judge the peoples, the tribes of the sanctified.
His words shall be like the words of the holy ones in the midst of sanctified peoples.
Blessed are those who will live in those days.
In that they shall see the good fortune of Israel which God shall bring to pass in the gathering together of the tribes.
May the Lord hasten His mercy upon Israel!
May He deliver us from the uncleanness of unholy enemies!
The Lord Himself is our king for ever and ever.

SOURCE: G. Buchanan Gray, "The Psalms of Solomon," in *The Apocrypha and Pseudepigrapha of the Old Testament in English*, vol. 2, ed. R. H. Charles (Oxford: Clarendon Press, 1913), 649–51, with modifications.

68

DUAL MESSIAHS AT QUMRAN

At least according to the first selection (ca. 100 BCE), the Qumran community—which was responsible for the Dead Sea Scrolls—seems to have anticipated two "messiahs," one priestly and the other royal. (Another Dead Sea Scroll [The Damascus Document] mentions the singular "Messiah of Aaron and Israel"). The second excerpt (mid-first century BCE) describes how the priest and the messiah will preside over the community's sacred meal "in the final days" (1QSa 1.1; cp. Mark 14:25; Luke 13:28-30; Rev 19:9).

Community Rule (1QS) 9.7–11

Only the sons of Aaron will have authority in the matter of judgment and of goods, and their word will settle the lot of all provision for the men of the Community and the goods of the men of holiness who walk in perfection. Their goods must not be mixed with the goods of the men of deceit who have not cleansed their path to separate from injustice and walk in a perfect behavior. They should not depart from any counsel of the law in order to walk in complete stubbornness of their heart, but instead shall be ruled by the first directives which the men of the Community began to be taught until the prophet comes, and the Messiahs of Aaron and Israel.

Rule of the Congregation (1QSa) 2.11–22

At [a ses]sion of the men of renown, [those summoned to] the gathering of the community council, when [God] begets the Messiah with them: [the] chief [priest] of all the congregation of Israel shall enter, and all [his] br[others, the sons] of Aaron, the priests [summoned] to the assembly, the men of renown, and they shall sit be[fore him, each one] according to his dignity. After, [the Mess]iah of Israel shall [enter] and before him shall sit the heads of the th[ousands of Israel, each] one according to his dignity, according to [his] po[sition] in their camps and according to their marches. And all the heads of the cl[ans of the congre]gation with the wise [men . . .] shall sit before them, each one according to his dignity. And [when] they gather [at the tab]le of the community [or to drink the n]ew wine, and the table of the community is prepared [and the] new wine [is mixed] for drinking, [no one should stretch out] his hand to the firstfruit of the bread and of [the new wine] before the priest, for [he is the one who bl]esses the firstfruit of bread and of the new win[e and stretches out] his hand towards the bread before them. Afterwar[ds,] the Messiah of Israel [shall str]etch out his hands towards the bread. [And afterwards, they shall ble]ss all the congregation of the community, each [one according to] his dignity. And in accordance with this precept one shall act at each me[al, when] at least ten me[n are gat]hered.

SOURCE: Florentino García Martínez and Eibert J. C. Tigchelaar, *The Dead Sea Scrolls Study Edition*, vol. 1 (Grand Rapids: Eerdmans, 2000), 91–93, 103. Used by permission of the publisher.

69

A JEWISH PROPHECY

Both the Jewish writer Josephus (writing around 75 CE) and the Roman writer Tacitus (writing around 105 CE) report a seemingly wide-spread Jewish expectation of a significant ruler based on a prophecy in the Jewish Scriptures (perhaps Mic 5:2-5a; cp. Matt 2:1-6). Both Josephus, who had

Roman sympathies, and Tacitus apply the prophecy to the Roman emperor Vespasian, in contrast to the Jews, who anticipated a Jewish ruler.

Josephus, *Jewish War* 6.312

What did the most to incite the Jews in undertaking this war (against the Romans) was an ambiguous oracle that was found in their sacred writings to the effect that about that time one from their own country would become ruler of the world. The Jews understood this prediction to mean someone from their own people, and many of their wise men were thereby deceived in their interpretation. Now this oracle, in fact, signified Vespasian, who was appointed emperor in Judea.

Tacitus, *Histories* 5.13

In the ancient records of their (the Jews') priests there was a prediction of how at this very time the East was to grow powerful, and rulers coming from Judea were to acquire a universal empire. These mysterious prophecies had pointed to Vespasian and Titus, but the common people, with the usual blindness of ambition, had interpreted these mighty destinies of themselves, and could not be brought even by disasters to believe the truth.

SOURCE: William Whiston, *The Works of Flavius Josephus* (Philadelphia: John E. Potter, 1895), 681, with modifications; Alfred John Church and William Jackson Brodribb, *The History of Tacitus* (London: MacMillan & Co., 1864), 199, with modifications.

※

70

A PROMISED CHILD

The *Eclogues* are a collection of ten pastoral poems (idealized portrayals of rural life) written by the Roman poet Virgil around 39–38 BCE. *Eclogue* IV describes the birth of a child whose life will inaugurate an anticipated time of peace and serenity (cp. Isa 11:6-9; Luke 1:26-35, 46-55). The intended identity of the child is debated, but the poem gets appropriated for the imperial ideology of the emperor Augustus. The poem is not influenced by the Jewish tradition, but demonstrates a broader Greco-Roman expectation of a divinely established peaceable rule through a divinely appointed agent.

Virgil, *Eclogue* IV

Muses of Sicily, sing us now a somewhat loftier task!
Not all men love coppice or lowly tamarisk:
If we sing woods, let them be woods worthy of a Consul.

Now has come and gone the last age by Cumae's Sibyl prophecy;
And the majestic roll of circling centuries begins anew.
Justice returns, returns the reign of Saturn:
A new breed of men comes down from heaven.
Only do thou, at the boy's birth in whom
The iron shall cease and the golden race arise,
Befriend him, chaste Lucina; it is thine own Apollo reigns.
And in thy consulate, O Pollio, this glorious age shall begin,
And the months begin their mighty march.
Under thy rule what traces remain of our old wickedness,
And the earth shall be free forever of fear.
He shall receive the life of gods,
And see heroes mingling with gods,
And himself be seen by them,
And with his father's virtue shall reign o'er a world at peace.

For thee, O boy,
First shall the earth, untilled, pour freely forth her childish gifts:
The gadding ivy spray with foxglove,
And Egyptian bean-flower mixed with laughing-eyed acanthus.
Untended will the she-goats bring home their udders swollen with milk,
And flocks in the fields shall not fear the monstrous lion.
Thy very cradle shall pour forth for thee caressing flowers.
The serpent too shall die, and die shall the treacherous poison plant,
And far and wide Assyrian spices spring.
But soon as you have the skill to read of heroes' fame and thy father's deeds
And to learn what virtue is,
The plain shall slowly grow golden waving corn crops,
From the wild briar shall hang the blushing grape,
And stubborn oaks sweat honeydew.
Nevertheless there shall lurk within some traces of ancient wrong,
Bidding tempt the deep with ships,
Girding towns with walls, with furrows cleave the earth.
There with a second Tiphys shall there be,
Her hero freight a second Argo bear;
New wars too shall arise, and once again
Some great Achilles to some Troy be sent.

Then, when the mellowing years have made thee man,
No more shall mariner sail, nor pine-tree bark ply traffic on the sea,
But every land shall all things bear alike:
The ground no more shall feel the harrow's grip, nor the vine the hook;
The sturdy ploughman shall loose yoke from steer,
Nor wool with varying colors learn to lie;
But in the meadows shall the ram himself,
Now with soft flush of purple, now with tint
Of yellow saffron, teach his fleece to shine.
While clothed in natural scarlet graze the lambs.
"Such still, such ages weave ye, as ye run,"
Sang to their spindles the consenting Fates
By Destiny's unalterable decree.
Assume thy greatness, for the time draws nigh,
Dear child of gods, great progeny of Jove!
See how the world's orbed mass totters,
Earth and wide ocean and the expansive sky;
Behold, all things are enraptured of the coming age!
Ah! may length of days be given to me,
And breath suffice me to rehearse thy deeds,
Nor Thracian Orpheus should not out-sing me then,
Nor Linus, though his mother this, and that
His sire should aid—Orpheus Calliope,
And Linus fair Apollo. Nay, though Pan,
With Arcady for judge, my claim contest,
With Arcady for judge great Pan himself
Should own him foiled, and from the field retire.
Begin to greet thy mother with a smile, O baby boy!
Ten months of weariness she bore for thee.
O baby boy, begin! For him, on whom his parents have not smiled,
Gods deem not worthy of their board or bed.

SOURCE: J. B. Greenough, *Vergil: Eclogues* (Boston: Ginn & Co., 1895), with modifications.

P. ROMAN IMPERIAL IDEOLOGY

Through architecture, sculptures, inscriptions, coins, texts, and religious and military rituals, the Romans promoted an ideology that the emperors were appointed by the gods to bring divine benefits to the inhabited world. These divine benefits included peace, harmony, and prosperity—the establishment of a hoped-for Golden Age.

✲

71

THE GOOD NEWS OF AUGUSTUS

Discovered in the ruins of the marketplace in the ancient city of Priene (Asia Minor), this inscription was set up around 9 BCE to announce a change in the calendar, with the New Year beginning on the birthday of the emperor Augustus, who is referred to as "savior" and "god." The inscription uses the term "good news" to describe the peace and welfare brought about by Augustus; it is the same term used for the "good news" of God and of Jesus in the New Testament (Rom 1:1, 3; 2 Cor 2:12; Mark 1:14; the verbal form of "good news" can be found in the Septuagint in Isa 52:7; 61:1-3). The inscription resonates particularly with Mark 1:1 and Luke 2:8-14.

Priene Calendar Inscription (*OGIS* 458)

Based on the motion of the high priest Apollonius, son of Menophilus of Azanitus, it was resolved by the Greeks of the province of Asia: Whereas divine Providence, who has ordered all things for our life and is earnestly interested in our life, has now set the world in perfect order by bringing into existence Augustus, whom she filled with virtue for the benefit of humanity, sending to us and to those after us a savior who ended war and put all things in order. And when he appeared, the Caesar surpassed the hopes of all those who anticipated such good news, not only going beyond those who were benefactors before him but not even the hope of surpassing for those coming after him. The birthday of the god (Augustus) was for the world the beginning of the good news that came about because of him.

SOURCE: Translation by Derek S. Dodson.

72

THE AENEID PROPHECY

The epic poem *Aeneid*, written between 29 and 19 BCE, tells the story of Aeneas, the legendary figure who escaped Troy and became the ancestor of the Romans. Virgil incorporates into this founding story a future vision of the reign of Augustus, which will fulfill the glorious destiny of Aeneas' Rome. This excerpt is part of the future vision, emphasizing renowned and divine ancestors, divine activity and plans, and the establishment of unprecedented glory and peace.

Virgil, *Aeneid* 6.777–797

See, in that line of ancestors the son of Mars,
Great Romulus, whose mother Ilia bore
From far-descended line of Trojan kings!
See from his helmet the twin plume,
And how his celestial father himself
Shows forth his divine birth! Of him, my son,
Great Rome shall rise, and favored by his star
Rome will have power worldwide and men of godlike mind;
And she will enclose her seven hills in single wall,
Proud mother of the brave! Just like Cybele,
The Berecynthian goddess, castle-crowned,
Who speeds her chariot through the Phrygian kingdoms,
Exulting in her hundred divine sons,
All numbered with the gods, all throned on high.

Let now thy visionary glance look
On thine own race, these Romans who are yours.
Here is Caesar, of Iulus' glorious seed,
Behold him ascending to the world of light!

Behold, at last, this is the man of whom
Was so often foretold to you:
Augustus Caesar, son of a god,
Who will again establish a golden age and restore
Old Saturn's reign to our Latin land.
He will extend his empire past the remote Garamant and India
To beyond stars and the sun's bright path,
Where Atlas' shoulder bears
The dome of heaven set thick with burning stars.

SOURCE: Theodore C. Williams, *The Aeneid of Vergil* (Boston: Houghton Mifflin Co., 1910), 214–15, with modifications.

73

THE AUGUSTAN PEACE

In 40 CE, the Jewish philosopher Philo was part of a delegation of Jews who went to the emperor Gaius (also known as Caligula) to report on the violence against Jews living in Alexandria and to petition for certain rights for Jews. This writing recounts those circumstances, as well as criticizes Gaius' reign and behavior. Philo draws upon the ideology of peace associated with Augustus' rule in order to contrast the rule of Gaius.

Philo, *On the Embassy to Gaius* 21.143–147

Again, why did you not pay similar honor to him who exceeded the common race of human nature in every virtue, who, by reason of the greatness of his absolute power and his own excellence, was the first man to be called Augustus, not receiving the title after another by a succession of blood as a part of his inheritance, but who was himself the origin of his successors, having that title and honor? He who first became emperor, when all the affairs of the state were in disorder and confusion; for the islands were in a state of war against the continents, and the continents were contending with the islands for the preeminence in honor, each having for their leaders and champions the most powerful and eminent of the Romans who were in office. And then again, great sections of Asia were contending against Europe, and Europe against Asia, for the chief power and dominion; the European and Asiatic nations rising up from the extremities of the earth, and waging terrible wars against one another over all the earth and over every sea with massive weapons, so that very nearly the whole race of mankind would have been destroyed by mutual slaughter and made utterly to disappear, if it had not been for one man and leader, Augustus, by whose means they were brought to a better state, and therefore we may justly call him the averter of evil. This is Caesar, who calmed the storms which were raging in every direction, who healed the common diseases which were afflicting both Greeks and barbarians, who descended from the south and from the east, and ran on and penetrated as far as the north and the west, in such a way as to fill all the neighboring districts and waters with unexpected miseries. This is he who did not only loosen but utterly abolished the bonds in which the whole of the habitable world was previously bound and weighed down. This is he who destroyed both the evident and the unseen wars which arose from the attacks of robbers. This is he who rendered the sea free from the vessels of pirates, and filled it with merchants. This is he who gave freedom to every city, who brought disorder into order, who civilized and made obedient and harmonious nations which before his time were unsociable, hostile, and brutal. This is he who increased Greece by many Greeces, and who Hellenized the regions of the barbarians in their most important regions: the guardian of peace, the distributor to every man of what was suited to him, the man who proffered to all the citizens favors with the most ungrudging liberality, who never once in his whole life concealed or reserved for himself anything that was good or excellent.

SOURCE: C. D. Yonge, *The Works of Philo Judaeus*, vol. 4 (London: H. G. Bohn, 1855), 131–32, with modifications.

Q. BIRTH STORIES

In the Greco-Roman world, stories of miraculous origins were sometimes connected with persons of extraordinary accomplishments and character. Ancients believed the greatness and superiority of such persons were signified by divine omens occurring around the time of birth. This superior status could also be articulated in terms of divine conception. See also readings §18, "The Birth of Cyrus" and §54, "Moses." Compare Matthew 1:1–2:23; Luke 1:5–2:52.

74

AUGUSTUS

Writing in the early second century CE, the Roman writer Suetonius relates traditions of various signs that accompanied the birth of the Roman emperor Augustus, including a story of divine conception by Apollo.

Suetonius, *Divus Augustus* 94.1–6

It is not improper to give an account of the omens, before and at Augustus' birth, as well as afterwards, which portended his future greatness, and the good fortune that constantly attended him. A long time ago, when part of the wall of (his home town) Velletri had been struck by lightning, the diviners predicted that a native of that town would some time or other come to have supreme power. Based on this prediction, the Velletrians, both then and several times afterwards, made war upon the Roman people, almost bringing about their own ruin. At last it appeared by the event that the omen had portended the reign of Augustus.

Julius Marathus informs us that a few months before his birth, there occurred at Rome an omen, which signified that Nature was in travail with a king for the Roman people. The senate became frightened and made a resolution that that no child born that year should be brought up. However, those among them whose wives were pregnant, thinking the prophecy might apply to their own family, took care that the decree of the senate was not obeyed.

I find in the theological books of Asclepias of Mendes that (Augustus' mother) Atia, when attending at midnight a religious solemnity in honor of Apollo and when the rest of the matrons retired home, fell asleep on her couch in the temple, and that a serpent immediately crept to her, and soon after withdrew. She awoke and purified herself in the usual manner as if coming from her husband's bed. Instantly there appeared upon her body a mark in the form of a serpent, which she never after could get rid of, and so she never attended public baths. Augustus, it was added, was born in the tenth month after, and for that reason was thought to be the son of Apollo. The same Atia, before her delivery, dreamed that her womb stretched to the stars and expanded over the whole of heaven and earth. His father Octavius, likewise, dreamed that the sun's radiance issued from his wife's womb.

. . . Afterwards, when marching with his army through the deserts of Thrace, (Augustus' father) Octavius consulted the oracle about his son in the grove of Father Bacchus with barbarous rites. He received from the priests an answer that confirmed Augustus' future greatness, because when they poured wine upon the altar a great flame shot up above the roof of the temple and reached up to the heavens. Such a portent had never happened to anyone but Alexander the Great, when he offered a sacrifice on the same altar. And the next night Octavius dreamed that he saw his son in appearance that was more than human: with thunder and a scepter and the other insignia of Jupiter, Optimus, Maximus, and having on his head a radiant crown and mounted upon a chariot decked with laurel and drawn by six pair of pure white horses.

While Augustus was still an infant, as Caius Drusus relates, he was laid in his cradle by his nurse in a low place. The next day he could not be found. And after he had been sought for a long time, he was finally discovered in a lofty tower lying with his face towards the rising sun.

SOURCE: Alexander Thomson, *Suetonius: The Lives of the Twelve Caesars* (London: George Bell & Sons, 1890), 138–39, with modifications.

75

PLATO

Consistent with the format of ancient biographies, Diogenes Laertius (writing ca. 200–250 CE) begins his account of the famous Greek philosopher Plato in terms of his ancestry and the circumstances of his birth (cp. Matt 1:1-25).

Diogenes Laertius, *Lives of Eminent Philosophers* 3.1–2

Plato was the son of Ariston and a citizen of Athens. His mother was Periktione (or Potone), who traced her descent back to Solon. Solon had a brother, Dropides, who was the father of Kritias, who was the father of Kallaischros, who was the father of Kritias (one of the Thirty), and Glaukon, who was the father of Charmides and Periktione. Thus Plato, the son of this Periktione and Ariston, was in the sixth generation from Solon. And Solon traced his descent to Neleus and Poseidon. His father too is said to be in the direct line from Kodros, the son of Melanthos, who, according to Thrasylus, trace their descent also from Poseidon.

Speusippos in the work entitled "Plato's Funeral Feast," Klearchos in his "Encomium on Plato," and Anaxilaïdes in his second book "On Philosophers," tell us that there was a story at Athens that Ariston made love to Periktione when she was ready to be pregnant, but he did not make her pregnant. When he had ceased his efforts, Apollo appeared to him in a dream, whereupon he abstained from sexual relations until her child was born. Apollodoros in his "Chronology" places the date of Plato's birth in the 88th Olympiad, on the seventh day of the month of Thargelion, which is the same day on which the Delians say that Apollo himself was born.

SOURCE: R. D. Hicks, *Diogenes Laertius: Lives of Eminent Philosophers*, vol. 1: *Books 1–5*, Loeb Classical Library 184 (Cambridge, Mass.: Harvard University Press, 1925), 277. Loeb Classical Library® is a registered trademark of the President and Fellows of Harvard College.

76

ALEXANDER THE GREAT

Writing around 100 CE, the biographer Plutarch includes traditions about the conception and birth of the Greek ruler Alexander the Great, including dreams, prophecies, and divine conception.

Plutarch, *Alexander* 2.1–3.2

As for the lineage of Alexander, on his father's side he was a descendant of Heracles through Caranus, and on his mother's side a descendant of Aeacus through Neoptolemus; this is accepted without any question. And we are told that (his father) Philip, after being initiated into the mysteries of Samothrace at the same time with (Alexander's mother) Olympias, he himself being still a youth and she an orphan child, fell in love with her and betrothed himself to her at once with the consent of her brother, Arymbas. Well, then, the night before the marriage was consummated, the bride dreamed that there was a peal of thunder and that a thunderbolt fell upon her womb, and that thereby much fire was kindled, which broke into flames that traveled all about, and then was extinguished. At a later time, too, after the marriage, Philip dreamed that he was putting a seal upon his wife's womb; and the device of the seal, as he thought, was the figure of a lion. The other diviners, now, were led by the vision to suspect that Philip needed to put a closer watch upon his marriage relations. But (the diviner) Aristander of Telmessus said that the woman was pregnant, since no seal was put upon what was empty, and pregnant with a son whose nature would be bold and lion-like. Moreover, a serpent was once seen lying stretched out by the side of Olympias as she slept, and we are told that this, more than anything else, dulled the desire of Philip's attentions to his wife, so that he no longer came often to sleep by her side, either because he feared that some spells and enchantments might be practiced upon him by her, or because he shrank from her embraces in the conviction that she was the partner of a superior being. . . .

Now, after his vision, as we are told, Philip sent Chaeroii of Megalopolis to Delphi, by whom an oracle was brought to him from Apollo, who exhorted him to sacrifice to Zeus-Ammon and hold that god in greatest reverence. He also told him he was to pluck out the eye with which he peered through the crack in the door to spy on the god in the form of a serpent sharing the couch of his wife. Moreover, Olympias, as Eratosthenes says, when she sent Alexander forth upon his great military campaign, told him, and him alone, the secret of his begetting, and exhorted him to have purposes worthy of his birth. Others, on the contrary, say that she repudiated the idea, and said: "Alexander must cease slandering me to Hera."

SOURCE: Bernadotte Perrin, *Plutarch: Lives*, vol. 7: *Demosthenes and Cicero, Alexander and Caesar*, Loeb Classical Library 99 (Cambridge, Mass.: Harvard University Press, 1919), 225–29. Loeb Classical Library® is a registered trademark of the President and Fellows of Harvard College.

R. PARABLES

Parables are short, fictional narratives that draw upon real-life scenarios for the purpose of metaphorical meaning. This metaphorical lesson can be moral and/or theological, depending on its literary context. The parables of Jesus have literary affinities with the Old Testament *mashal* (e.g., Jdg 9:7-20; 2 Sam 12:1-4; Isa 5:1-6) and rabbinic material, as well as the fable tradition of the Greco-Roman world.

77

PARABLES OF THE KINGDOM

The Gospel of Thomas, a noncanonical text, is a collection of Jesus' sayings (logia). The collection contains a mix of familiar material found in the canonical Gospels but also material that is unique. Dating the document has proved to be difficult, but the early second century CE is probable. The parable of the Empty Jar is only found in the Gospel of Thomas, and its meaning is obscure. Is it a cautionary story about missing the kingdom or about self-assuredness? Or, like the parable of Leaven (Matt 13:33//Luke 13:20-21) and the Mustard Seed (Mark 4:30-32//Matt 13:31-32//Luke 13:18-19), is it a story about the kingdom's modest initiation but surprising eventuality? The parable of the Lost Sheep has parallels in the Gospels of Matthew and Luke, but scholars differ on which one represents the earliest version of the parable, an identification usually attempted by comparing the three versions (cp. Luke 15:1-7; Matt 18:11-14).

Gospel of Thomas

Logion 97

Jesus says, "The kingdom of the father is like a woman carrying a jar full of flour. As she was walking a far distance on a road, the handle of the jar cracked and the flour leaked out behind her onto the road. She did not know it and was unaware of the mishap. When she entered into her house, she put the jar down and found it empty."

Logion 107

Jesus said, "The kingdom is like a shepherd who had a hundred sheep. One of the sheep, the largest, went astray. He left the ninety-nine and searched for that one until he found it. After such trouble, he said to the sheep, 'I love you more than the ninety-nine.'"

Source: Translation by Derek S. Dodson.

78

PARABLE OF THE LOST COIN

The following parable was told by a certain Rabbi Phineas (second century CE). Both this parable and the parable of Luke 15:8-10 draw upon the scenario of searching for a lost coin to teach a lesson.

Song of Songs Rabbah 1.1.9

If [a person] should lose a penny or a pin in his house, [he] will light any number of candles, any number of wicks, until he finds them. . . . If to find these, which are useful only in the here and now of this world, a person will light any number of candles, any number of wicks, until he finds them, as to words of Torah, which concern the life of the world to come as much as this world, do you not have to search for them like treasures?

SOURCE: Jacob Neusner, *A Theological Commentary to the Midrash*, vol. 3: *Song of Songs Rabbah* (Lanham, Md.: University Press of America, 2001), 36. Used by permission of the publisher. All rights reserved.

�

79

AESOP'S FABLES

The Hellenistic fable tradition is connected with the legendary Aesop (sixth century BCE), but his fables have come to us through various collections, like those of the Phaedrus (first half of the first century CE) and Babrius (second half of the first century CE). Though most of Aesop's fables are fantastic in nature with talking animals, a number of them relate stories of human of interaction and are quite comparable with the Gospel parables. Compare "The Brother and the Sister" to Luke 15:11-32; compare "The Farmer and the Tree" to Luke 13:6-9.

The Brother and the Sister
(Phaedrus, *The Fables of Aesop* 3.8)

A man had a very ugly daughter, and also a son, remarkable for his handsome features. These, while playing as children do, happened to look into a mirror, as it lay upon their mother's chair. He praises his own good looks; she is infuriated and cannot endure the teasing of her boasting brother, construing everything (and how could she do otherwise?) as an insult against herself. Accordingly, she runs off to her father to get revenge on him, and with great malice she makes a charge against the son, how that he, though a male, has been meddling with a thing that belongs to women. Embracing them both, kissing them, and dividing his tender affection between the two, the father said: "I wish you both to use the mirror every day: you (the son), that you may not spoil your beauty by vicious conduct; you (the daughter), that you may make amends for your looks by your virtues."

The Farmer and the Tree
(Babrius, *Fables of Aesop in Iambics* Appendix 299)

A farmer had in his garden a tree that did not bear fruit but only served as a place for the sparrows and grasshoppers. He decided to cut it down, and taking his axe in his hand he made a bold stroke at its roots. The grasshoppers and sparrows begged him not to cut down the tree that sheltered them but to spare it, and they would sing to him to lighten his labors. He paid no attention to their request, but gave the tree a second and a third blow with his axe. When he reached the hollow of the tree, he found a hive full of honey. Having tasted the honeycomb, he threw down his axe, and looking on the tree as sacred he took great care of it.

SOURCE: Henry Thomas Riley, *The Comedies of Terence and the Fables of Phaedrus* (London: George Bell & Sons, 1880), 398, with modifications; George F. Townsend, *Three Hundred of Aesop's Fables* (London: Routledge & Sons, 1871), 194, with modifications.

S. MIRACLE STORIES

The belief in and experience of miracles were prevalent in the ancient world, where the lines between magic, medicine, and miracle were often blurred. Deliverance from calamities and maladies were often sought from various deities, which could be accessed through temples or divine agents such as prophets, priests, diviners, philosophers, or rulers.

80

A JEWISH BOY CALMS THE SEA

Illustrating ways in which God is ever present and hears the prayers of his people, the following story from the Jerusalem Talmud, of a Jewish boy who calms a sea storm, is attributed to Rabbi Tanhooma (ca. 350 CE). The story also contains a polemic against gentile idolatry. Compare Mark 4:35-41//Matthew 8:23-27//Luke 8:22-25; also Jonah 1:4-10.

Jerusalem Talmud Tractate Berakhot 9.1

Rabbi Tanhooma relates that a Jewish boy was once on board a ship filled with gentiles, and it was sailing for the great sea (Mediterranean). A great storm arose, and everyone, seized with fear, took his idol in his hand and invoked it; but it was in vain. Seeing this, they said to the young boy, "My son, get up, and invoke your God; for we have learned that he hears you when you pray to him, and that he is all-powerful." The child immediately arose, and prayed with such fervor that God heard him favorably. The sea became calm, and they were able to disembark.

Source: Moses Schwab, *The Talmud of Jerusalem* (London: Williams & Norgate, 1886), 154–55, with modifications.

⁂

81

MIRACLES BY VESPASIAN

The Roman historian Tacitus (writing around 105 CE) provides an account of the newly declared Roman emperor Vespasian (69 CE). The miracles attributed to Vespasian—healing a blind man and healing a crippled hand—function to demonstrate his divine destiny of becoming the emperor. Compare Mark 8:22-26; John 9:1-7; Mark 3:1-6//Matthew 12:9-14//Luke 6:6-11.

Tacitus, *Histories* 4.81

In the months during which Vespasian was waiting at Alexandria for the return of the season of summer winds and calm seas, many wonders occurred which seemed to demonstrate that he was the object of favor from heaven and had a share in the divine. One of the common people of Alexandria, well-known for his blindness, threw himself at the emperor's knees, and implored him with groans to heal his infirmity. He did this by the advice of the god Serapis, whom this nation, devoted as it is to many superstitions, worships more than all other deities. He begged Vespasian that he stoop to moisten his cheeks and eyeballs with his saliva. Another person with a crippled hand, who was ordered by the same god, prayed that the Caesar would step on the limb with his foot. At first Vespasian ridiculed and resisted them, but they persisted. And though he was initially afraid of scandal if he failed, he was ultimately more hopeful because of the prayers of the men and by flattery of the people. At last he ordered that physicians should be consulted, as to whether such blindness and infirmity were within the reach of human skill. They discussed the matter from different points of view. In the one case, they determined that the faculty of sight was not completely destroyed, and it might return if the obstructions were removed. In the other case, the hand, which had fallen into a deformed condition might be restored, if a healing influence were applied. This, they suggested, was perhaps the pleasure of the gods, and the emperor might be chosen to be the minister of the divine will. At any rate, all the glory of a successful healing would be Caesar's, while the ridicule of failure would fall on the sufferers. And so Vespasian, supposing that all things were possible to his good fortune, and that nothing was any longer incredible, with a joyful countenance, amid the intense expectation of the multitude of bystanders, accomplished what was required. The hand was instantly restored to its use, and the light of day again shined upon the blind man. Persons actually present attest to both facts, even now when nothing is to be gained by falsehood.

SOURCE: Alfred John Church and William Jackson Brodribb, *The History of Tacitus* (London: MacMillan & Co., 1864), 258–59, with modifications.

82

THE HEALING GOD ASCLEPIUS

The Greek god Asclepius was primarily known as a healing deity. Asclepius temples attracted people with all sorts of ailments with the hope of being cured. The healing process included spending the night in a "sleep room," where the petitioner would have a dream. The dream either was the means of healing or provided information for the dream-interpreter priest of what procedures were needed for healing. If healing occurred, the person would pay to have his or her testimony inscribed on the temple columns or erected stone slabs. The following accounts are two such inscriptions from the most famous Asclepius temple in Epidaurus, Greece, dating from the third century BCE. Compare Mark 8:22-26; John 9:1-7.

Epidaurian Inscriptions

Stele A 18

Alketas of Halieis. This man, though suffering from blindness, saw a dream. It seemed that the god came to him and opened his eyes with his fingers, and he initially saw (in the dream) the trees in the temple complex. When day came he left well.

Stele B 2

Hermon of Thasos. This man, though he came blind, was healed. But after this, when he did not pay the healing fees, the god made him blind again. When the man returned and slept there again, the god restored his health.

SOURCE: Translation by Derek S. Dodson.

83

MIRACLES BY APOLLONIUS

Writing in the third century CE, the biographer Philostratus writes to defend the Pythagorean philosopher Apollonius (first century CE) against accusations of magic. The first excerpt presents the miracles of Apollonius, along with his disciples, as originating from the philosopher's holiness and virtue (cp. Matt 11:2-6//Luke 7:18-23; Mark 8:22-26; John 9:1-7; Mark 2:1-12//Matt 9:1-8//Luke 5:17-26; Mark 3:1-6//Matt 12:9-14//Luke 6:6-11; John 5:1-9). The second selection recounts an exorcism performed by Apollonius (cp. Mark 5:1-20//Matt 8:28-34//Luke 8:26-39).

Philostratus, *Life of Apollonius of Tyana*

3.39

There also arrived a man who was lame. Already thirty years old, he was a keen hunter of lions; but a lion had sprung upon him and dislocated his hip so that he limped with one leg. However, when Apollonius and his disciples massaged his hip, the young man immediately was able to walk properly. And another man had had his eyes put out, and he went away having recovered the sight of both of them. Yet another man had his hand paralyzed, but left their presence in full control of his hand.

4.20

Now while he was discussing the question of libations, there happened to be present in his audience an older teenage boy who had such a bad a reputation for licentiousness, that his conduct had once been the subject of vulgar street-corner songs. His home was Corcyra, and he traced his pedigree to Alcinous the Phacacian who entertained Odysseus. Apollonius then was talking about libations, and was urging them not to drink out of a particular cup, but to reserve it for the gods, without ever touching it or drinking out of it. But when he also urged them to have handles on the cup, and to pour the libation over the handle, because that is the part of the cup at which men are least likely to drink, the youth burst out into loud and coarse laughter, drowning out Apollonius' voice. Then Apollonius looked up at him and said: "It is not yourself that perpetuates this insult, but the demon, who drives you on without your knowing it." And in fact the youth was, without knowing it, possessed by a demon; for he would laugh at things that no one else laughed at, and then he would start weeping for no reason at all, and he would talk and sing to himself. Now most people thought that it was the boisterous humor of youth which led him into such excesses; but he was really the mouthpiece of a demon, though it had only seemed a drunken frolic in which on that occasion he was indulging. Now when Apollonius gazed on him, the spirit in him began to utter cries of fear and rage, such as one hears from people who are being branded or racked; and the spirit swore that he would leave the young man alone and never take possession of any man again. But Apollonius addressed him with anger, as a master might speak to a devious, rascally, and shameless slave, and he ordered him to leave the young man and show by a visible sign that he had done so. "I will throw down that statue over there," said the demon, pointing to one of the images which was in the king's portico, for there it was that the scene took place. So when the statue began by moving gently and then fell down, it would defy anyone to describe the hubbub which arose thereat and the way they clapped their hands with wonder. But the young man rubbed his eyes as if he had just woke up, and he looked toward the rays of the sun, and won the consideration of all who now had turned their attention to him; for he no longer showed himself licentious, nor did he stare madly about, but he had returned to his own self, as thoroughly as if he had been treated with medicine; and he gave up his dainty dress and summery garments and the rest of his luxurious way of life, and he fell in love with the austerity of philosophers, and donned their cloak, and stripping off his old self modelled his life in future upon that of Apollonius.

Source: F. C. Conybeare, *Philostratus: The Life of Apollonius of Tyana*, Loeb Classical Library 16 (Cambridge, Mass.: Harvard University Press, 1912), 317–19, 389–91. Loeb Classical Library® is a registered trademark of the President and Fellows of Harvard College.

84

A SYRIAN EXORCIST

A Greek writer from Syria writing in the mid-second century CE, Lucian is a satirist who critiques those who believe in the supernatural. In the following selection, his dialogue partner Ion shares a story about a presumably well-known exorcist in Syria. Compare Mark 5:1-20//Matthew 8:28-34//Luke 8:26-39.

Lucian, *The Lover of Lies* 16

"You act ridiculously," said Ion, "to doubt everything. For my part, I should like to ask you what you say about those who free possessed men from their terrors by exorcising the spirits so manifestly. I need not discuss this: everyone knows about the Syrian from Palestine, how skilled he was in this, taking many in hand who fall down in the light of the moon and roll their eyes and fill their mouths with foam. He restores them to health and sends them away normal in mind, delivering them from their predicament for a large fee. When he stands beside them as they lie there and asks the demons: 'Whence came you into his body?' the patient himself is silent, but the spirit answers in Greek or in the language of whatever foreign country he comes from, telling how and whence he entered into the person; whereupon, by adjuring the spirit and if he does not obey, threatening him, he drives him out. Indeed, I actually saw one coming out, black and smoky in color."

Source: A. M. Harmon, *Lucian*, vol. 3, Loeb Classical Library 130 (Cambridge, Mass.: Harvard University Press, 1921), 345. Loeb Classical Library® is a registered trademark of the President and Fellows of Harvard College.

T. ASCENSION STORIES

Ascension stories—also known as translation stories—depict persons being taken into heaven (the company of God or the gods), usually without experiencing death. These accounts function to contribute to the exceptional status of the person. In the Jewish tradition, the person's remarkable faith and standing before God results in an ascension. The only ascension story in the Hebrew Bible is the departure of Elijah (2 Kgs 2:1, 11-12). In the Greco-Roman tradition, the ascension is also an apotheosis, an elevation to divine status. Compare Luke 24:50-51; Acts 1:6-11.

85

MOSES

In his retelling of the biblical story, the Jewish writer Josephus (writing in the later first century CE) incorporates the ascension tradition in the end of Moses' life. The Bible records the death of Moses (Deut 34:7-8), a fact Josephus needs to reconcile, and so Josephus' inclusion of an ascension functions to promote the honorable status of Moses.

Josephus, *Jewish Antiquities* 4.320–326

When Moses had spoken thus at the end of his life, and had foretold what would happen to each of their tribes afterward, with the addition of a blessing to them, the multitude fell into tears. . . . Now as Moses went to the place where he was to vanish out of their sight, they all followed after him weeping. But Moses gestured with his hand to those who were at a distance from him and directed them to stay behind quietly, and he exhorted those who were near him that they would consider his departure so lamentable. They decided that they ought to grant him that favor, to let him depart according to his wishes. So they restrained themselves, though they continued weeping among themselves. All those who accompanied him were the elders, Eleazar the high priest and Joshua their commander. Now as soon as they had come to the mountain called Abarim (which is a very high mountain situated over against Jericho, providing a view of the greatest part of the excellent land of Canaan), he dismissed the elders. He embraced Eleazar and Joshua, and while he was still speaking with them a cloud suddenly came over him, and he disappeared in a certain chasm. Now he wrote in the holy books that he died, because he was concerned that they would say that he went to God on account of his extraordinary virtue.

SOURCE: William Whiston, *The Works of Flavius Josephus* (Philadelphia: John E. Potter, 1895), 116–17, with modifications.

86

ENOCH

Enoch is a very minor character in the Bible, yet he garnered much attention because of the description, "Enoch walked with God; then he was no more, because God took him" (Gen 5:24). The apocalyptic text 2 Enoch (written late first century CE) fills out this terse account with conventional features of ascension stories.

2 Enoch 67

When Enoch had talked to the people, the Lord sent darkness upon the earth, and there was darkness; and it covered those men standing and talking with Enoch. And angels took Enoch up to the highest heaven, where the Lord is; and he received him and placed him before his face. And the darkness departed the earth, and light came again. And the people saw and understood that Enoch had been taken, and they glorified God. And they found a scroll in which was written "The Invisible God," and all went to their homes.

SOURCE: N. Forbes, "2 Enoch," in *The Apocrypha and Pseudepigrapha of the Old Testament in English*, vol. 2, ed. R. H. Charles (Oxford: Clarendon Press, 1913), 469, with modifications.

87

ROMULUS

In his history of Rome (written late first century BCE), Livy concludes his account of the Romulus, the founding king of Rome, with an ascension story. The ascension story also includes Romulus' apotheosis, an idea promoted by the inability to find his body and the witness of his appearance. Some interpreters suggest that the empty tomb tradition and post-resurrection appearances in the Gospels have a similar background (cp. Mark 16:1-8; Matt 28:1-20).

Livy, *History of Rome* 1.16

When these remarkable deeds had been done, as the king (Romulus) was reviewing his army near the swamp of Capra at Campus Martius, suddenly a storm came up with loud claps of thunder and enveloped him in a cloud so thick that he was hidden from the sight of the assembly; and from that moment Romulus was no more on earth. When the Roman soldiers recovered from their panic after this hour of wild confusion had been succeeded by a sunny calm, they saw that the royal seat was empty. Although they believed the assertion of the senators, who had been standing next to Romulus, that he had been caught up on high in a whirlwind, they nevertheless remained for some time grieving and silent, as if filled with the fear of being orphaned. Then, when a few men had taken the initiative, they all together hailed Romulus as a god, born of a god, and the king and father of the city of Rome; and they with prayers asked his favor that he would graciously protect his children. However, I believe that even then there were some who secretly asserted that the king had been torn limb from limb by the senators, though this rumor was spread in very obscure terms. The other version (narrated above) gained popularity based on the men's admiration for the hero and the intensity of their panic. And one man's clever device is also said to have added credibility to the story. As tradition tells, Proculus Julius, whose advice was greatly respected, seeing how the people were upset by the loss of their king and how they were enraged with the senate, addressed the group as follows: "People of Quirites, the father of this city, Romulus, descended suddenly from the sky at dawn this morning and appeared to me. Filled with fear, I stood reverently before him, praying that I might be allowed to look upon his face without offense. 'Go,' said he, 'and declare to the Romans that it is the will of Heaven that my Rome should be the capital of the world. So, let them cherish the art of war, and let them know and teach their children that no human strength can resist Roman arms.'" He concluded, "Romulus departed on high." It is wonderful what confidence the people placed in that man's story, and how the grief for the loss of Romulus, which the people and the army felt, was quieted by the assurance of his immortality.

SOURCE: Benjamin O. Foster, *Livy: History of Rome*, vol. 1: *Books 1–2*, Loeb Classical Library 114 (Cambridge, Mass.: Harvard University Press, 1919), 57–61. Loeb Classical Library® is a registered trademark of the President and Fellows of Harvard College.

88

HERACLES

As part of his ambitious history of the world (written mid-first century BCE), the Greek writer Diodorus recounts the ascension and apotheosis of the legendary hero Heracles. The tale of Heracles' death varied little, but Diodorus accentuates his full apotheosis with the ascension tradition.

Diodorus of Sicily, *Historical Library* 4.38.3–5

As Heracles continued to suffer more and more from his malady he dispatched (his companions) Licymnius and Iolaus to Delphi to inquire of Apollo what he must do to heal the sickness. Meanwhile, (Herakles' wife) Deianira was so traumatized by the magnitude of Heracles' misfortune that, knowing that it was her fault, she ended her life by hanging herself. The god gave the reply that Heracles should be carried with his armor and battle gear to Oetê and that they should build a huge pyre near him. What remained to be done, he said, would rest with Zeus. Now when Iolaus had carried out these orders and had withdrawn a distance to see what would take place, Heracles, having abandoned hope for himself, ascended the pyre and asked each one who came up to him to light the pyre. And when no one had the courage to obey him, Philoctetes alone was moved to obey. And he, having received in return for his obedience the gift of the bow and arrows of Heracles, lighted the pyre. And immediately lightning fell from the heavens and the pyre was wholly consumed. After this, the companions of Iolaus came to collect the bones of Heracles, but they did not find a single bone anywhere. They supposed that, in accordance with the words of the oracle, he had passed from among men into the company of the gods.

SOURCE: C. H. Oldfather, *Diodorus of Sicily: Library of History*, vol. 2: *Books 2.35–4.58*, Loeb Classical Library 303 (Cambridge, Mass.: Harvard University Press, 1935), 465–67. Loeb Classical Library® is a registered trademark of the President and Fellows of Harvard College.

U. DOUBLE DREAM/VISION REPORT

The double dream/vision report is an elaborate literary convention that involves two persons who have their own dream or vision. The dreams/visions create a situation where the two persons interact and benefit from the subsequent circumstance. Because dreams/visions were understood as divine messages, the subsequent circumstance that benefits each party is presented as the will of the divine. Dream/vision reports are usually utilized for significant, dramatic developments within a narrative. Compare Acts 9:1-19; 10:1-48.

89

DREAMS OF AENEAS AND LATINUS

In his history of Rome (written late first century BCE), Dionysius describes how the legendary Aeneas and his people came to be allies with the inhabitants of Latium (named for their ruler Latinus), where Rome would be established. The account certainly has embellishments, promoting the idea that such peace was the work of the gods. Both Aeneas and Latinus have made plans to attack each other the following day, but both have dreams that move each man to make peace with the other.

Dionysius of Halicarnassus, *Roman Antiquities* 1.57. 4

Now when Latinus had determined these things, a certain deity of that region appeared to him in his sleep and said to him the Greeks should be received into his land to dwell with his own subjects, adding that their coming was a great advantage to him and a benefit to all the original inhabitants as well. And the same night Aeneas' household gods appeared to him and admonished him to persuade Latinus to grant them of his own accord a settlement in the part of the country they desired and to treat the Greek forces as allies

220

rather than enemies. Thus the dream prevented both of them from initiating a battle. And as soon as it was day and the armies were drawn up in order of battle, messengers came to each commander from the other with the same request that they should meet for a discussion; and so it came to pass.

SOURCE: Earnest Cary, *Dionysius of Halicarnassus: Roman Antiquities*, vol. 1: *Books 1–2*, Loeb Classical Library 319 (Cambridge, Mass.: Harvard University Press, 1937), 191. Loeb Classical Library® is a registered trademark of the President and Fellows of Harvard College.

90
DREAMS OF JADDUS AND ALEXANDER THE GREAT

The Jewish writer Josephus (writing in the later first century CE) provides the only account of Alexander the Great entering Jerusalem with his army. By utilizing the double dream/vision report, Josephus embellishes the event to create a peaceful encounter (one in which the Jews do not simply submit to Alexander) and to promote Alexander's empire-expanding success as the will of Israel's God.

Josephus, *Jewish Antiquities* 11.326–335

The high priest Jaddus decreed that the people should make prayers, and should join with him in offering sacrifice to God, whom he sought to protect that nation and to deliver them from the perils that were coming upon them. As a result, after he had offered sacrifice, God commanded him in a dream to take courage, to adorn the city with wreaths, and to open the gates; that the people should be in white garments, and he himself with the priests should meet the king in the robes prescribed by the laws; and that they should not dread any ill consequences, for the providence of God was watching over them. When he rose from his sleep, he greatly rejoiced, and declared to all the command that he had received from God. He acted in every way in accordance to the dream, and so waited for the coming of the king. . . .

Alexander, when he saw the multitude at a distance in white garments, with the priests standing clothed with fine linen and the high priest in purple and scarlet clothing with his liturgical headdress on his head, which had a golden plate whereon the name of God was engraved, he approached by himself and revered that name, and first saluted the high priest. The Jews also did all together, with one voice, saluted Alexander, and gathered around him. And seeing this, the kings of Syria and the rest were surprised at what Alexander had done, and thought that he had lost his mind. However, (Alexander's general) Parmenio alone went up to him, and asked him why, when all others revere him, he should adore the high priest of the Jews? Alexander replied, "I did not revere him, but the God who has honored him with his high priesthood. For I saw this very person in a dream, in these very vestments, when I was at Dios in Macedonia, when I was considering with myself how I might obtain the dominion of Asia, and he exhorted me not to delay but confidently to cross over the sea, for he himself would lead my army, and would give me the dominion over the Persians. Since, therefore, I have seen no other in these vestments, but now seeing this person in it and remembering that vision, and the exhortation which I had in my dream, I believe that I am making this military expedition under the divine guidance, and that I will conquer Darius (the Persian king) and destroy the power of the Persians, that I will succeed in all things which I have in mind."

SOURCE: William Whiston, *The Works of Flavius Josephus* (Philadelphia: John E. Potter, 1895), 282–83, with modifications.

V. EARLY CHRISTIAN WORSHIP AND RITES

The following selections provide material for considering early Christian worship and the two most prominent Christian rites, baptism and Eucharist/Lord's Supper. The first selection describes a polytheistic religious group, providing an interesting comparison (and contrast) to early Christian communities. The remaining selections are "snapshots" of how some Christians in particular places and times were practicing their sacred rites. The New Testament does not offer a lot of explicit details about Christian worship, but 1 Corinthians does provide some information, at least for Pauline churches. First Corinthians assumes a gathering of Christians that begins with "the Lord's supper" (11:17-34; esp. 11:20), a sacred, commemorative meal based on Jesus' last supper with his disciples (Mark 14:12-25//Matt 26:17-29//Luke 22:7-20). After the meal, the gathered Christians then participate in a time of teaching, exhortation, and encouragement by the exercising of spiritual gifts (14:26-33). Christian baptism is an initiation rite with various imagery and meaning associated with it (Acts 2:38; 10:44-48; Rom 6:3-11; 1 Cor 6:11; 12:12-13; Gal 3:27-28; Titus 3:5-7; 1 Pet 3:20-22).

91

INSTRUCTIONS FOR A RELIGIOUS ASSOCIATION

Dating from the late second century to early first century BCE from the city of Philadelphia (Asia Minor), this inscription contains instructions for a religious association that meets in the house of a certain Dionysios. Comparison with Christian house churches can reveal how early Christianity participated in some broader socioreligious patterns of the times, particularly social makeup, moral instruction, and community discipline. Compare

Acts 5:1-11; 1 Corinthians 5:1-20; 11:17-22, 27-32; 1 Thessalonians 4:1-12; 1 Timothy 3:1–4:10; Titus 1:3–2:14.

LSAM 20 (=*SIG*³ 985)

For good fortune! For health, common salvation, and the best reputation, the instructions that were given to Dionysios in his sleep were written down, giving access into his house (*oikos*) to men and women, free people and house-hold slaves. For in this house altars have been set up for Zeus Eumenes and Hestia his consort, for the other Savior gods, and for Eudaimonia ("Prosper-ity"), Ploutos ("Wealth"), Arete ("Virtue"), Hygeia ("Health"), Agathe Tyche ("Good Fortune"), Agathos Daimon ("Good Spirit"), Mneme ("Memory"), the Charitae ("the Graces"), and Nike ("Victory"). Zeus has given instructions to this man for the performance of the purifications, the cleansings, and the mysteries in accordance with ancestral custom and in accordance with what has now been written here.

When entering this house let men and women, free people and household slaves, swear by all the gods that they do not know about any deceptive action against a man or a woman or about any drug harmful to people, and that they neither know nor use harmful spells, a love charm, an abortive drug, or a contraceptive. Nor should they use any other thing fatal to children, or give advice or connive with another person about such things. Now no one should withdraw their goodwill toward this house, and if anyone should do any of these things or plan them, the others are neither to look the other way nor remain silent, but shall expose and avenge the violations.

Beyond his own wife, a man is not to seduce someone else's wife, whether free or slave, nor a boy, nor a virgin girl. Nor shall he advise someone else to do so. Should he connive at it with someone, they shall expose such a person, both the man and the woman, and not conceal it or keep silent about it. Let the woman and the man, whoever does any of the things written above, not enter this house. For the gods set up in it are great, and they watch over these things and will not tolerate those who transgress the instructions.

A free woman is to be pure and not know the bed of another man, nor have intercourse with anyone except her own husband. But if she does know the bed of another man, such a woman is not pure, but defiled, full of endemic pollution, and unworthy to revere this god whose sacred things have been established here. She is not to be present at the sacrifices, nor cause offence at the purifications and cleansings, nor see the mysteries being performed. If she does any of these things after the instructions have been inscribed, she will have evil curses from the gods for disregarding these instructions. For the god does not want these things to happen at all, nor does he wish it. Rather, he wants obedience.

The gods will be merciful to those who obey and will always give them all good things, whatever things gods give to people whom they love. But if any transgress, the gods will hate such people and inflict upon them great punishments. These instructions were stored with the goddess Agditis, the holiest guardian and mistress of this house. May she create good thoughts in men and women, free people and household slaves, so that they may obey the things written here. During the monthly and annual sacrifices, may those men and women who have confidence in themselves touch this stone on which the instructions of the god have been written, so that those who obey these instructions and those who do not obey these instructions may become evident.

Zeus Soter ("Savior"), accept the touch of Dionysios mercifully and kindly, and be gentle with him and his family. Provide good rewards, health, salvation, peace, safety on land and sea . . . likewise. . . .

Source: Richard S. Ascough, Philip A. Harland, and John S. Kloppenborg, *Associations in the Greco-Roman World: A Sourcebook* (Waco: Baylor University Press, 2012), 82–84.

92

INSTRUCTIONS ON BAPTISM, EUCHARIST, AND THE LORD'S DAY

The Didache is an anonymous Christian text written around 100 CE, probably in Syria. It is a "church manual" providing both ethical and community instructions. The Didache here describes the practice of baptism, the observance of the Eucharist, and brief instructions on gathering for worship.

The Didache

Chapter 7

Now concerning baptism, baptize in this way: Having first rehearsed all these things, baptize in the name of the Father and of the Son and of the Holy Spirit in running water. But if you do not have running water, baptize in other water. And if you cannot baptize in cold water, then do it in warm. But if you have neither, pour water three times on the head in the name of the Father, Son, and Holy Spirit. And before the baptism let the baptizer and the one who is to be baptized fast, and any others who are able. And you will charge the one who is to be baptized to fast one or two days before. . . .

Chapter 9

And now concerning the Eucharist, observe the Eucharist in this way: First concerning the cup, "We give thanks to you, our Father, for the Holy Vine of David your child, which you made known to us through Jesus your child; to you be glory forever." And concerning the broken bread: "We give you thanks, our Father, for the life and knowledge which you made known to us through Jesus your Child. To you be glory forever. As this broken bread was scattered upon the mountains, but was brought together and became one, so let your church be gathered together from the ends of the earth into your kingdom, for yours is the glory and the power through Jesus Christ forever." But do not let anyone eat or drink of your Eucharist except those who have been baptized in the Lord's Name. For concerning this also did the Lord say, "Give not that which is holy to the dogs." And after you are filled with food, give thanks in this way: "We give thanks to you, O Holy Father, for your Holy Name which you made to tabernacle in our hearts, and for the knowledge and faith and immortality which you made known to us through Jesus your Child. To you be glory forever. You, Lord Almighty, created all things for the sake of your name, and you gave food and drink to people for their enjoyment so that they might give thanks to you. But you have blessed us with spiritual food and drink and eternal light through your Child. Above all we give thanks to you because you are mighty. To you be glory forever. Remember, Lord, your church, to deliver it from all evil and to make it perfect in your love; and gather it together in its holiness from the four winds to your kingdom which you have prepared for it. For yours is the power and the glory forever. Let grace come, and let this world pass away. Hosanna to the God of David. If anyone is holy, let them come. If anyone is not, let them repent. Maranatha! Amen." . . .

Chapter 14

On the Lord's Day come together, break bread, and observe the Eucharist, after confessing your transgressions so that your offering may be pure. Do not let anyone who has a quarrel with their fellow believer join in your meeting until they are reconciled, so that your sacrifice may not be defiled. For this is that which was spoken by the Lord, "In every place and time offer me a pure sacrifice, for I am a great king," says the Lord, "and my name is wonderful among the nations" (Mal 1:11, 14).

SOURCE: Kirsopp Lake, *Apostolic Fathers*, vol. 1, Loeb Classical Library 24 (Cambridge: Harvard University Press, 1912), 319–21, 323, 331. Loeb Classical Library® is a registered trademark of the President and Fellows of Harvard College.

93

A ROMAN REPORT ON CHRISTIAN GATHERINGS

Pliny the Younger was the Roman governor of Bithynia-Pontus, Roman provinces in northern Asia Minor. The following excerpt is from a letter written to the emperor Trajan in 112 CE, in which Pliny describes his approach to judging and punishing Christians who have been brought to him (see reading §105, "Pliny the Younger's Examination of Christians"). As a result of his interrogations, he learns some details about the gathering of Christians and relates them to the emperor.

Pliny the Younger, *Letters* 10.96 (To Trajan)

They declared that the sum of their guilt or error only amounted to this: It was their custom to gather on a stated day before daybreak and to recite a hymn to Christ, as though he were a god; and that they bound themselves by oath not to commit any crime, but rather to abstain from theft, robbery, and adultery, and to not break faith nor to deny money placed in their keeping when called upon to deliver it. When this gathering was concluded, it was their custom to depart and meet again to eat a meal, though it was quite harmless. They even ceased this practice after the edict in which, in accordance with your orders, I banned all secret societies.

SOURCE: J. B. Firth, *The Letters of the Younger Pliny*, vol. 1 (London: Walter Scott, 1900), 378–79, with modifications.

94

AN EXPLANATION OF BAPTISM, EUCHARIST, AND WORSHIP

Writing around 150 CE to the emperor Antoninus, the Christian intellectual Justin Martyr defends Christianity and attempts to explain its beliefs and practices. The following excerpts describe the meaning and process of baptism, the observance of the Eucharist, and the activities of a worship service.

Justin Martyr, *1 Apology*

Chapter 61

I will also relate the manner in which we dedicated ourselves to God when we had been made new through Christ; lest, if we omit this, we seem to be unfair in the explanation we are making. As many as are persuaded and believe that what we teach and say is true, and undertake to be able to live accordingly, these are instructed to pray and to entreat God with fasting for the remission of their past sins; we pray and fast with them. Then they are brought by us where there is water, and are regenerated in the same manner in which we ourselves were regenerated. For, in the name of God, the Father and Lord of the universe, and of our Savior Jesus Christ, and of the Holy Spirit, they then receive the washing with water. For Christ also said, "Unless you are born again, you shall not enter into the kingdom of heaven" (John 3:5). Now, that it is impossible for those who have once been born to enter into their mothers' wombs, is manifest to all. And how those who have sinned and repent will escape their sins is declared by Isaiah the prophet, as I wrote above; he thus says: "Wash yourselves, make yourselves clean; put away the evil of your doings from your souls; learn to do well; judge the fatherless, and plead for the widow: and come and let us reason together, says the Lord. And though your sins be as scarlet, I will make them white like wool; and though they be as crimson, I will make them white as snow. But if you refuse and rebel, the sword shall devour you: for the mouth of the Lord hath spoken it" (Isa 1:16-20). And for baptism we have learned from the apostles this reason. Since at our birth we were born without our own knowledge or choice, by our parents coming together, and were brought up in bad habits and wicked training. In order that we may not remain the children of necessity and of ignorance, but may become the children of choice and knowledge, and may obtain in the water the remission of sins formerly committed, there is pronounced over the one who chooses to be born again and has repented of their sins the name of God the Father and Lord of the universe. . . . And this washing is called illumination, because they who learn these things are illuminated in their understandings. And in the name of Jesus Christ, who was crucified under Pontius Pilate, and in the name of the Holy Spirit, who through the prophets foretold all things about Jesus, he who is illuminated is washed. . . .

Chapters 65–67

After we have washed the one who has been convinced and has agreed to our teaching, we bring him to the place where those who are called brothers are gathered, so that we may offer sincere prayers together for ourselves, for the baptized [illuminated] person, and for all others in every place: that we may be counted worthy now that we have learned the truth, and that by our works we may be found to be good citizens and keepers of the commandments, so that we may be saved with an everlasting salvation. After the prayers, we greet one another with a kiss. Then bread and a cup of wine mixed with water is brought to the presider of the assembly; and he takes them, gives praise and glory to the Father of the universe through the name of the Son and of the Holy Spirit, and offers thanks at some length for our being counted worthy to receive these things from God's hands. And when he has concluded the prayers and thanksgivings, all the people present express their agreement by saying Amen. This word Amen corresponds in the Hebrew language to "so be it." And when the presider has given thanks and all the people have expressed their agreement, those who are called by us deacons give to each of those present to partake of the bread and wine mixed with water over which the thanksgiving was pronounced, and to those who are absent they take a portion.

And this food is called among us the Eucharist, of which no one is allowed to partake but the person who believes that the things which we teach are true, and who has been washed with the washing that is for the remission of sins and for regeneration, and who is so living as Christ has commanded. For we do not receive these as common bread and common drink. But in a similar way as Jesus Christ our Savior, having been made flesh by the Word of God, had both flesh and blood for our salvation, so likewise have we been taught that the food which is blessed by the prayer of His word, and from which our blood and flesh by transformation are nourished, is the flesh and blood of Jesus who was made flesh. For the apostles in the memoirs composed by them, which are called Gospels, have delivered to us what was directed to them: that Jesus took bread, gave thanks, and said, "Do this in remembrance of me; this is my body." And after in the same way, he took the cup, gave thanks, and said, "This is my blood." And he gave it to them alone. The wicked demons have imitated this in the mystery rites of Mithras, commanding the same thing to be done; for bread and a cup of water are used in the mystic rites of one who is being initiated with certain incantations, which you either know or can learn. . . .

And on the day called Sunday, all who live in cities or in the country gather together in one place, and the memoirs of the apostles or the writings of the prophets are read as long as time permits. Then, when the reader has finished, the presider verbally instructs and exhorts that these good things are to be imitated. Then we all rise together and pray, and, as we before said, when our prayer is ended bread and wine and water are brought out. The presider in like manner offers prayers and thanksgivings according to his ability, and the people give their agreement by saying Amen. Then there is a distribution of these things to each, and a partaking of them over which thanks have been given; and to those who are absent a portion is sent by the deacons. And those who are well-to-do, and willing, give what each thinks is appropriate; and what is collected is placed with the presider, who assists the orphans and widows, those who through sickness or any other cause are in need, those who are in prison, and the strangers staying with us—in a word he takes care of all who are in need. And Sunday is the day on which we all hold our common assembly, because it is the first day on which God, having brought about a change in the darkness and matter, made the world; and Jesus Christ our Savior on the same day rose from the dead. For he was crucified on the day before the day of Saturn (Saturday); and on the day after that of Saturn, which is the day of the Sun, he appeared to his apostles and disciples and taught them these things, which we have submitted to you for your consideration.

SOURCE: Marcus Dods and George Reith, *Justin Martyr: The First Apology*, in *Ante-Nicene Fathers*, vol. 1, ed. Alexander Roberts, James Donaldson, and A. Cleveland Coxe (Buffalo: Christian Literature Publishing Co., 1885), 247, 250–51, with modifications.

W. EARLY CHRISTIAN LEADERSHIP

The New Testament reveals a diversity of leadership in the earliest Christian movement. Apostles and prophets are prominent, including more than the Twelve (1 Cor 15:5-9) and including women (Rom 16:7; 1 Cor 11:5; Acts 21:9). At least for Pauline churches, leadership is characterized by individual Christians exercising their spiritual gifts (1 Cor 12:4-11, 27-28; Rom 12:3-8). Given the setting of houses for most groups of Christians, the structure of the Greco-Roman household most likely provided "ready-made" leadership structures, with the head of the household—which could include women (Acts 16:11-15; Col 4:15)—hosting, providing, and giving oversight to the congregation (Rom 16:1-2, 3-5a; Phlm 1b-2). The following selections (1) provide a parallel to the deacon Phoebe in Romans 16:1-2 and (2) reveal developments from this earliest diversity to a more formal structure.

95

A DECREE HONORING IUNIA THEODORA

In the mid-first century CE, several cities of the region of Lycia (Asia Minor) and the Lycian federation itself sent decrees and letters to the city of Corinth to honor a certain Lycian woman named Iunia Theodora, who resided in Corinth. Though published and sent at different times, the decrees and letters (five in all) were at some point inscribed on a single stele, most likely at the death of Iunia. The inscriptions acknowledge the many ways Iunia, a woman of stature and means, had acted on behalf of the Lycian people. In one of the decrees, Iunia is described as a "benefactor," the same term used for Phoebe in Romans 16:2. The following decree gives an overview of Iunia's activism for the Lycian people. We can imagine Phoebe, whom

Paul commends to the Roman church (Rom 16:1-2), doing similar acts of goodwill for Christians living in and traveling through Achaia. Compare also Luke 8:1-3; Acts 16:11-15; Colossians 4:15.

SEG 18, no. 143

It was resolved by the people of Patara: Whereas Iunia Theodora, a Roman residing in Corinth, a woman of the greatest honor, living according to the virtue of modesty, who is a friend of the Lycians, who has dedicated her own livelihood for the gratitude of all Lycians, and has provided much benefit for many of our citizens; exhibiting her own magnificent character from acts of goodwill, she does not cease offering hospitality to all Lycians and welcoming them in her house; and she never ceases to act on behalf of our citizens regarding all favors, so that most of our citizens come before the civic assembly to testify to her—therefore our people, being grateful, thought it proper to commend Iunia and to testify about her that she has affirmation and goodwill from our native city; and to invite her to extend goodwill to the people, knowing that our people will not show any neglect in its goodwill and favor to her and will do everything for the distinction and glory that she deserves. Because of this, with good fortune, it was decided to commend her because of all the things previously mentioned. So that Iunia herself and the city of Corinth might know the goodwill of our city to her and the decree passed for her, the secretary of the city council sends a copy of this decree, having sealed it with an official seal, to the people of Corinth.

SOURCE: Translation by Derek S. Dodson.

96

INSTRUCTIONS ON PROPHETS, BISHOPS, AND DEACONS

The Didache is an anonymous Christian text written around 100 CE, probably in Syria. It is a "church manual" providing both ethical and community instructions. The Didache presents church leadership as one centered on the teaching ministry of traveling apostles/prophets (cp. Matt 10:7-15//Luke 10:3-12), though the text does recognize that an apostle/

prophet could reside with the community. It also mentions the supporting ministry of bishops and deacons. The Didache is particularly concerned with how to recognize a false prophet; similar concerns are found in 1 John 4:1-3 (cp. also 1 Cor 14:29).

The Didache

Chapters 11–13

Therefore, whoever comes and teaches you all these things previously stated, receive him. But if the teacher himself turns and teaches another doctrine in order to destroy these things, do not listen to him. But if his teaching increases righteousness and knowledge of the Lord, receive him as the Lord. Now concerning the apostles and prophets, act according to the principles of the gospel. Let every apostle who comes to you be received as the Lord. He should not stay more than one day, or if need be a second day. But if he stays three days, he is a false prophet. And when an apostle departs he should take nothing but bread until he reaches his next place of lodging; but if he asks for money, he is a false prophet. And do not test or examine any prophet who speaks in the spirit, "for every sin will be forgiven, but this sin will not be forgiven" (Matt 12:31). But not everyone who speaks in the spirit is a prophet, but he who has the habits of the Lord. Therefore, the false prophet and the true prophet will be known from his habits. No prophet who orders a meal in the spirit will eat of it; otherwise he is a false prophet. And every prophet who teaches the truth; if he does not do what he teaches, is a false prophet. And no prophet who has been tried and is genuine, though working for a worldly mystery of the church, if he does not teach others to do what he does himself, will be judged by you; for his judgment lies with God, as did the prophets of old. But whoever says in the spirit, "Give me money, or something else," you will not listen to him. But if he tells you to give for others who are in need, let no one judge him. . . .

Now every true prophet who wishes to reside with you is worthy of his food. Likewise a true teacher is himself worthy of his food, even as a laborer is. Therefore you will take every firstfruit of the produce of the winepress, of the threshing floor, and of oxen and sheep, and give them as the firstfruits to the prophets, for they are your high priests. But if you do not have a prophet, give to the poor. If you make bread, take the firstfruits and give it according to the commandment. In the same way, when you open a jar of wine or oil, give the firstfruits to the prophets. And also of money, of clothes, and of all your possessions, take the firstfruits, as it seems good to you, and give according to the commandment.

Chapter 15

Therefore, appoint for yourselves bishops and deacons worthy of the Lord, men who are meek, not lovers of money, and true and approved, for they also minister to you the ministry of the prophets and teachers. Therefore do not despise them, for they are honorable among you with the prophets and teachers. Do not admonish one another in anger, but in peace as you find in the gospel. And let no one speak to anyone who has wronged another, nor let him hear a word from you until he repents. But practice your prayers and alms and all your acts as you find in the gospel of our Lord.

SOURCE: Kirsopp Lake, *Apostolic Fathers*, vol. 1, Loeb Classical Library 24 (Cambridge, Mass.: Harvard University Press, 1912), 325–31. Loeb Classical Library® is a registered trademark of the President and Fellows of Harvard College.

97

THE ROLE OF THE BISHOP

Ignatius was the bishop of Antioch in the late first century CE. While under arrest and in route to Rome, where he would be martyred (107 CE), Ignatius wrote letters to seven churches about various issues of faith, doctrine, and community practices. In his letter to the church at Smyrna, he promotes the centrality and authority of the bishop for the unity and faithfulness of the church. The Pastoral Epistles in the New Testament reflect a development of this hierarchical structure (cp. 1 Tim 3:1-7; Titus 1:5-9). Ignatius also refers to the Lord's Supper as a "love feast" (or agape meal), which is also referenced in Jude 12.

Ignatius, *To the Smyrneans* 7.2–8.2

Flee divisions as the beginning of evils. See that all of you follow the bishop as Jesus Christ follows the Father; and follow the elders as the apostles; and pay respect to the deacons as you would the command of God. Let no one do anything pertaining to the church without the bishop. Let that be deemed a valid Eucharist which is administered by the bishop or by someone appointed by him. Wherever the bishop appears, let the congregation also be present; just as wherever Jesus Christ is, there is the catholic church. It is not permitted either to baptize or hold a love feast without the bishop. But whatever he approves, this is also pleasing to God, so that everything you do may be secure and valid.

SOURCE: Kirsopp Lake, *Apostolic Fathers*, vol. 1, Loeb Classical Library 24 (Cambridge, Mass.: Harvard University Press, 1912), 261. Loeb Classical Library® is a registered trademark of the President and Fellows of Harvard College.

X. HOUSEHOLD RELATIONS

Instructions and guidelines about household relations were a common topic for moral and political writings of the Greco-Roman world, including Jewish and Christian writings. Such teachings were referred to as household management, and they dealt with relations between husbands and wives, masters and slaves, and fathers and children. The following selections come from elite men, and so reflect the values and perspectives of upper-class, educated males. It is difficult to know if and how these ideals reflect actual lived experiences, but we can imagine that the ideals created standards by which society judged what was appropriate and inappropriate. The New Testament contains instructions for household relations, and in general they reflect the larger patriarchal assumptions of the larger culture. But some interpreters note that these instructions are also grounded in the Christian gospel, which may also undermine the values of that culture. Compare Ephesians 5:22–6:9; Colossians 3:18–4:1; 1 Peter 2:18–3:7; also 1 Corinthians 7:1-7; 1 Timothy 2:11-15; 3:4-5, 11-12; 5:14-15.

98

HOUSEHOLD MANAGEMENT

As part of his political theory, the ancient Greek philosopher Aristotle (384–322 BCE) discusses household management, for it was believed that the household was a microcosm of the state. Aristotle's discussion of the hierarchy of household relations expresses the ideals that would continue for the larger Greco-Roman world.

Aristotle, *Politics* 1.1253b–1254b

And now that it is clear what the component parts of the state are, we have first of all to discuss household management; for every state is composed of households. Household management falls into departments corresponding to the parts of which the household in its turn is composed; and the household in its perfect form consists of slaves and freemen. The investigation of everything should begin with its smallest parts, and the primary and smallest parts of the household are master and slave, husband and wife, father and children. We ought therefore to examine the proper constitution and character of each of these three relationships . . .

. . .

Authority and subordination are conditions not only inevitable but also expedient. . . . In every composite thing where a plurality of parts . . . is combined to make a single common whole, there is always found a ruling and a subject factor. . . . Between the sexes, the male is by nature superior and the female inferior, the male ruler and the female subject. And the same must also necessarily apply in the case of mankind generally; therefore all men that differ as widely as the soul does from the body and the human being from the lower animal . . . these are by nature slaves, for whom to be governed by this kind of authority is advantageous. For he is by nature a slave who is capable of belonging to another (and that is why he does so belong), and who participates in reason so far as to apprehend it but not to possess it; for the animals other than man are subservient not to reason, by apprehending it, but to feelings. And also the usefulness of slaves diverges little from that of animals: bodily service for the necessities of life is forthcoming from both, from slaves and from domestic animals alike.

SOURCE: H. Rackham, *Aristotle*, vol. 21: *Politics*, Loeb Classical Library 264 (Cambridge: Harvard University Press, 1932), 13, 19–23. Loeb Classical Library® is a registered trademark of the President and Fellows of Harvard College.

99

HUSBAND AND WIFE RELATIONSHIP

The Greek writer Plutarch (late first century CE) promotes the ideal duties and virtues of wives and husbands. Plutarch's direction that a wife should worship only the god(s) of her husband—a fairly standard notion—would make for an interesting negotiation for Christian wives of non-Christian husbands (cp. 1 Pet 3:1-6).

Plutarch, *Advice to Bride and Groom* 139C–142E

. . . Whenever the moon is at a distance from the sun we see her conspicuous and brilliant, but she disappears and hides herself when she comes near him. In the reverse, a virtuous woman ought to be most visible in her husband's company and to stay in the house and hide herself when he is away.

Herodotus was not right in saying that a woman lays aside her modesty along with her undergarment. On the contrary, a virtuous woman puts on modesty in its stead, and husband and wife bring into their mutual relations the greatest modesty as a token of the greatest love.

Whenever two notes are sounded in accord the tune is carried by the bass; and in like manner every activity in a virtuous household is carried on by both parties in agreement, but discloses the husband's leadership and preferences. . . .

Just as a mirror, although embellished with gold and precious stones, is good for nothing unless it shows a true likeness, so there is no advantage in a rich wife unless she makes her life true to her husband's and her character in accord with his. If the mirror gives back a gloomy image of a glad man, or a cheerful and grinning image of a troubled and gloomy man, it is a failure and worthless. So too a wife is worthless and lacking in sense of fitness who puts on a gloomy face when her husband is bent on being sportive and gay, and again, when he is serious, is sportive and mirthful. The one smacks of disagreeableness, the other of indifference. Just as lines and surfaces, in mathematical parlance, have no motion of their own but only in conjunction with the bodies to which they belong, so the wife ought to have no feeling of her own, but she should join with her husband in seriousness and sportiveness and in soberness and laughter.

Men who do not like to see their wives eat in their company are thus teaching them to stuff themselves when alone. So those who are not cheerful in the company of their wives, nor join with them in sportiveness and laughter, are thus teaching them to seek their own pleasures apart from their husbands.

The lawful wives of the Persian kings sit beside them at dinner, and eat with them. But when the kings wish to be merry and get drunk, they send their wives away, and send for their music girls and concubines. Insofar they are right in what they do, because they do not concede any share in their licentiousness and debauchery to their wedded wives. If therefore a man in private life, who is incontinent and dissolute in regard to his pleasures, commit some indulgence with a lover or a female slave, his wedded wife ought not to be indignant or angry, but she should reason that it is respect for her which leads him to share his debauchery, licentiousness, and wantonness with another woman. . . .

A wife ought not to make friends of her own, but to enjoy her husband's friends in common with him. The gods are the first and most important friends. Wherefore it is becoming for a wife to worship and to know only the gods that her husband believes in, and to shut the front door tight upon all strange rituals and outlandish superstitions. For with no god do stealthy and secret rites performed by a woman find any favor.

. . .

Pheidias made the Aphrodite of the Eleans with one foot on a tortoise, to typify for womankind keeping at home and keeping silence. For a woman ought to do her talking either to her husband or through her husband, and she should not feel aggrieved if, like the flute player, she makes a more impressive sound through a tongue not her own.

Rich men and princes by conferring honors on philosophers adorn both themselves and the philosophers; but, on the other hand, philosophers by paying court to the rich do not enhance the repute of the rich but lower their own. So is it with women also; if they subordinate themselves to their husbands, they are commended, but if they want to have control, they cut a sorrier figure than the subjects of their control. And control ought to be exercised by the man over the woman, not as the owner has control of a piece of property, but, as the soul controls the body, by entering into her feelings and being knit to her through goodwill. As, therefore, it is possible to exercise care over the body without being a slave to its pleasures and desires, so it is possible to govern a wife, and at the same time to delight and gratify her.

SOURCE: Frank Cole Babbitt, *Plutarch: Moralia*, vol. 2, Loeb Classical Library 222 (Cambridge, Mass.: Harvard University Press, 1928), 305–15, 323. Loeb Classical Library® is a registered trademark of the President and Fellows of Harvard College.

100

SPHERES FOR MEN AND WOMEN

As part of his systematic exposition of the Ten Commandments, the Hellenized Jewish philosopher Philo (ca. 20 BCE–ca. 50 CE) reflects the prevailing Greco-Roman ideal of the proper spheres of activity for men and women.

Philo, *Special Laws* 3.169–170

Men are suited for marketplaces, council halls, courts of justice, large companies, and assemblies of numerous crowds, and a life in the open air full of arguments and actions relating to war and peace. But taking care of the house and remaining at home are the proper duties of women. The virgins have their bedrooms in the center of the house within the innermost doors, and the full-grown women do not go beyond the foyer and outer courts. For there are two kinds of states, the greater and the smaller. The larger ones are really called cities, and the smaller ones are called houses. And the superintendence and management of these is allotted to the two sexes separately: the men have the government of the greater, which government is called politics; and the women that of the smaller, which is called household management. Therefore let no woman busy herself about those things that are beyond the province of household management, but let her cultivate solitude and not be seen to be going about like a woman who walks the streets in the sight of other men, except when it is necessary for her to go to the temple, if she has any proper regard for herself. And even then let her not go at noon when the market is full, but after the greater part of the people have returned home—like a well-born woman, a real and true citizen, performing her vows and her sacrifices in tranquility, so as to avert evils and to receive blessings.

SOURCE: C. D. Yonge, *The Works of Philo Judaeus*, vol. 3 (London: H. G. Bohn, 1855), 345, with modifications.

101

MARRIAGE AND PARENTHOOD

Writing in the early second century CE, the Jewish writer Josephus defends Judaism against the polemical writing of a Hellenized Egyptian named Apion. In this selection, Josephus sets forth the ideals of marriage. Josephus' reference to the "law" is somewhat ambiguous—whether he means Scripture, tradition, or even his interpretation of Scripture—for some of his descriptions are not found in the Hebrew Bible (e.g., that women are inferior to men, or the act of abortion).

Josephus, *Against Apion* 2.199–205

So, what are our laws about marriage? That law maintains no other mixture of sexes but that which nature has appointed, that of a man with his wife, and that this be used only for the procreation of children. It abhors the mixture of a male with a male; and if anyone does that, death is its punishment. It also commands us that when we marry not to have regard for a dowry, nor to take a woman by violence, nor to persuade her deceitfully and fraudulently; but to seek her marriage by him who has power to arrange her and who is fit to give her away according to who is next of kin. The law says that a woman is inferior to her husband in all things. Let her, therefore, be obedient to him; not so that he should abuse her, but because he is the ruler, for God has given the authority to the husband. A husband, therefore, is to lie only with his wife whom he has married, but to make an attempt on another man's wife is unholy and punishable by death. The same penalty is for the one who forces a virgin engaged to another man or entices another man's wife. The law, moreover, charges us to bring up all our offspring, forbidding women to cause abortion of what is begotten or to destroy it afterward. And if any woman appears to have so done, she will be a murderer of her child, by destroying a living creature and diminishing humankind. If anyone, therefore, proceeds to such fornication or murder, he cannot be clean. Moreover, the law charges that after the man and wife have laid together in a regular way they will wash themselves, for there is a defilement contracted both in soul and body, as if they had gone into another country. For indeed the soul, by being united to the body, is subject to miseries, and is not freed from there but by death, at which point the law requires this purification to be entirely performed. The law certainly does not permit us to make festivals at the births of our children, which might afford the occasion of drinking to excess, but it ordains that the very beginning of our education should be immediately directed to sobriety. It also commands us to bring up those children in education and the things in the laws, and to inform them of the acts of their ancestors so that they might imitate them, and so that they might be nourished in the laws from their infancy, and might neither transgress them nor have any pretense for their ignorance of them.

SOURCE: William Whiston, *The Works of Flavius Josephus* (Philadelphia: John E. Potter, 1895), 738, with modifications.

102

TREATMENT OF SLAVES

Seneca was a stoic philosopher and Roman statesman, who late in his life (64 or 65 CE) wrote many letters on various moral and philosophical topics to Lucillius, governor of Sicily. Stemming from his Stoic philosophy, Seneca describes and critiques the normal attitude toward and treatment of slaves. Compare 1 Corinthians 7:22-23; Ephesians 6:9; Colossians 4:1.

Seneca, *Moral Epistles* 47.1–11

I am glad to learn, through those who come from you, that you live on friendly terms with your slaves. This befits a sensible and well-educated man like yourself. "They are slaves," people declare. No, rather they are men. "Slaves!" No, comrades. "Slaves!" No, they are unpretentious friends. "Slaves!" No, they are our fellow slaves, if one reflects that Fortune has equal rights over slaves and free men alike.

That is why I smile at those who think it degrading for a man to dine with his slave. But why should they think it degrading? It is only because purse-proud etiquette surrounds a householder at his dinner with a mob of standing slaves. The master eats more than he can hold, and with monstrous greed loads his belly until it is stretched and at length ceases to do the work of a belly; so that he is at greater pains to discharge all the food than he was to stuff it down. All this time the poor slaves may not move their lips, even to speak. The slightest murmur is repressed by the rod; even a chance sound—a cough, a sneeze, or a hiccup—is visited with the lash. There is a grievous penalty for the slightest breach of silence. All night long they must stand about hungry and dumb. . . .

We maltreat them, not as if they were men, but as if they were beasts of burden. When we recline at a banquet, one slave mops up the disgorged food, another crouches beneath the table and gathers up the leftovers of the tipsy guests. Another carves the priceless game birds; with unerring strokes and skilled hand he cuts choice morsels along the breast or the rump. Hapless fellow, to live only for the purpose of cutting fat capons correctly. . . . Another, who serves the wine, must dress like a woman and wrestle with his advancing years; he cannot get away from his boyhood; he is dragged back to it; and though he has already acquired a soldier's figure, he is kept beardless by having his hair smoothed away or plucked out by the roots, and he must remain awake throughout the night, dividing his time between his master's drunkenness and his lust; in the chamber be must be a man, at the feast a boy. Another, whose duty it is to put a valuation on the guests, must stick to his task, poor fellow, and watch to see whose flattery and whose immodesty, whether of appetite or of language, is to get them an invitation for tomorrow. Think also of the poor purveyors of food, who note their masters' tastes with delicate skill, who know what special flavors will sharpen their appetite, what will please their eyes, what new combinations will rouse their gorged stomachs, what food will excite their loathing through sheer satiety, and what will stir them to hunger on that particular day. With slaves like these the master cannot bear to dine; he would think it beneath his dignity to associate with his slave at the same table! Heaven forbid! . . .

Kindly remember that he whom you call your slave sprang from the same stock, is smiled upon by the same skies, and on equal terms with yourself breathes, lives, and dies. . . . I do not wish to involve myself in too large a question and to discuss the treatment of slaves, towards whom we Romans are excessively haughty, cruel, and insulting. But this is the kernel of my advice: Treat your inferiors as you would be treated by your betters.

SOURCE: Richard M. Gummere, *Seneca*, vol. 1: *Epistles 1–65*, Loeb Classical Library 75 (Cambridge, Mass.: Harvard University Press, 1917), 301–7. Loeb Classical Library® is a registered trademark of the President and Fellows of Harvard College.

103

INTERCESSION FOR A FORMER SLAVE

Pliny the Younger (61 CE–ca. 113 CE) was a Roman statesman. In the following letter, Pliny writes to his friend Sabinianus to intercede on behalf of a former slave, who has offended Sabinianus in some way. The second letter indicates that Pliny's intercession was successful. Many interpreters compare Pliny's letter of intercession with Paul's letter to Philemon, in which Paul intercedes on behalf of Philemon's slave Onesimus (cp. Phlm 1-25).

Pliny the Younger, *Letters*

9.21 (To Sabinianus)

Your freedman, with whom you told me you were angry, came to me and begged for my pardon, as earnestly as he would have done from you. He shed many tears; he made many pleas; and, at times, he kept a modest silence. He convinced me of his penitence. I really and truly believe that he has turned over a new leaf, because he is conscious of having done wrong. I know you are angry, and I also know you are justly angry, but clemency deserves most praise just when the cause of anger is most unimpeachable. You have in the past entertained some affection for the man, and I hope you will again. In the meantime, it will be enough for you to allow yourself to be won over to forgiveness. Make some consideration for his youth, for his tears, and make some also for your own good nature. Do not distress him any longer, nor yourself either. I am afraid that, if I join my appeals to his, you will think that I am not so much asking as forcing you to forgive. Yet join them I will fully and unreservedly, just as I have sharply and severely reprimanded him and given him a plain warning that I will never ask such a favor again. That is what I told him, for it was necessary to frighten him. But, of course, I do not use the same language to you, for it may be that I will have to repeat my present request. Indeed, I certainly will, provided that the case be one in which it is becoming for me to ask and for you to grant the favor.

Farewell.

9.24 (To Sabinianus)

You have done well to take back into your household and favor, on the intercession of my letter, the freedman who was once dear to you. This will afford you great satisfaction. It certainly pleases me, because, first, I see that you are able to control your passions; even when you are angry, you are open to guidance. And, secondly, because you pay me the fine compliment either of yielding to my influence or of indulging my requests. That is why I applaud your conduct, and thank you. At the same time I advise you for the future to be ready to pardon the faults of your household, though there be no one to intercede on their behalf.

    Farewell.

SOURCE: J. B. Firth, *The Letters of the Younger Pliny*, vol. 1 (London: Walter Scott, 1900), 308–9, 311, with modifications.

Y. PERSECUTION AND SOCIAL HARASSMENT OF CHRISTIANS

Persecution of Christians during the times of the New Testament (first century and early second century CE) is best described as local and sporadic. The suffering of Christians during this time was not empire-wide or a policy of the emperor. If and when it happened (sporadic), it happened at the hands of civic leaders and/or the local populace (local). Christians were harassed and at times maltreated primarily because of their refusal to worship any god except their own. In the eyes of their neighbors, this refusal to worship other gods—with the subsequent belief that the gods would respond in anger—was an act of subversion and hatred of family, humanity, and the empire. This suspicion and dislike created an environment of verbal and social harassment, which in turn could result in random acts of violence.

104

NERO'S PERSECUTION

In 64 CE, much of the city of Rome was destroyed by a fire that raged for six days. Nero blamed Christians for the fire, a move—according to Tacitus—intended to squelch rumors that Nero himself was responsible for the fire. In addition to describing Nero's extreme torture of Christians, which was limited to those Christians living in Rome (thus not empire-wide), this reading also reveals Tacitus' own prejudice against Christians.

Tacitus, *Annals* 15.44

Consequently, to get rid of the rumor, Nero fastened the guilt and inflicted the most excruciating tortures on a class of people despised for their vices, called Christians by the populace. Christus, from whom the name had its origin, suffered the extreme penalty during the reign of Tiberius at the hands of one of our procurators, Pontius Pilatus; and this most destructive superstition, thus checked for the moment, again broke out not only in Judea, the origin of the evil, but even in Rome, where all things hideous and shameful from every part of the world collect and become popular. Accordingly, an arrest was first made of all who confessed to being members of the sect; then, upon their information, an immense multitude was convicted, not so much of the crime of burning the city, as of hatred of humanity. Mockery of every sort was added to their deaths. Covered with the skins of beasts, they were torn by dogs and perished, or were nailed to crosses, or were doomed to the flames and burnt, to serve as nightly lamps when daylight had ended. Nero offered his gardens for the spectacle, and gave an exhibition in the Circus, mingling with the people dressed as charioteer or mounted on a chariot. Hence, even for these criminals who deserved extreme and exemplary punishment, there arose a feeling of compassion; for it was not, as it seemed, for the public good, but for the excess of one man's cruelty that they were being destroyed.

Source: Alfred John Church and William Jackson Brodribb, *Complete Works of Tacitus* (London: MacMillan & Co., 1876), 304–5, with modifications.

105

PLINY THE YOUNGER'S EXAMINATION OF CHRISTIANS

Pliny the Younger was the Roman governor of Bithynia-Pontus, Roman provinces in northern Asia Minor. The following selection is a letter written to the emperor Trajan in 112 CE, in which Pliny describes his approach to judging and punishing Christians, and Trajan's response. It should be noted that Pliny is not seeking out Christians, but they are being brought to him, presumably by city leaders or the general populace (cp. Acts 19:21-41); the emperor Trajan in his response explicitly instructs that Christians are not to be sought after. One feature of Pliny's considerations is whether Christians should be punished simply by having the name Christian, an issue reflected in 1 Peter 4:12-16.

Pliny the Younger, *Letters*

10.96 (To Trajan)

It is my custom, Sir, to refer to you in all cases where I have uncertainty, for who can better direct my doubts or inform my ignorance? I have never been present at any examination of Christians, and therefore I do not know what are the usual penalties passed upon them, or the extent of those penalties, or how far to take an investigation. I have hesitated a great deal in considering whether any distinctions should be made according to the ages of the accused; if the weak should be punished as severely as the stronger; if they renounce their faith they should be pardoned; or if once confessed as a Christian, he should gain nothing by recanting; if the name itself, even though crimes are absent, should be punished, or only the crimes that go with the name.

In the meantime, this is the method that I have adopted with those Christians who have been brought before me. I ask them whether they are Christians; if they say yes, then I repeat the question a second and a third time, warning them of the penalties it entails, and if they still persist, I order them to be led away. For I have no doubt that, whatever the character of the crime may be which they confess, their pertinacity and inflexible obstinacy certainly ought to be punished. There were others of similar madness whom I sent to Rome, for they were Roman citizens. Subsequently, as is usually the case, my dealing with this problem led to a great increase of accusations, and a variety of cases were brought before me. A pamphlet was published anonymously, containing the names of a number of people. Those who denied that they were or ever had been Christians, when they called upon the gods in the usual formula, reciting the words after me, and offered incense and wine before your image— which I had given orders to be brought forward for this purpose—together with the statues of the deities, and cursed the name of Christ—which, it is said, those who are really Christians cannot be induced to do—I considered that these should be acquitted. Others, whose names were given me by an informer, said that they were Christians but had lapsed, declaring that they had been but were so no longer. Some of them had recanted many years before, and more than one so long as twenty years back. They all worshiped your image and the statues of the deities, and cursed the name of Christ. . . . I thought it all the more necessary to find out what was truth about their meetings by submitting two slave women, who were called deaconesses, to the torture, but I found nothing but a disgusting superstition carried to great lengths. So I postponed my examination, and immediately consulted you. The matter seems to me worthy of your consideration, especially as there are so many people involved in this danger, for many persons of all ages and of both sexes are being brought to trial by their accusers, and the process will go on. The contagion of this superstition has spread not only through the cities but also into the villages and the rural districts, and yet it seems to me that it can be checked and set right. It is beyond doubt that the temples, which were almost deserted, are beginning again to be filled with worshipers, that the sacred rites which have for a long time been allowed to lapse are now being renewed, and that the food for the sacrificial meats are once more finding a sale, whereas, up to recently, a buyer was hardly to be found. From this it is easy to infer what vast numbers of people might be reclaimed, if only they were given an opportunity of repentance.

10.97 (Trajan's Response)

You have taken the proper course, my dear Pliny, in examining the cases of those who have been accused before you as Christians, for no hard-and-fast rule can be laid down to address an issue of such wide extent. These people are not to be hunted out. If they are brought before you and the accusation is proved, they are to be punished, but with this reservation: that if any one denies that he is a Christian and makes it clear that he is not by offering prayers to our gods, then he is to be pardoned because of his recantation, however suspicious his past conduct may have been. But pamphlets published anonymously must not carry any weight whatsoever, no matter what the charge may be, for they are not only a precedent of the very worst type, but they are not in keeping with the spirit of our age.

SOURCE: J. B. Firth, *The Letters of the Younger Pliny*, vol. 1 (London: Walter Scott, 1900), 377–80, with modifications.

106

ALEXAMENOS GRAFFITO

This graffito was discovered on the Palatine Hill in Rome in a room connected with the imperial palace; the room seems to have been a housing area for servants. The dating of the graffito is debated, but most interpreters give a general estimation of around 200 CE. The inscription reads, "Alexamenos worships [his] god." Because the object of worship is a crucified figure with the head of a donkey (probably related to anti-Jewish sentiments), it is generally agreed that the meaning or intent of the graffito is to ridicule a certain Christian named Alexamenos. Compare 1 Corinthians 1:18–2:5.

SOURCE: https://commons.wikimedia.org/wiki/File:AlexGraffito.svg, with modifications.

107

CELSUS' POLEMIC AGAINST CHRISTIANS

Celsus was a Greek philosopher, whose work *The True Word* (ca. 175 CE) gave a sustained critique of Christianity. Celsus' writing only survives in extensive quotations in the Christian writer Origen's *Against Celsus*, which is a defense of Christianity in response to Celsus. In this selection, Celsus reveals an elitist prejudice against Christians, who seem to gain most of their adherents from the lower class. He also suggests that Christians represent a subversive threat to the social order of the household (cp. 1 Pet 2:18–3:6, which seems to offer instructions to slaves and wives on how to avoid such allegations).

Origen, *Against Celsus* 3.55

We see, indeed, in private houses (Christians) who work with wool and leather, and fullers, and persons of the most ignorant and least cultured character. They dare not utter a word in the presence of their elders and wiser heads of households. But as soon as they get hold of the children privately or certain women who are as ignorant as themselves, they incessantly speak wonders, to the effect that they should not listen to their father and their teachers, but should obey them. These Christians are foolish and stupid, neither knowing nor performing anything that is really good; they are preoccupied with frivolous matters. They alone know how people ought to live, and that, if the children obey them, they will both be happy themselves, and will make their home happy as well. And while they thus are speaking, if they see one of the instructors of youth approaching or one of the more intelligent class, or even the father himself, the more timid among them becomes afraid. The ones who are more bold, however, incite the children to throw off the yoke, whispering in the presence of father and teachers that they neither will nor can explain to them any good thing, that they should turn away with repugnance from the silliness and stupidity of such persons as being altogether corrupt and far advanced in wickedness, and that they would inflict punishment upon them. If they really wish to know the truth, they must leave their father and their instructors, and go with the women and the children to the women's quarters, or to the leather shop, or to the fuller's shop, that they may learn perfection. By words like these they gain them over.

Source: Frederick Crombie, *The Writings of Origen*, vol 2: *Origen Contra Celsum, Books II–VIII*, ed. Alexander Roberts and James Donaldson, Ante-Nicene Christian Library (Edinburgh: T & T Clark, 1872), 135–36, with modifications.

Z. APOCALYPTIC LITERATURE

Apocalyptic literature originated in times of crisis and oppression, though it later was adapted to other situations, such as cultural accommodation. Its purpose was to instill hope and confidence in God's sovereignty over earthly situations and in God's ultimate accomplishment of justice and peace. An apocalypse is revelatory literature, and its visions and related symbols purport to unveil the future and/or the realm of heaven. These revelations, however, are intended to connect with and interpret the circumstances of the original readers in order to give them the proper perspective on reality. The two apocalyptic texts in the Bible are Daniel and Revelation.

108

2 BARUCH

Written in Palestine in the late first century CE, this Jewish apocalyptic text is a response to the Roman destruction of the temple in Jerusalem in 70 CE. The following selection represents a common theme found in apocalyptic literature: a time of tribulation, often schematized, at the end times and before God's grand intervention to make all things right, including judgment. In the case of 2 Baruch, God's messiah is the agent of that intervention. Compare Mark 13:1-37//Matthew 24:1-44; Revelation 6:1–11:19; 15:1–16:21; 19:11–20:15; see also Revelation 12:1–14:5.

---

2 Baruch 25–30

And (the Lord) answered and said to me: "You too will be preserved till that time when that sign which the Most High will work for the inhabitants of the earth in the end of days. This therefore will be the sign: when a stupor shall seize the inhabitants of the earth, and they will fall into many tribulations, and again when they shall fall into great afflictions. And it will come to pass that they will say in their thoughts because of their much tribulation: 'The Mighty One no longer remembers the earth'—yes, it will come to pass when they abandon hope that the time will then awake." And I answered and said: "Will that coming tribulation last a long time, and will that necessity embrace many years?" And He answered and said to me: "That time is divided into twelve parts, and each one of them is reserved for its appointed purpose. In the first part there will be the beginning of commotions. And in the second part there shall be slayings of the great ones. And in the third part the fall of many by death. And in the fourth part the drawing of the sword. And in the fifth part famine and drought. And in the sixth part earthquakes and terrors. [There is no seventh part in the text.] And in the eighth part a multitude of ghosts and attacks of demons. And in the ninth part the fall of fire. And in the tenth part seizure of property and much violence. And in the eleventh part wickedness and sexual immorality. And in the twelfth part disorder from the mingling together of all those things that have been before. These parts of that time are reserved, and will be mingled one with another and facilitate one another. For some of these parts will withhold some of their own, and receive in their stead from other parts; and some will complete their own and that of others. Consequently, those who are upon the earth in those days may not understand that this is the consummation of the times. Nevertheless, whoever understands will be wise at that time. For the measure and reckoning of that time are two parts: weeks of seven weeks." And I answered and said: "It is good for a man to come this far and see, but it is better that he should not come lest he fall. But I will say this also: Will he who is incorruptible despise those who are corruptible, and will he despise what happens with those things who are corruptible, so that he might look only to those who are not corruptible? But when, O Lord, those things surely come to pass which you have foretold to me, let me know this also if indeed I have found grace in your sight: Is it in one place or in one part of the earth that those things are come to pass, or will the whole earth experience them?" And He answered and said to me: "Whatever will happen then will happen in the whole earth, therefore all who live will experience them. For at that time I will protect only those who are found in this land at that time. And it will come to pass that when all that which should come to pass in those parts has been accomplished, that the messiah will then begin to be revealed. And Behemoth will be revealed from his place, and Leviathan will ascend from the sea; those two great monsters, which I created on the fifth day of creation and have kept until that time, then they will be food for all who are left. The earth also will yield its fruit ten thousandfold. And on each vine there will be a thousand branches, and each branch will produce a thousand clusters, and each cluster produce a thousand grapes, and each grape produce 230 liters of wine. And those who have hungered will rejoice: moreover, also, they will see marvels every day. For winds will go forth from before me every morning to bring the fragrance of aromatic fruits, and at the close of the day clouds to distill the dew of health. And it will come to pass at that same time that the treasury of manna will again descend from on high, and they will eat of it in those years, because these are they who have come to the consummation of time.

"And it will come to pass after these things, when the time of the coming of the messiah is fulfilled, that he will return in glory. Then all who have fallen asleep in hope of him will rise again. And it will come to pass at that time that the treasuries will be opened in which is preserved the number of the souls of the righteous, and they will come forth, and a multitude of souls will be seen gathered together in one accord; and the first will rejoice and the last will not be grieved. For they know that the time has come of which it is said, that it is the consummation of the times. But the souls of the wicked, when they see all these things, will then waste away the more, for they will know that their torment has come and their damnation has arrived."

SOURCE: R. H. Charles, "2 Baruch," in *The Apocrypha and Pseudepigrapha of the Old Testament in English*, vol. 2, ed. R. H. Charles (Oxford: Clarendon Press, 1913), 496–98, with modifications.

109

4 EZRA

Written in Palestine near the end of the first century CE or early second century CE, 4 Ezra is a Jewish apocalypse written in response to the destruction of the Jerusalem temple by the Romans in 70 CE. Apocalyptic literature often addresses the rise and fall of world empires and their kings, which are represented with symbolic or mythic creatures (cp. Dan 7:15–8:27). This excerpt is an account of the rise of the Roman Empire, represented by the eagle, and its judgment by God's messiah. Compare Revelation 18:1–19:21, and also Revelation 13:1-18.

4 Ezra 11–12

On the second night I had a dream: I saw rising from the sea an eagle that had twelve feathered wings and three heads. I saw it spread its wings over the whole earth, and all the winds of heaven blew upon it, and the clouds were gathered around it. I saw that out of its wings there grew opposing wings; but they became little, puny wings. But its heads were at rest; the middle head was larger than the other heads, but it too was at rest with them. Then I saw that the eagle flew with its wings, and it reigned over the earth and over those who inhabit it. And I saw how all things under heaven were subjected to it, and no one spoke against it—not a single creature that was on the earth. Then I saw the eagle rise upon its talons, and it uttered a cry to its wings, saying, "Do not all watch at the same time; let each sleep in its own place, and watch in its turn; but let the heads be reserved for the last."

. . .

Then I heard a voice saying to me, "Look in front of you and consider what you see." When I looked, I saw what seemed to be a lion roused from the forest, roaring; and I heard how it uttered a human voice to the eagle, and spoke, saying, "Listen and I will speak to you. The Most High says to you, 'Are you not the one that remains of the four beasts that I had made to reign in my world, so that the end of my times might come through them? You, the fourth that has come, have conquered all the beasts that have gone before; and you have held sway over the world with great terror, and over all the earth with grievous oppression; and for so long you have lived on the earth with deceit. You have judged the earth, but not with truth, for you have oppressed the meek and injured the peaceable; you have hated those who tell the truth, and have loved liars; you have destroyed the homes of those who brought forth fruit, and have laid low the walls of those who did you no harm. Your insolence has come up before the Most High, and your pride to the Mighty One. The Most High has looked at his times; now they have ended, and his ages have reached completion. Therefore you, eagle, will surely disappear, you and your terrifying wings, your most evil little wings, your malicious heads, your most evil talons, and your whole worthless body, so that the whole earth, freed from your violence, may be refreshed and relieved, and may hope for the judgment and mercy of him who made it.'"

. . . Then I woke up in great perplexity of mind and great fear, and I said to my spirit, "You have brought this upon me, because you search out the ways of the Most High. I am still weary in mind and very weak in my spirit, and not even a little strength is left in me, because of the great fear with which I have been terrified tonight. Therefore I will now entreat the Most High that he may strengthen me to the end." Then I said, "O sovereign Lord, if I have found favor in your sight, and if I have been accounted righteous before you beyond many others, and if my prayer has indeed come up before your face, strengthen me and show me, your servant, the interpretation and meaning of this terrifying vision so that you may fully comfort my soul. For you have judged me worthy to be shown the end of the times and the last events of the times." He said to me, "This is the interpretation of this vision that you have seen: The eagle that you saw coming up from the sea is the fourth kingdom that appeared in a vision to your brother Daniel. But it was not explained to him as I now explain to you or have explained it. The days are coming when a kingdom shall rise on earth, and it shall be more terrifying than all the kingdoms that have been before it. And twelve kings shall reign in it, one after another. But the second that is to reign shall hold sway for a longer time than any other one of the twelve. This is the interpretation of the twelve wings that you saw." . . .

"And as for the lion whom you saw rousing up out of the forest and roaring and speaking to the eagle and reproving him for his unrighteousness, and as for all his words that you have heard, this is the messiah whom the Most High has kept until the end of days, who will arise from the offspring of David, and will come and speak with them. He will denounce them for their ungodliness and for their wickedness, and will display before them their contemptuous dealings. For first he will bring them alive before his judgment seat, and when he has reproved them, then he will destroy them. But in mercy he will set free the remnant of my people, those who have been saved throughout my borders, and he will make them joyful until the end comes, the day of judgment, of which I spoke to you at the beginning. This is the dream that you saw, and this is its interpretation. And you alone were worthy to learn this secret of the Most High. Therefore write all these things that you have seen in a book, put it in a hidden place; and you shall teach them to the wise among your people, whose hearts you know are able to comprehend and keep these secrets. But as for you, wait here for seven days more, so that you may be shown whatever it pleases the Most High to show you." Then he left me.

Source: NRSV.

SCRIPTURE INDEX

257

New Testament